Chrysalis

Chrysalis

Awakening to God's Path, Protection, and Power in Your Life

Guy W. Gane Jr.

Gane Wisdom LLC

ISBN: 979-8-218-95197-9
Library of Congress Cataloging-in-Publication Data available upon
This work is non-fiction.
Gane, Guy W. Jr.

Chrysalis: Awakening to God's Path, Protection, and Power in Your Life

Published: May 2023

CONTENTS

CONTENTS

To my granddaughters...............
Giuliana, Gabriela and Grazia

"Eye has not seen, nor ear heard,
Nor have entered into the heart of man
The things which God has prepared
for those who love Him"
I Corinthians 2:9

If you're like me, when I am excited to read a new book, you may be tempted to skip the Introduction and get right into the red meat within those pages! I hope you won't do that this time!

Although our thinking - as human beings and as Christians - has become more influenced by technology, one thing that can never change is the influence that God has over our lives. It is easy, very easy in fact, to disregard the teachings, lessons and stories found in the Bible. The "modern" world seems to believe that it can navigate the world without God's compass. The New Testament proclaims the good news of Jesus Christ while the Old Testament exposes us to the announcements, prophecies and preparations that would give way and make possible the coming of the Savior. It is those words that are found in God's Holy Book that I relied on to guide me and center me in my writing. I also realize that what *I found* not only to be enlightening but instructive may not be interrupted in the same manner by every reader.

Over the years, I have noticed that there are those who try to make Scripture say something that it does not. There is no doubt that Scripture speaks to each of us in different ways. A passage may have tremendous effect on one person and has no meaning to another, however there are instances where a speaker or an author tries to create a theology that they like. I once read a quote that said, "Whenever possible, let Scripture interpret Scripture." In Chrysalis I took God's words at face value.

I prayed as I wrote this book and I asked for His guidance in putting together a manuscript that might help those who find it difficult to achieve the goals and dreams for their future as well as living a life with peace. However, this is not a manual in how to manipulate God in the hope of granting our wishes – which wouldn't be possible anyway. What I hoped to convey is the joy of a relationship of living a life fully according to His will. Matthew quoted Jesus that "with God all things are possible". Do we dare not take Jesus at His word?

Our God is a God of love, a God of Supreme Truth, and a God of second and twentieth and hundredth chances - and for that I am personally grateful. You see, as I wrote this book, I was a guest of the United States. As a stockbroker for many years, I was blessed with not only a significant income but a sterling professional reputation in Western New York where I lived. After organizing a start-up company toward the end of my career I came under the gaze of the Federal government and despite vehemently proclaiming my innocence I eventually spent nearly a decade in prison. I relate this story in more detail in my book "Unchained and Unbroken: Life Lessons and Strength Training from a Jailhouse GymRat". I wrote both Chrysalis and Unchained and Unbroken while I was incarcerated. My plans were to edit and publish Chrysalis as soon as I could after my release, however when I came home it seemed that people were fascinated to know what prison was like and I was encouraged to publish Unchained and Unbroken first. I equate that with the observation that everyone wants to go to heaven, but nobody wants to die to go there! It appeared that people felt the same way about prison - everyone wants to know about it, but no-one wants to go there! For that I totally understand. Prison is not a place you ever want to be.

Prison is terrifying. I tried to constantly remind myself that I should not fear – after all God said so 365 times in the Bible – but living in a living hell was a constant struggle emotionally, mentally, and spiritually.

I have always believed however, that when handed a bag of lemons you make lemonade, and it was shortly after entering prison that I began to practice writing. For many years prior I wanted to write a book. I wanted to share what (I thought) I knew with the world, but I could just never get going, never really find the words, never find the time or become motivated enough to do so.

In the first few months of my bid (prison slang for sentence) I started out simply, constructing in words, observations of my life, of my then-surroundings and eventually graduating to writing down what truly happened with my firm and the events that surrounded our, and my, becoming a target of the Securities and Exchange Commission, and eventually the United States Attorney's Office. As the years passed, I kept having the feeling that I should write a book (while my cherished friend Walter Blair constantly prodded me as well!). A book that would inspire, motivate, ruminate, and illuminate the process by which to achieve a goal. That in itself was a bit crazy since there I was sitting in a place I did not want to be at and prayed continually to be free of! As those prayers (seemingly) went unanswered, I came to understand how in fact, things *really* worked. No matter how much I visualized, spoke affirmations, or focused on my objective - my freedom - it just wasn't coming about. Why?

Like you, I read the "positive-thinking" books, those by the popular and famous and by the not-so-popular and the not-so-famous, authors. How could it happen that I did not reach my goal? How could it be that my objectives were continually eluding me? Through introspection, long contemplations, and sincere prayer I came to find the reasons. It was still difficult to be sure – waiting on the Lord is never easy. I came to find however, the absolute truths. And although the many inspirational and motivational books I had read over my lifetime were on the right track, they missed THE MOST important ingredient crucial to success in any endeavor. I believe you will find that ingredient within these pages.

In writing a book with scripture as it's backbone I was constantly aware that I am just an average guy. I have no Doctorate in Divinity; I am not a Theologian, nor am I ordained in any religious denomination. "Who" I would think to myself, "*are you* to write about God's path, protection, or power in anyone's life?" But whatever small voice spewed out discouragement and disparagement, a much larger one encouraged me onward. In prison it was a constant chore to retain any reference material. Usually, it was not possible. I would read something, somewhere, anywhere and if it made sense and gave me comfort, encouragement or a different way to look at things I would write it down - usually on whatever scrap of paper was lying around - and try to fit it into my tiny locker. If it would fortify me in some way, I realized that that was not a bad thing, and it was worth saving. That's how it went for years. Then finally in 2016 I felt compelled to write this book. It took two years. A few years later I then wrote Unchained and Unbroken.

As you will read, this book is a bit different than others of its genre. I include historical correlations that allowed me to make a specific point. I've also pointed out some of the biological and genetically imparted reasons why we say, act and do the things we do as human beings. While this information is certainly not meant to be a scientific expose, it does help, I believe, to explain, in laymen's terms, why we behave and react to outside influences like we do.

I know that in order to become the dynamic person each of us hope to become, we need to begin from a strong base. A strong foundation. Starting out easily is the best way to meet with success and it was with this thought in mind that I structured the words you are about to read. Beginning simply with basic ideas and concepts in the first few chapters while continually building through each succeeding chapter, eventually bringing you by the final pages, to a place where dreams transform into reality and where goals truly are reached.

Many of those who I quote here were God's mighty servants. Some who I quote were not believers. All of them however imparted wisdom that is as relevant today as it was hundreds and thousands of years ago when they were pronounced. We are after all, all God's children, and each of us have something to offer to our neighbor, and it was with that thought that I felt inspired to include them. Also, where I felt led to, I repeated themes to ensure that you would know *that they were that important* to brand into your subconscious. I also repeated a scriptural verse if it helped make a point.

It is a common assumption by the public that when a guy goes to prison, he gets a tattoo, and he finds Jesus. Of course, that happens but not nearly as much as Urban Legend would have you believe. Personally, I became much stronger in my relationship with Christ through my ordeal, but it wasn't until I came home that I truly realized how much and how awesome that connection was and how grateful I am for the opportunity. Home has many distractions while prison is monotonous. It is Groundhog Day. Every day. In many ways however prison allows someone who searches for life's meanings to find it easier than is possible in the outside, free world. As crazy as it sounds, in a messed-up way I miss prison, the *only reason* being that I spent so much time being in His company and in His arms. The human mind is, I think, much like riding a bicycle – if you don't keep moving forward you fall. What I found in lockdown is this: your faith either became stronger, you were completely apathetic, or you blamed God for your predicament and loathed Him. I observed it all.

As I began to organize my thoughts, I began to sense another presence. Words began flooding into my mind with ideas I had really not thought of. I constantly questioned myself, asking "do you really want to write this?" I decided early on to just let go and write down what came into my mind and if it "felt" right to do so and if I felt I was being led to do so I put it on paper. It was a bit ironic (and, to a degree humorous) that as I would study and contemplate scripture verses, think on the point that I was trying to make using God's words, that I would hear some of the most vulgar, some of the filthiest language imaginable. "But" I would realize, "this is prison"! I also knew however, that I began to understand that putting the words on paper would be my responsibility and if anyone questioned my authority (or even 'right') to write them they were entitled to their opinions and beliefs. I also realized that if by putting my thoughts on paper could help just one person on their life's journey it was certainly worth it.

It is my hope that you come to realize that the source of your power can only come from God. It is up to you to transform God's power into your life. You *can not* do this on your own – only by invoking the Holy Spirit will this be possible. If you have until now, been distant from Him it will take commitment by you to allow this power to permeate into your being. How? By constant prayer. How to pray like this will also be found in these pages.

Every human being faces challenges and obstacles in their life but fortunately we also find successes too. We encounter defeats and misfortunes and do our best to find a way out of them. But in order to benefit from those setbacks we need to accept them as *set-ups* for the life that God has planned for us. Do NOT buy the garbage that man is made to suffer. That somehow God punishes us. Suffering is different than learning and learning is what we must do to keep moving ahead. What father "sets up" his children to punish them? Whatever answer you come up with, *"not a very nice father"* would probably be included. I choose to believe that Our Father in Heaven can be nothing but an awesome, loving, and fantastic Father who adores and cherishes *all* His children. I believe the adage that "God loves you so much, He has your picture on His refrigerator!"

You may find my opinions, observations, theories, and words comforting. You may find my words empowering. You may even find issue with those written words, but it is my hope that you find them thought provoking.

During the years I spent writing Chrysalis, I thought of you. I prayed for you. I wrote in the hope of emboldening you. I encourage you to accept that nothing just happens in your life and that you will always know that no matter how dark the night, how lonely the walk, how impossible the quest seems, God is there, with you, by you and for you.............

May the grace of our Lord Jesus Christ be with you all.
Guy W. Gane, Jr.

1

God's Energy

Point to yourself.

Seriously, put this book down, stand up, and point to yourself. Where are you pointing?

If you're like most people, you're pointing toward your heart.

Interesting isn't it? Why do most of us point to our heart? The answer is because that's where we identify our "selves" to be. When Solomon wrote, "For as he thinks in his heart, so is he," he knew that was where human beings believe themselves to reside. (Proverbs 23:7)

Referring to sports, we'll hear "he shows a lot of heart" to mean grit and determination. When we're told to "put your heart into it," we take that to mean "get enthused."

Scripture says that God doesn't look at a man's appearance but at what is in his heart.(1 Samuel 16:7) So we see that the heart is not only the organ that propels blood throughout our body but where our moral, ethical, and ethereal body is centered.

In 1991, scientists found that within every human heart resides approximately 40,000 unique and specialized cells configured to create a neural network of sorts. This network is akin to brain-like cells, which is why they are called "the little brain of the heart." It was found that these cells think independently from the brain. They feel independently as well. This means that everything that we experience is registered in two separate places—the brain and the heart. Attempting to heal upsets or trauma by simply thinking or talking to our mind will usually feel incomplete due to our only addressing one half of ourselves. [1]

Grit and determination are two qualities we admire in others and work toward having in ourselves. Most of us equate those two words with hard work and firmness of mind.

Some will compare the words to fighting our way into achieving a goal. But is elbowing our way into achievement necessary? Or even successful? What if by your thoughts you could achieve any goal and reach any objective? Physical struggle need not be involved as we've demonstrated to ourselves over our lifetime. Examples of those demonstrations will be clear as we go through this book. How to make those occurrences work for you and not against you will also become apparent.

When we try to reconcile this premise with our past experience, we find it difficult, if not impossible, to believe. Henry Ford once said, "Whether you think you can, or you think you can't—you're right."

Why is it that what we want in our lives appears now and then, but what we don't want in our lives usually shows up regularly? It really is quite simple; it's all in our emotions. The feeling we put into it—whatever 'it' happens to be.

There are two basic emotions that govern our human lives: pain and pleasure.

We all want the nicer things in life—the nice car, the most comfortable, beautiful home, stylish clothes. We want, even crave, pleasurable experiences. This emotion of pleasure is different from happiness, as you'll discover. Pleasure is a quest, a goal, something hoped for—but not a mandatory achievement that can even be transitory before we bring it to pass.

Pain, on the other hand, is something every living creature tries to avoid. If we have a headache, we take an aspirin. That's simple. More complex however is having a toothache. It hurts but we'll avoid going to the dentist until the pain becomes unbearable when we then rationalize that the initial pain of filling a cavity is less than the constant agony of the toothache.

Pain can also be emotional where fearful and torturous thoughts occupy every waking moment. It is just this feeling of fear—visualizing an unhappy outcome that creates the realization of that result.

You have probably heard about or read about visualization in the past and may not have believed it or thought that it sounded "New Age," but the scripture plainly describes it: "What I feared has come upon me,"said Job. Fear only comes about by thinking about it first. (Job 3:25)

Fear is so powerful that we usually dwell on the unhappy scenario we picture in our mind. We visualize in dramatic fashion that very thing we want to avoid. We add feeling into the movie and get caught up emotionally and like Job we lament the realization of what we didn't want into our life.

In order to successfully achieve our desires, we need to understand how our thoughts affect our outcomes. You've been in situations where you 'knew' what someone else was about to say. That is considered by some a transfer of energy. In this instance thought energy.

Everything in the universe is energy. Energy permeates everything in both the physical world—that which we see and feel—and the non-physical world (think radio waves).

Mankind is on the verge of discovering what is actually going on in the non-physical world. In the coming years, it's not inconceivable that we will have the ability to observe the interactions of the startling forces at work in the unseen world. Could we be where the intellectuals of the 15th century were? Convinced that the world was flat? Only an idiot believed otherwise. In 1492, Christopher Columbus' forethought and courage overcame their disbelief. The multiple dimensions written about by science fiction writers could be confirmed in the future and as scientific and intellectual discovery has proven in the 20th century—anything is possible.

2,000 years ago, as Paul sat in a Roman prison, he reached out to the church in Colossae (located in today's modern Turkey) writing that God, Himself invisible, created visible and invisible things in heaven and on the earth (Colossians 1:16).

Our connection to God's energy began before birth and once born, we learned how to think, reason, and adapt to our surroundings. We began to process outside information to make choices. As a newborn we had no need to think or worry. We cried and our mother responded. We smiled, slept, played, and went with the flow. All of this was completely natural. Our lives were pure, simple, and innocent. As we learned to respond to certain signals our mind began to split from the essence of who we really are. Such is the progression of life on planet Earth.

In order to live in this world, we must be aware of the basic workings of it. It is our longing for more than just the empty stimulation of loving a day-to-day existence that eventually calls to us to reach out to God, to learn how abiding in Him, and in His words causes our lives to elevate.

In some lives this rise takes hold and takes place, while others not at all. You reading this book is not by chance.

Energy comes to us in two ways: physiologically—that which deals with living matter. Physiological energy is brought into our bodies as a result of food digestion. Universal energy—God's universe, is that which is unlimited in scope but only by the degree that we perceive to be worthy of. This perception is centered in the mind. Problems arise when we feel unworthy—consciously or subconsciously, to receive it. We impede this reception with thoughts such as "I don't deserve it;" "That's for other people not me;" "God doesn't love me and has abandoned me." Like a clogged drainpipe, the flow becomes obstructed, hindering our ability to be our best.

This ever-present force of nature, energy "behaved," according to the ancients, like the weather and air. To the early Chinese this invisible force was known simply as "the air" or 'Chi.' In the other Asian dialects —Japanese or Korean, for instance—this same word is spelled KI, QI, KEI, and so on. This energy came to be identified with our life energy and that each of us are born with the life force. Each of us part of God yet unique and different as each person transformed that life energy within their own life.

No matter where on earth we reside, there is a universal acknowledgement of a superior intelligence or being that we look to that we are a part of. We know, honor, and fear Him as God. However, to the Chinese He is "The Tao" To the Muslim He is Allah. To the Hindu He's known as the Brahmin.

It is beyond question that the lifeless corpse of the person you once knew is not the real person because "they" are no longer there. Regardless of one's religious beliefs, we are not human beings with a spirit but spiritual beings who are temporarily human.

For some people, blaming God for ill health or misfortune is easy as it absolves them of any responsibility and while we acknowledge that sometimes bad things happen to good people, we must recognize our being accountable for the results of our choices in life.

As we'll see, we are capable of harmonizing with our Creator to bring balance to our body and our lives. It is our challenge and our privilege to accept, coexist and thrive with the free-choice He so lovingly gives us to live for His glory.

Unfortunately, our 21ˢᵗ Century lives encourages us to look toward 'outside' pleasures and accomplishments instead of valuing the core of who we really are. It is by going inward that we find true reward, not only foundationally but with our relationship to the world. As you'll see, this is attainable but first you must become a true child, open to new thoughts and ideas as well as a new way of living.

This can not happen by just having the best of intention. It won't happen by reading words on a page. It can only come about by our soul's firm commitment to become completely immersed in the presence of God in our lives. It is with integrity and honesty to ourselves that will allow this journey to not only be possible, but for the results to be inevitable.

Jesus spoke about the care that God gives to His creation when He spoke to His disciples. Jesus spoke of the freedom the birds enjoyed from worry to illustrate the truth that nature (God) is stability, perfection, tranquility. At its very core nature is excellence. (Matthew 6:26)

In our lives trouble, problems and challenges arise. As much as we look for peace in our life, we realize that things will come up to upset that peace. Our growth depends on how we handle these situations. But at the very center of the universal presence we know as God, is peace and serenity.

"How," you might ask, "can you prove that?" If there is a pond or any body of water nearby take a stone and throw it into the water. What do you notice, especially if it is a placid body of water? The stone hits the water creating turbulence. Waves generate forcefully outward. But within moments the water settles down, the commotion vanishes and once again calm returns, as if nothing happened. Peace, serenity, "normal."

We observe the same results with the weather. Violent thunderstorms, tornadoes, hurricanes or natural disasters like earthquakes and tsunamis. Thankfully like the storms in our lives, peace eventually returns.

Life has a tendency to go in unplanned directions. Instead of us controlling it, 'life' controls us. If we persist in living by chance only, not putting Him first, not having goals or having no plan for where we want to be, we risk losing the favor God has for us. We end up constantly putting out fires instead of fulfilling the destiny God has for us.

Each of us needs to "recharge our batteries" now and again. We need to go inward at times to reconnect with our true selves. We need to find that special place in nature, to become an observer, to become aware, maybe for the first time in our life.

Notice the air around you. The birds singing, the crickets chirping, the waves crashing. Become one with it. Observe the feeling. Empty your mind—just for these precious moments—of the anxious thoughts rushing into your head. This is your opportunity to reconnect with God. You will notice that there is always something going on around you. Expand your love, your very being into every sight and sound. Really love it. Really experience the moment. Because now you have become aware of God on a physical level. Feel the branches sway gently in the breeze. Hear the rustle of the leaves. Observe the individual snowflake. Become a part of everything around you. Breath in His love. Hold it inside you. Live the words "Be still and know that I am God." (Psalm 46:10)

"In the beginning God created the heavens and the earth...." (Genesis 1:1) With these words Moses begins to describe God's creation of the world and the special people He chose to populate it. The world in which we know and live in was *spoken* by Him into existence. Not only is this a bold statement but an amazing one; however it is at the basis of who we are and answers the great question "Where did I come from?"

We know that to speak creates vibratory waves, yet those vibrations are unseen.

We now know that nothing is solid. Not a rock, not a book, not even a body. All of it, all of us are made up of matter—energy vibrating at a certain level. In the beginning matter's presence existed in its purest vibratory form—that which we call hydrogen. As the atoms of hydrogen began to gravitate toward each other they expanded into a complex state. As this hydrogen took on density, it began to heat and burn and eventually became a star. In an endless cycle of expansion, the star exploded sending forth new elements into the universe, creating an untold number of atoms until the basic elements formed and scattered everywhere. Hydrogen—the simplest form of energy, caused matter to evolve to carbon. As each star sent these gases into the universe eventually pockets of matter became our sun and then our planets. The true majesty of it is that He created it all.......

There are those who hold firmly to the doctrine that evolution and the age of the Earth are absurd. This book, if for nothing else, is foundational, something in which the reader can use as a guidepost on their own life path so therefore nothing will be purposefully omitted. The topic of our planet's age has been discussed in the past by some who have been led to believe that in order to comply with Biblical teachings the proposition of the Earth's development must be a literal interpretation. I believe that this thinking short-changes our God by trying to conform Him to our own human understanding. The grandeur of what He brought about throughout nature is truly miraculous, and in order to accept all that God has in store for us we need to have our minds open. The age of the Earth and the rejection of evolution are not central Christian convictions. Jesus never taught them neither do they appear in the Nicene or Apostles Creeds. Christianity has always focused on our relationship with God through Jesus' death and resurrection. The age of the Earth has been proven through DNA evidence and not on what was once "ambiguous" fossil evidence. We may live on a four-billion-year-old planet, yet we experience God's magnificence in our every waking moment now.

As we go about our lives we think, if we consider it at all, that we are solid physical beings. Why wouldn't we? Each of our senses perceive it so. Our consciousness controls our bodily moves for the most part. But on another level, one more subtle, we are aware that our internal organs function beyond our conscious will. We pay no attention to the continuous biochemical reactions in each cell of our body. But even these reactions are not the ultimate reality that takes place in the physical.

There is no such thing as a solid object. Particles that make up the chair you're sitting on are moving at immeasurable speed and the free space between those particles make up more than the mass of the particles themselves. You could realistically and correctly conclude that you're sitting on nothing. Now consider that in like manner your body, relative to every solid mass, is made up of these same free-moving particles widely divided by free space, moving in hyper speed. We are made up of the same substance as every essence of matter we see, the only difference between us and the object being form and consciousness, with consciousness being the awareness of our divine connection to God.

Mass is potential energy and energy is potential mass. Scientific research has shown, despite our logical thinking, that there is only one substance from which energy is made, that being a single proton of hydrogen. We can also consider that space is consisting of vibration and that similar vibrations are attracted to each other to form a unit. And yes, it is possible that we pick up these vibrations from one human to another.

Every physical manifestation is made of this energy, and it is infinite in time and space—no beginning and no end. All time everywhere and anywhere at any time.

The formed atom has its own vibration seeking out corresponding vibration bringing together the physical manifestation of matter. Therefore, matter is formed from intelligence and most significantly, intelligence is matter. Since intelligence must be conscious there can be no argument that we are enveloped by a living universe and beyond that, there can only be consciousness in all things. When Jesus said, "God is not a God of the dead but the God of the living". He was revealing the basic truth of a living universe. (Luke 20:38)

"In the beginning was the Word, and the Word was with God, and the Word was God." (John 1:1) Words, vibrations, energy, all hold God's presence. Being sensitive to the world around us is the first step in the journey of living a full life both physically and spiritually. The evidence of God's presence in our lives is overwhelming—just look around.

Words have meaning and as you'll read throughout the following pages, words have power. As Solomon wrote "Death and life are in the power of the tongue" (Proverbs 18:21) Repeating falsehoods such as "I can't," "I never will," "I'm doomed to fail," and so on have more effect on your life then perhaps you realize. Fortunately, "I can," "I will," and "I am blessed by God's favor," do too.

The Holy Spirit's presence is around and in each of us. Whether you accept or believe that is not critical. (1 Corinthians 3:16). Like the air we breathe, unseen, it's there. God's words have never changed nor will they. Throughout scripture God, through His prophets and His son Jesus Christ, has assured us that nothing is too big, or too small, for Him.

Whether it was being thrown in a pit, then a prison and coming out as the second in command, staring down a den of lions, or inviting someone to touch their side, God's word in our lives will not be left undone.

Fill yourself with the moment around you and as you do—love.

Love each and everything you observe. Hold that feeling, love, inside of you. Speak it, feel it, live it for as John wrote, "God is love and he who abides in love abides in God and God in him." (1 John 4:16)

If you're like most people, you want your life to be one of happiness, comfort, peace, wealth, and of course, love. You want to be healthy and be free of problems.

Yet it seems that despite our best intentions the opposite of our desires appears. After we experience frustration and something less than success, we can feel desperate which may in turn lead to making wrong choices. Not wanting to accept our own responsibility for these choices, some of us blame God, too often bitterness settles in and soon a negative spirit and outlook becomes part of our personality. We need to open our minds to the knowledge that we are God's children and He loves us. God is Omnipotent. He is Omnipresent and He is Omniscient —Almighty, everywhere and aware of everything.

There is a very fine line between knowing what we want for our lives and discerning what is God's will for our lives. For many people this is a challenge. Waiting on God can be difficult (I know, believe me). Maybe difficult is an understatement. Painful might be more appropriate. We want what we want and we want it now, however the demand of 'I want it now' not only causes us to think without comprehension but can cause separation from God. We lose patience, deciding to take matters into our own hands, perhaps even achieving our goal only to discover that it wasn't what we hoped or maybe even wanted.

Some years ago, Garth Brooks made popular a song entitled (Thank God for) "Unanswered Prayers." I'm sure you've thought those words a time or two. This kind of gratitude can only occur when, after our petitions we step back and put His will before ours.

We honor a God, who with a word, created the universe. As human beings we will never fully be able to grasp His true Supremacy. Quite simply it is too overwhelming to contemplate, overpowering our ability to comprehend who He is. Is it any wonder that many of us feel unworthy of His favor? Hopefully before the end of this book you will become comfortable, as well as convinced that God will not only open doors you didn't know were there but that He will guide you straight through those obstructions, difficulties, restraints and limitations that once prevented you from being all He wants you to be. You'll be assured through God's own words that with faith and belief *nothing* is impossible.

It is now time to decide what you want for your life. You can spend the rest of your time on earth struggling and fighting for your place under the sun or you can choose a different approach, one that has been available to us all along—through the words found in Holy Scripture. Choosing is not wishing, nor is it hoping for your dreams to come true. It is your birthright as an heir to His Royal Bloodline to choose to accept God's good pleasure in giving you the Kingdom (Luke 12:32).

Many of us look for the physical affirmation that God is guiding us, leading us and watching over us. As Christians we look for God to approve our actions as well as forgive our transgressions. Throughout the Bible the encounters between God and His people are often described as covenants notably to illustrate how God manifests His glory to His people. In the end we are left to interpret and then institute what we know and what we see, what we discern, what we read and what we think, with and in, our relationship with God.

Whether you are Baptist or Methodist, Lutheran or Catholic, or any of the various Christian denominations, we need to realize that there is no "corner" in God's grace. *Jesus did not die for a religion, He died so that we would have a relationship with God!*

How we see the hand of God at work in our lives begins with a conscious decision to do so. "Your ears shall hear a word behind you saying, 'This is the way, walk in it,' whenever you turn to the right hand or whenever you turn to the left." (Isaiah 30: 21)

The following pages puts forward proposals to do just that.

2

It All Begins With A Word

"You'll never amount to anything...."

It starts too early in life. Most people from the moment they start to walk begin to be told, be warned, and be threatened. This does not mean that well-intentioned caregivers, be they parents or grandparents purposely intend to destroy a child's self-esteem but unfortunately these sorts of words do exactly that. We learn by example and many of us have been brought up hearing these things said to us at one time or another.

The difference we face however is that hearing negatives continually, we come to accept and believe them. "You're worthless"—I always embarrass myself and my family. "You never do anything right"—I am nothing but a failure. Worse still is when you decide to make positive changes in your life and tell others about that decision; chances are good that those very people who've discouraged you are the exact ones you're confiding in and their reaction is typical (if not predictable) "Yea, right!" This is a good reason to keep quiet and keep your business to yourself. I'll have more to say about keeping your own counsel later, but for now and going forward keep the following in mind: Silence is Golden.

Accepting your own worthiness can be difficult to some people due to false dogma they accepted over the years. Not only have they been exposed to verbal put downs, but some even equate humility with humiliation! When Jesus spoke about turning the other cheek, He was not avowing degradation. Being a Christian does not mean you have to be a doormat! Feeling reprehensible and undeserving are not the qualities people look for in others and are certainly not Christ-like!

One of the simplest ways to bring about a feeling of self-worth is by asking yourself empowering questions. We chatter constantly during any given moment. Our inner voice has an endless variety of topics on any subject. Some are pertinent to what we're occupied with at that particular moment, but many others are random—"I can't believe I left the car window opened when it rained last week" "When we went on vacation last year, I forgot to pack my boots" Sometimes they are oddball thoughts or questions but in too many instances they become down right cruel—"I am such a loser!"

When was the last time you gave yourself a compliment?

It seems easy to castigate ourselves for our 'perceived' shortcomings. I use the word perceived because most of us are our own worst critics. It is too easy to beat ourselves up. Brain chemistry, genetics, coping skills and our life experiences can predispose us to thinking excessively negative thoughts of ourselves. Additionally, once we begin down this road, we seem to root ourselves with the same thoughts over and over.

According to scientists, a thought is made up of an intricate pattern of movement between proteins and other chemicals, gene expressions and neural connections in our brain. As we continue to dwell on the thought, the stronger this circuit grows. It's no accident (or deficiency on our part) that as we think of a hurt let's say, we begin to feel even worse!

According to neuroscientist and author Alex Korb, a well-developed thought is like a ski track in the snow. In his book *The Upward Spiral,* he writes that "the more you ski down a path, the easier it is to go down that path and not another."

Thoughts are truly amazing things. You can't see them, yet they're real. You can't touch them, yet they have the power to touch lives. You can't hear them however their power is heard in every spoken word. We can never turn them off and without effort (through meditation for example) it's difficult to stop thinking about something or other.

Faults are regularly veiled in questions and statements—"How could I have been so wrong?" "I'm going to run to the store." "I can't believe I did that!" We constantly chatter.

I had been in prison for about a year when one day I allowed my thought process to go where it willed. It was a Monday, my wife's birthday and after seeing her the previous day and along with not being with her on her special day I was feeling pretty low. I laid down on my bunk contemplating my life to that point—how things got out of control, where I could have made changes and improvements and so on. Although many years have now passed, as I look back to that day, I recall going into what I can only describe as a semi-conscious state, half awake and half asleep. There happened to be a pencil and pad next to me and for the next 90 minutes I wrote down 93 (I still have them) of the most hurtful, destructive, venomous and injurious questions and observations any person could pile on themselves. It was, as I now think on it, the very beginning of my healing process, however it is still tough to look at. But yet I'm thankful that by writing those thoughts down I could begin to work on reconstituting and reconstructing myself.

Psychologists tell us that with intent and practice we can create another path for our thoughts. The technique is called Cognitive Reappraisal and can result in a stronger neural network devoted to positive thoughts. Throughout this book, you'll find how the inner operations of our body, most especially our brain, impact our daily and long-term lives. Much of the way we behave and react has been passed down, genetically speaking, from our distant ancestors. We'll examine that truth later.

Scripture and science have been consolidating of late in such a way as to prove factually what was written thousands of years ago. Until recently prayer for instance, was considered by science to be a benefit to the emotions and not the body. God's people have always believed otherwise but now it has been proven, as you'll see, to have a direct effect on the body. In using science to validate what we as Christians have innately known, we are now overcoming the doubt that so many have had in accomplishing our goals.

We need to reframe our thoughts, our self-talk and questions we ask ourselves. We need to step out of ourselves and become observers, describing our own selves in a non-judgmental way. We need to be able to recognize quickly when our thoughts turn negative. As you begin the transformation of becoming a non-judgmental observer of yourself, give yourself a break! You may have spent a lifetime being critical of yourself, beating yourself up with self-condemnation. As you'll read here constantly—words have meaning, and they have power. We will put our focus on using words that will allow us to fulfill God's destiny for us. This new way of thinking will take time. Be patient with yourself. When you fall just pick yourself up, dust yourself off and start running again. We serve a God of not only second chances but seventy-fifth chances.

For the next two days, carry a notepad with you and observe what you say to yourself. Write down whatever statements or words come to mind. By committing this mission to yourself you are resolving to make positive changes in your life. After these 48 hours of introspection, you'll be ready to begin a dedicated program of self-improvement, not because 'you should' but because you'll want to.

A November 2014 study in the journal "Behavior Research and Therapy" revealed that people who practiced the Cognitive Reappraisals we spoke of a minute ago, were able to reduce their negative emotions significantly in 16 weeks! In four months, they effectively decreased a lifetime worth of self-worthlessness. Like any habit formed, there are instances where old patterns re-emerge. Take immediate steps to counter these reappearances. I realize there is a bit of comfort in telling the world "Leave me alone and let me be happy being miserable" but backsliding is detrimental to your progress! Be aware and prepare your-self to meet these challenges when this happens.

3,500 years ago, David began to write and talk to God, and he did this in a very personal way. The book of Psalms is a songbook composed of prayers, praise and complaints to God. When you read these verses, it's striking to discover the similar concerns and personal issues that those of us living in the 21st-century share with our Biblical forefathers.

For now, let's focus on those verses that empower and uplift us. For our purposes let's focus on some key words and declarations that impart protection and love to us.

With these affirmations we can directly influence circumstances and conditions that affect our daily life. You'll feel truth in the core of your spirit, empowering you with a kind of unstoppable energy and strength. Although we will never completely silence the running nega-tive inner dialogue that periodically occupies our mind, we can limit it by replacing those expressions with powerful spiritual assertions.

As God's children we know He is always with us and by acknowl-edging Him in our lives we promote ourselves beyond our mortal perceptions to an awareness beyond our natural comprehension to supernatural understanding. For instance, in Psalm 8 David wrote;

"O Lord, our Lord, how excellent is your name in all the earth!" (Psalms 8:9)

How easily could these words be adopted into your vocabulary?

"The Lord is my rock and my fortress and my deliverer; my God, my strength, in whom I will trust; my shield and the horn of my salvation, my stronghold." (Psalms 18:2)

It's impossible to deny the Omnipotence of these words. My for-tress, my strength, my shield, my salvation, my stronghold! These are declarations that are muscular, stout, and powerful. By inserting and invoking His promotion and protection into your life you are reframing your reality in an absolute and purposeful way. This is how you affirm your trust. By invoking God's Holy words in a personal way, you begin an immediate transformation.

As you know there are psalms that complain, lament, and bemoan and although there are times that we need to vent, as David did, our focus should be on unlimited favor and dynamic praise.

Do not take these words of scripture slightly. You are calling upon the Creator of the universe to transmit His protection and guidance on you. With ceaseless repetition you'll begin to observe changes not only in communicating with others but will notice a perceptible change in your character.

Read through the Book of Psalms. Find those words that have meaning to you, don't worry, the Holy Spirit will guide you. By absorbing these words into your very being, you will never be the same. As Paul wrote "If God is for us, who can be against us?"(Romans 8:31). Who indeed?

God's Spirit is with us wherever we are, whatever challenges we face, whatever happiness we experience. Each of us have been through the desert—money all gone, job outsourced, friends disappeared. We've stood in line for handouts, soup kitchens, and food pantries. We've been told "I wish I had it to give to you;" "I would've been there to help you, but I just couldn't get away;" and "This just isn't working, I'm leaving;" and then when we just can't do it anymore, go through anymore with our face in the dirt we notice a pair of feet and look up to realize God is there. He never left, its just that we thought our strength was enough to get us to the goal line. Through tears, through exhaustion, through just plain giving up we reach out just that one more time and find Him, finally understanding that He's never been far from us all along.[6]

Carefully consider your attitude toward taking this next step in your personal evolution. By this I mean don't force yourself to practice using these power words because doing something because "you have to" loses its excitement pretty quickly. Actually, using words that sound great but have little meaning is ineffective as well as a waste of time. By being passionate in calling God's strength and authority you become emotional about the success of your objective. You project images of that success onto your subconscious mind where only feeling and emotions are successful in imprinting those images there.

Once you feel the excitement and start the belief process, you are open to God's favor on you. As you continue to think on achievement, your inner dialogue changes from "I hope" to "I am." Becoming comfortable with these feelings, you notice that they've now become part of you and who you are.

And then be prepared for abundance. Wonders appear and coincidences that you can't explain become unmistakably obvious. Things become calm, problems become manageable, questions generate answers, wisdom replaces confusion.

It's crucial that you set aside alone time. Every engine needs to cool down and have maintenance performed in it for optimal productivity. Our mind needs tranquility to accept new stimulus into it. Some people unwind with a book, some with exercise. Others relax with music while some are content to look out the window at the clouds. Whatever way you find a few moments of inner peace, go to that place, and reside there for a while.

"Wisdom is the principal thing; therefore get wisdom, And in all your getting, get understanding." (Proverbs 4:7) That is a pretty bold statement. Solomon seems to be saying "If you're gonna ask for one you better ask for the other because you're gonna need both."

How does someone get wisdom? How about understanding? One obvious way is through life. A five-year-old doesn't have the good judgement to know how much the value of a dollar is, nor does he understand what the costs of living are. There is a saying "Wisdom comes more from living than from studying" and when you consider that life is with us longer than schooling, we accept that life is the greatest teacher. In order to grow in wisdom and understanding, we need to keep our focus on uprightness and justness. Nelson Mandela once said, "A good head and a good heart are always a formidable combination." Knowledge awaits us to make educated decisions but having a sense of righteousness puts the light on our pursuit of wisdom. In life however, it's not always easy to recognize the noble path. Our interaction with others, who have their own interests and objectives can, and usually do, cause us to put aside a set agenda as to how we want our lives to be. Wisdom is also knowing how to relate to others and how we wish them to identify with us.

People have one over-riding motivation, and it is so subtle. They usually don't take conscious notice of it—that of being personally significant! In order to become agreeable to others, let them talk about themselves. When you show attention toward others you become interesting because you 're actually being exceptional. Most people want to flaunt their attributes and accomplishments, leaving little time for those who they're speaking to, to share theirs. As you go about your day, control the urge to talk about yourself because to the other person it's not how interesting you are, but rather how valuable you could be as an acquaintance or associate to them. This sounds harsh but it is accurate. Consciously and subconsciously, people make an evaluation of how well you'd fit their profile of who they imagine themselves to be. What most people want, what is of greatest importance to them, is their feeling of significance they get from socializing with you. The way to become valued in another person's life is to allow them to be important, to be significant. When you are sincere in showing interest in another's life and their experiences you become inestimable because again, most people are centered on themselves. Think about the qualities you look for in a new acquaintance because those are the general qualities others look for too. It's a feeling of like-mindedness that Paul wrote about to the believers in Rome. (Romans 15:5)

When you allow others to talk about themselves you become distinguished in their eyes. I had a friend, Al, who had this characteristic. He was always genuine in his interest in others. He listened, asked questions and before long the other person seemed to crave his presence. He had that quality that too many ignore – he truly cared about the other persons beliefs and opinions. Al passed away many years ago but he taught me the valuable art of listening with sincerity.

As you listen to others, ask questions, express interest for the essence of what they're talking about, and avoid the temptation to feel "What's in it for me?" Mark Zuckerberg recognized the value people put on their personal significance when he launched Facebook in 2004.

When you ask questions of another person, do so sincerely. Be curious about that person and remember what they've spoken about. Keep in mind that they are allowing you to partake in their lives by showing their personal feelings, insights, opinions, and experiences.

Use the person's name often in your conversation.

Ask people their thoughts on a subject "Jim, let me ask you your opinion...." When we first learn of another, we'll notice such things as their personality, intelligence, manners, temperament and so on. They of course do the same. Proverbs reminds us that to have friends we must be friendly and if you'd like someone to get to know you, talk to them about things that interest them (Proverbs 18:24).

Accept the reality that you have flaws and limitations. Accept that you can't be knowledgeable in everything or an expert on every topic. We all know people who "know" everything about everything. Not only are these people foolish and ill-mannered but they make those listening uncomfortable and embarrassed. You may not be the best athlete, you may not have any type of interest in athletics or whatever topic your discussing, but you do have other virtues. Focus on those instead.

Avoid trying to be someone you're not just to meet with someone else's approval. Talking in a manner you usually don't is belittling to you as well as your own self-esteem. Being (or trying to be I should say) someone you are not is demeaning and should always be avoided. When you speak to others let it be graceful and courteous but never phony.

It would be great if we could surround ourselves with people who are always positive and uplifting. When we're feeling down, we could rely on someone to brighten us up with a cheerful word, sage advice and a spirit of happiness. In the real world however, we encounter many different types of personalities during our lifetime—those who bring out our best, those who do their best to bring us down and every disposition in between! It's up to us who we choose to spend our time with.

Yes, Proverbs advises us that to have friends we must also be friendly, but in another sense, we need to be discerning in our choice of companions. "Like" really does attract 'like' and when our parents told us we're judged by the company we keep they were spot on. In order to fly with the eagles, as the saying goes, you can't stay up with the owls. Or in this case, hang around with the negative buzzards!

Before we leave this chapter, there are a few things I'd like you to consider that will not only elevate your qualities and virtues but increase the significance people attach to you.

The word friend has become a catchphrase of sorts, loosely thrown around by most of us. Plato wrote "the word 'friend' is common, the fact is rare." It was true for Plato 2,400 years ago, and it is true today. I'm not sure that there is a word we use in the English language that conveys both acquaintance and associate. In Italian, the word 'COMPARE' is something like that. In Spanish 'COMPADRE'. Most of the time when we say that someone is a 'friend' we know little more of them than their name and some superficial knowledge of theirs.

I knew Peter for a number of years. Some of the qualities of his I admire is that he is forthright, direct, and honest—brutally honest when need be. In other words, he gives it to you straight, and tells it like it is! A few months before my legal challenges began, I was sitting in his living room and the subject of friends came up. Although born and brought up in England, Peter, when he grew older moved to Australia for ten years. He related how the Aussies view each other. Introducing someone, an Australian will present them as "an acquaintance of mine." The term 'friend' is reserved for that very special person, the one you could call at 2 a.m. and would come to pick you up when your car stalled out. The one who, no matter what others say (or write) stays by your side.

That afternoon in his living room, Peter said "Guy, if anything were to ever happen, you would be lucky to count your 'friends' on one hand." (I had dozens of "friends" at the time.) Even now, years later, I am awestruck as to why, ten weeks before my world was to be shaken— we just happened to talk about friendship. Certainly (at least that I was aware) there was nothing on the horizon that would test those many 'friendships' I thought I had. Thankfully Peter and his wife Jan are still in my life, in every way exemplifying the meaning of friends, but his words and counsel that day so long ago proved to be prophetic.

There is a saying in Iceland "You don't really know your friends from your enemies until the ice breaks." François de La Rochefoucauld, the French essayist, once wrote, "What men have called friendship is merely association, respect for each other's interests, and exchange of good offices, in fact nothing more than a business arrangement from which self-love is always out to draw some profit.... Rare though true love may be true friendship is rarer still."

As you think about who among your friends is a true friend, ask yourself: *"Who am I a true friend to?"* True friendship is more than just about dollars and cents. It's about being available. Someone who is a friend, a true friend, will stand by you in the good times and the bad. You would be right to think that friendship is a serious commitment.

Keep in mind however that you are born with your family, but *you choose* your friends. Be very discerning in choosing who you associate with. Pythagoras wrote "Make him your friend who distinguishes himself by his virtue and take example from his virtuous and useful actions."

Pay close attention to someone's character and honor before you make the commitment of sincere friendship. This sounds like common sense, but we have all allowed people that we know on a superficial basis to get close to us only to realize that we don't share the same values. When that 'still small voice' puts us on guard, we need to pay attention.

Married couples are especially susceptible to the various personalities previously known by one of the partners. As a young couple my wife and I began to keep company with neighbors of hers who had been married for a few years. Although well-meaning and amiable, they were totally disrespectful to one another. What was initially shocking to my wife and I, too—soon became amusing. Before long we were shocked to realize that we were beginning to emulate them! Influences like that can destroy relationships as well as marriages.

Emerson said, "Go often to the house of thy friend, for weeds choke the unused path." What Emerson meant when he penned this verse was don't take friendships lightly. Or for granted.

As I wrote a moment ago, "Who can count on me?" True friendship can never be a one-way street. Whether it's you or the other person who must work too hard to maintain the relationship, it becomes a heavy burden and can no longer feel peaceful. Simply because a person is a friend, a real friend, I caution you to avoid treating that relationship casually or neglectful. Set the standard—that only you can do—of who you consider a friend or a mere acquaintance.

You may be wondering by now "What does friendship, communicating and self-evaluation have to do with achieving goals?" In a word: foundational. You've probably met with some degree of happiness and success from time to time, but when you've reached that point where you've achieved your objective you became complacent. You may have coasted or drifted with the tide and before you knew it old patterns reappeared. It's time to create new patterns. Build a new foundation. The old habit that we had can be replaced with a new way of thinking and instead of being satisfied with the achieved status quo, you embrace the fact that God is changing you. You are redeemed, restored, and wonderfully made.

Your character will always be on display and first impressions are lasting ones. In a study done at Harvard University, researchers Nalini Ambady and Robert Rosenthal found that we make snap judgements *in the first two seconds* of meeting someone! We decide, before we hear them speak, if we like and trust them! What's more, we rarely adjust that conclusion even when we get more information from or about them.

Hand gestures have an impact on how people perceive you. These gestures have an ability to show intention and what your motives are. The way we use our hands and the perceptions of those who we're talking to may be a carry-over from our ancient ancestors. When a stranger approached the cave entrance, what was in their hand told a lot about their intentions. A club or spear usually communicated a hostile intention which sharpened our forebearers power of observation. The way a person stood, their eyes, their hands—what today we call body language—were indications that became inbred in our species. In order to improve your first impression to others, keep your hands visible. Crazy but accurate.

Today in our society the most common greeting is the handshake. It was once thought to be ill mannered for a man to reach for a woman's hand first to shake it. It was for a woman to first reach out, but the increased numbers of women in the workforce seems to have removed that restriction of men reaching to shake a woman's hand.

The result of touching skin-to-skin causes our body to produce the hormone known as Oxytocin. Oxytocin has been discovered to facilitate trust and is actually known as "the connection hormone." Once again science has validated a phrase, in this case "Keep your hands where I can see them!"

How you stand impresses others in how they perceive you. By standing, you allow people to look for indications of confidence—or the lack of it. We all want to be with winners, not losers. Each of us have a natural inclination to associate with those who we think can watch out for us, protect us and who we can count on in times of danger or adversity. "Seest thou a man diligent in his business? He shall stand before Kings" (Proverbs 22:29, KJV)

The dictionary defines "diligent" as "characterized by steady, warmest and energetic effort" three words that convey leadership. And what do we look for, demand even, in our leaders? A winner!

We are innately programmed to interpret non-verbal signals. Our body language broadcasts WINNER—LOSER—VICTOR—FAILURE. When we're feeling pride, we tend to seek notice, we take up space. When we feel defeated, we don't want anyone to see it. We try to hide so to speak, by taking up as little space as possible—head bowed, shoulders slumped, arms tight to the side.

Contrast that to the feeling of success—chest out, head tilted toward the sky. If you want to make a positive impression, walk with purpose—shoulders back, chin, chest, and forehead straight ahead and slightly up. Walk *knowing* that you are God's pride and joy.

"He can't look me in the eye" is a comment generally attributed to mean that person is deceitful and untrustworthy. Eye contact is another non-verbal signal we all notice immediately. When you're speaking to someone your eyes project goodwill (or not). We tend to look more at a person's eyes when we like them, and it's perceived that the eyes are the mirror of the soul. In Proverbs 15:30 its written "The light of the eyes rejoices the heart"and we all subconsciously conclude a person's motives, honesty and sincerity by what we see in their eyes.

When you meet someone for the first time what are some questions you ask? "How are you?" "What brings you here?" "How do you know (our host, our mutual friend, etc.)?" "What do you do?" and so on. Most people ask the same routine (boring) questions. But think about the last time you met someone who actually stands out among the people you've been introduced to. What did they say or talk about that causes you to remember them even now? Or to look forward to seeing them again? Chances are good that they asked questions that were out of the ordinary. Most likely they were questions and topics that were fresh, and they showed a genuine attitude of interest in your responses and views.

The way to become memorable is to cause a chemical pleasure in another!

I know that sounds a bit strange (even sterile and clinical!) but the human body and mind is, physically speaking, composed of sensory neurons that induce chemical reactions in it. The chemical compound released in our brain allowing us to feel pleasure is called Dopamine. Chances are you're familiar with the word, but did you know that Dopamine also helps to root experiences in our long-term memory? This also explains why we tend to remember the good things that have happened in our lives and usually forget the disappointments. We'll discuss how Dopamine and other neurotransmitters as well as various functions of our brain help us to achieve our goals in more detail later but for now let's continue to explore how we can become significant in people's eyes.

First impressions, as we've discussed, are lasting ones but it is actually instinctive (as so much of our lives as human beings are) to react to what we see and hear. This is part of the fight/ flight response that our ancestral predecessors needed in order to handle uncertainty and peril. If you want someone to feel comfortable with you, you'll need to 'win them over' quickly. You need to become interesting. Asking routine, dull, and tiresome questions like "Where are you from?" puts you in the category of "just like everybody else."

What response might you get by asking "So what's the best thing that happened to you today?" What answer would you think you'd receive by asking "What are some things you find inspiring?" Questions like these will cause a person to remember a happy event or a pleasant mental picture (triggering Dopamine) and would quickly associate you with enjoyment. "What project are you working on now?" "Do you have anything new coming up soon" "Where do you get your ideas for your work from?" Asking uplifting and original questions that bring up a feeling of joy causes you to become notable. But do that sincerely. Most people can spot a phony eventually.

Don't be typical. Stand out. Let God's light shine like a beacon from you.

As you proceed to metamorphosis into your true destiny, the life that God has planned for you, you need to be aware that your future is what you decide to make it. Through God's unselfish, unconditional love He gives us free will—as well as free choice. We can choose to allow people to put us down or we can choose to associate with people who lift us up.

You can be the person that everyone avoids because of your negative and sour attitude, or you can be the person who everyone takes pleasure in being with, always uplifting, optimistic and in good spirits.

As you'll discover, you can live in mud, or you can live in clover. You are free to choose any destiny you like. God gives each of us that freedom. Most people never use that right because they don't really understand what "to choose" means. Before you finish this book, you will understand exactly what it means.

3

Just A Closer Walk With Thee

What can we effectively do in our lives to allow the best to happen in it?

How can we live a life of abundance, happiness, and peace? Would the answer be to always think happy thoughts? To pray continually? To avoid sin? How do we reach a point where we accept and carry out God's will without blaming God?

Gottfried Wilhelm Leibniz, the 17th-century philosopher gave the view that every apparent good and bad was part of God's plan. Voltaire however attacked religion in his poem "An Inquiry into the Maxim 'Whatever Is, Is Right.'" Taking the position that faith was nothing more than self-deception. Bad things, he insisted, just happen.

In 1755 Lisbon was the fourth largest city in Europe. On November 1—All Saints Day in the Catholic Church—most of the city's population of 275,000 were at church when an earthquake hit killing 60,000. Two-thirds of the city was leveled.

How could a loving God allow such a catastrophe even as his people were praying to Him? The question abounded as they had before and since, how can God allow tragedy?

Jean Jacques Rousseau observed that instead of blaming God, the death toll in Lisbon was caused by poor building decisions. He put forth that the right approach was for man to realign his relationship with nature. In other words, to adapt design with the knowledge that earthquakes occur and build on that knowledge.

Unfortunately, some people think of prayer as a type of guarantee of fulfillment or a protection against something. Some have a misconception of scripture that if they bombard God with prayer and petition, He'll get exhausted from listening to them and grant their request. When the widow pestered the judge for justice in Luke (18:5), Jesus was illustrating the point that our prayers need to be one of faith, knowing that they will be answered in God's time. Living by faith and not giving up was what allowed the widow to realize her objective.

Effective prayer is having a definite sense of purpose, not using meaningless and empty words. Praying when everything else has failed, most people pray with their emotions filled with fear and doubt. Not having faith - belief actually - that their prayer will be answered affirmatively, what they don't want to see happen, does. It can't be any other way. Praying negative brings negative. Praying definite, positive prayers produces definite, positive results.

Having a definite goal, and faith in the realization of that goal or purpose, allows God to transmute that dominant desire and feeling into your life. Screaming, shouting, wailing in Biblical terms, will not bring about the desired result. The only thing it brings is attention.

Jesus is usually portrayed as a pretty serious guy. The many paintings and icons that we notice always look somber. We have a tendency to forget that Jesus was a man, a human being with feelings and emotions, who interacted with brothers and sisters (imagine that household— "You never holler at Jesus, you think He's perfect!") and a mother and father. He laughed, He played, He had fun and lived a life.

Jesus had little respect for hypocrites and phonies as we know (Matthew 23: 1-30). If we were to use 21st century language for Jesus' observation of those who liked to be noticed maybe it would sound like this "You see those guys there? The ones with their arms in the air praying? Don't be like those fools. They are as phony as a three-dollar bill. They only want everyone to think that they're better than them because they pray. They need to be seen. They've done that, so they got what they wanted."

God knows what's in our heart. Thankfully. No matter what others say or think of us, or believe our motives are, God knows. Keeping a constant dialogue with Him, even for brief moments throughout the day results in a connection that can only be called Divine.

The author Richard Rohr in his book 'The Naked Now' makes an outstanding observation regarding prayer, repetition and our relation-ship with God. Allow me to paraphrase:

"Then Moses said to God, "Indeed when I come to the children of Israel and say to them, "The God of your fathers has sent Me to you" and they say to me 'What is His name?' What shall I say to them?" and God said to Moses, "I AM who I AM." And He said, "Thus you shall say to the children of Israel, I AM has sent me to you" Moreover God said to Moses "Thus you shall say to the children of Israel: 'The Lord God of your fathers, the God of Abraham, the God of Israel and the God of Jacob, has sent me to you.' This is my name forever, and this is My memorial to all generations!" (Exodus 3:13-15)

Yahweh is derived from the Hebrew word for I AM, the Jewish revelation of the name of God. Yahweh, to those who speak Hebrew is known in the sacred Tetragrammaton YHVH (YOD, HE, VAU and HE). For Jews, it was considered an unspeakable word. When speaking or writing they used the word ELOHIM or ADONAI. The reason we see LORD and GOD in our Bibles is due to the Jewish tradition whereby the name YAHWEH could not and should not be spoken for fear that His name be blasphemed. God allowed His divine identity to be kept mysterious and unavailable to the human mind.When Moses, barefoot and hiding his face asked for His name, he received the phrase that translates to "I AM WHO AM.... This is My Name forever, and this is My memorial to all generations" That we now know the word 'GOD' was unspeakable is beyond doubt. However, we also know that this goes much deeper: The word was not uttered from man's lips—But *breathed*! The correct pronunciation of the word, many are convinced, is the attempt to replicate and imitate the exact sound of inhalation and exhalation. What we—the entire human family—do every moment of our lives is speak the name of God. It is the first word—and the last— that we utter in our lives."

Think on the amazing implication of Rohr's words above. Knowing that in every moment of our lives, we share a connection with every living thing—breath. Unseen but undeniable. Rohr also observed that like Jesus in the desert, our minds need to be still, at peace and in silence.

Like a never-ending stream, our minds chatter constantly, and it takes firm dedication and commitment, as well as time, to cut it back or at least transform, the negative expressions into empowering thoughts and words.

Going inward, in silence and in prayer can't help but bring us into a closer relationship with God. This is called contemplation by Christians, meditation, sitting or practicing by Buddhists, Prayer of the Heart by Hesychastic Orthodoxy, Ecstasy by Sufi Islam, Living from the Divine Spark within by Hasidic Jews, Non-dual knowing—or just simply breathing by Vedantic Hinduism, and Communion with nature itself or the Great Spirit through dance rituals by Native Americans.

In the last twenty years scientific research has clinically confirmed the effectiveness of prayer. Dr. Mitchell Krucoff, a cardiologist at Duke University selected 150 heart patients at random for a pilot research project. After dividing the patients into five groups, he selected one of them to receive standard cardiac care. Three others received their treatments from a bedside therapist using imagery stress—relaxation and touch therapy. The last group received distant "off-site intercessory prayer."

Improvement of over 50% was observed by the patients who received prayer therapy! "There may be a benefit to these therapies" said Dr. Krucoff. He since has expanded the study to include fifteen hundred patients.

William Harris PhD at St. Luke's Hospital in Kansas City also found positive results from a study in intercessory or distant prayer. Dr. Harris, a cardiac researcher conducted the study with one thousand heart patients with serious prior cardiac conditions. Randomly assigning patients into two groups, group one received daily prayer for two weeks. Group two did not receive prayer. *Those cardiac patients who were prayed for fared 11% better than those who did not receive prayer!* What made this study impressive was the fact that the group prayed for had *no knowledge* they were being prayed for! In 1988 a similar study was performed at San Francisco General Hospital. Those patients who received prayer were able to leave the hospital sooner.

Duke University's Dr. Harold Koenig, associate professor of medicine and psychiatry, stated that some twelve hundred studies on the effects of prayer and health were conducted at universities such as Duke, Dartmouth, and Yale. In his book 'Handbook of Religion and Health' he discussed some of the results of these studies. For instance it was discovered that hospitalized people who attended church regularly had an average stay three times shorter than those who were not regular church goers. Cardiac patients who participated in religion were 14% more likely to survive after surgery than those who did not. Elderly church attendees were 50% less likely to suffer strokes than those who don't attend church. In Israel it was found that devout practitioners were 40% less likely to die from cardiovascular disease and cancer than those who were not religious.

Dr. Koenig was also quoted in USA Today as observing, "Healthy senior citizens who said they rarely or never prayed ran about a 50% greater risk of dying from their cardiac condition!"

Effective prayer works.

But what is "effective prayer?" How do we separate what we want and pray for, receive it, then call it effective and God's will?

Dr. Norman Vincent Peale said "If you expect the worst, you get the worst. And if you expect the best, you will get the best."

When we pray there is a feeling, a hunch, an intensity almost of that which we're praying about. If we were praying for the misfortune of someone, hoping they break their leg let's say, we would 'feel' that is wrong, yet praying for someone's recovery would 'feel' right. So, much of what we pray for, and about, has much to do with what we know—or are led to believe—about a particular person or thing. But how do you know really? To be in that space of knowing requires being connected.

Being "connected" is to have a deep relationship with God. In Paul's letter to the church in Thessalonica, he wrote "Pray without ceasing" (1 Thessalonians 5:17). Paul wasn't advising those Christians in Northern Greece to constantly ask for things. He was talking about having a continual dialogue with God. A relationship.

We all experience that relative or acquaintance who only calls when they need or want something from us. It's the only time we hear from them. There is no bond there, no relationship. Realistically that person doubts we'll help them anyway, but being desperate, they give it a try none the less. We know where their heart is (and they know we know) so they don't hold much hope of our help. Their own past actions (toward us) and their inner feeling of rejection gives them what they don't want—being rejected.

In order to pray effectively, we need to 1.) Have a strong relationship with God. 2.) We need to have the wisdom and the reverence to discern His guidance and 3.) Belief. Knowing that what we have chosen, in wisdom, will manifest in our life. This kind of connection can only come about through unceasing prayer.

To perform this type of constant connection you may have to re-adjust your lifestyle, rethink your priorities and commit to foundational change. This could involve reexamining your current relationships, letting go of past hurts and slights, removing any bitterness from your life, and living in thankfulness.

Don't wait until you overcome profanity, remove bad influences, or conquer bad habits—you may never get started! Pray for strength to surmount them. We serve a loving God who sees what's in our hearts. It is what's in that heart that God will work with. As you initiate any changes, remember it's not God who needs to be convinced of your intentions—it's you! The most absolute and most liberating feeling you'll ever experience is knowing that no matter what happens in this world, only you and God know what is in your thoughts and your mind.

If you are serious about your journey, you'll overcome the need for approval, or fear of disapproval, from others. When you come to that place, you will know you are ready and prepared to move beyond what once was into what will be.

To begin an effective prayer life, especially if you've never had one, you'll need to "get in the zone" as it were, building a foundation of sacred words, phrases, and affirmations. This can easily be done through a devotion known as "The Jesus Prayer."

The Jesus Prayer is used in the Eastern Orthodox Church and is a powerful invocation that is short and concise— *"Lord Jesus, have mercy on me."*

In the monasteries on Mt. Athos, Greece, the priests can be found exclaiming this prayer on a continual basis as they go about their daily tasks. [2]

Prayer is about us. Praying is something we do to elevate our awareness to something so much more magnificent than us. I once read that prayer is where we ask God, meditation is where we hear God. The greatest most profound understanding is to comprehend that we are part of the Divine and there is absolutely nothing – nothing - that can or will ever take that away. The false assumption that we are separate from God is the basis of every anguish, torment, anxiety, and misery we suffer. Once we accept that nothing can separate us from Him our lives transform.

Growing up we learn various prayers, the prayer Jesus taught us, known as the Lord's Prayer being probably the first. Every word, every sentence is sublimely profound.

In order for us to move into a relationship with other human beings, we rely on personalized conversation. When we are bonding with another, we are natural, unassuming and candid with no walls or barriers in our speech. Moving beyond what's known as "rote" prayer—a mechanical, unfeeling repetition of words—effective praying consists of conversations with God in our minds. This is the type of conversation you'd have with your closest friend.

As you mindfully talk to Him, you allow the Holy Spirit to permeate your consciousness. Being able to discern the difference between chatter and wisdom takes time—but it will happen if you're faithful to the pursuit. As in weightlifting where you're training your muscles, here you are training your thought process and receptivity. You become still, silent and alert to what you're feeling. You pay attention to the words and maybe images that go through your spirit. You focus on prompts or cues as the voice of God. This practice has been written about in Tanya Luhrmann's book 'When God Talks Back.'

After four years of studying the prayer life of various believers, Luhrmann observed "I do think that if God does speak to someone, God speaks through the human mind."

In 2007 Luhrmann, wanting to better understand how the mind is impacted by spiritual practice, divided Christian volunteers into two groups. The first group listened to lectures on the Gospels for 30 minutes a day on their I-PODS. The second group participated in a more interactive, emotion-filled, imagination - rich way. The recordings given the second group invited them to see, hear, and touch God in their mind's eye and to also carry on a dialogue with Jesus. "I found that after a month of prayer practice, people reported more vivid mental imagery than those who listened to the lectures" Luhrmann wrote.

She went on to say, "They used mental imagery more readily and had somewhat better perceptual attention, and they reported more unusual sensory experience. In short, they attended to their inner experience more seriously, and that altered how real that experience became for them."

Through Luhrmann's study as well as countless others, we now know the massive impact our mind—consciously and subconsciously—has on our prayer life and the impact of our imagination. It is just no longer possible to dismiss the role that faith and belief have on our lives, and the important part our imagination plays in accomplishing our wishes, dreams and goals. I'd like to share an illustration of the power of imagination that I read many, many years ago. Perhaps you're familiar with this illustration but it is worth revisiting.

If I were to lay a 24-inch-wide plank on the floor (and for argument's sake, let's say it's twenty feet long) and I were to ask you to walk end to end without falling off could you do it? After all a two-feet wide plank is pretty big. Chances are good you could do so without a problem. Actually, it would not only be uneventful but boring.

Now, after you've easily strolled across that board, I place that same piece of wood between two fifty story buildings, roughly 600 feet off the ground, and ask you to walk across it. Could you?

Most people would immediately imagine falling off, plunging down into the abyss. The dilemma is in the knowledge that you just walked on that same piece of wood as it lay on the ground, however you visualize—imagine—falling! There is an irrefutable lesson here. When your desire and your imagination are in conflict your imagination most always prevails.

Let's stay with this thought for a minute. Every bridge you've ever driven across has guardrails. Certainly, an occasional car is prevented from plunging over the side by them, but could we agree that that type of accident is rare?

What if the bridge you travelled on every day suddenly was without those guardrails? IF you or any of your fellow-commuters had the "courage" to cross how fast would you go? 2 miles per hour? 5 maybe, at the most? Why? Why would you, who has crossed that bridge at 55 MPH dozens of times, with never a problem, suddenly become full of anxiety? Because your imagination of pitching over the side would outway your desire to cross over the bridge. Glance at the railings the next time you cross a bridge, and you'll understand what I'm saying!

How we talk to ourselves, what we say, the core beliefs we hold to be true and the outlook we visualize for ourselves shapes who we are and what shows up in our lives. If this is true—and it has been verified in study after study—doesn't it make sense to maintain an effective prayer life? To, as Paul said, pray without ceasing?

David spoke to God in a most personal way as we learn in Psalms. Written as songs, the Psalms are prayers, praise and complaints but all of them centered to God directly. But looking more deeply, the Book of Psalms was not only petitions but Declarations!

According to the dictionary, a declaration is "to make known explicitly, announce, to state emphatically, affirms." Listen to what probably is the most well-known of the Psalms – 23:

'The Lord is my shepherd; I shall not want. He makes me to lie down in green pastures; He leads me beside the still waters. He restores my soul; He leads me in the paths of righteousness for His name's sake. Yea, though

I walk through the valley of the shadow of death, I will fear no evil, for you are with me; Your rod and Your staff they comfort me. You prepare a table before me in the presence of my enemies; You anoint my head with oil; My cup runs over. Surely goodness and mercy shall follow me all the days of my life; and I will dwell in the house of the Lord forever.'

There are no words like hope or might or maybe. There are no phrases like "If only You would" or "I wish that He would allow me..." These are instead, bold statements affirming, while also attesting to, God's favor. But further, think about who is writing this praise-verse. A man. One who fell down many times yet never gave up or gave in to be anything but the apple of God's eye.

Jesus always considered prayer to be important and significant. Prayer to Him was not just words spoken over and over without meaning. Prayer to Jesus was His whole life. He made clear to those who heard His words that prayer was communion with God. It was through prayer as a source of power that He was able to perform miracles. Casting out demons, healing the sick and raising the dead were all based on the importance of prayer in Jesus' life.

For us, prayer allows us to deal with everyday life. It gives us the strength to deal with disappointments, the earnestness to make requests and the humility to give thanks. Prayer, Jesus showed, was a way for us to avoid temptations and have the fortitude to do so at any given moment.

Jesus confronted sin for the reason that it put distance between God and us. It puts distance between each other. *Our true nature* as God's children could only be made up of love and Jesus knew that this would put a feeling of aloofness in our relationship with God. Prayer then becomes a way to re-energize ourselves to become vessels of God's grace.

There are times in our lives that are unbearable, where we just cannot endure another loss, misfortune, rejection, or sorrow. When (it seems) we are alone in a battle against Satan and his dark forces, we must set aside a period of intense supplication.

Effective prayer is an attitude *and* a commitment. It is also an action. You must ask and you must *act*.

In the gospel of Mark, Jesus was approached by a man, a father broken-hearted and exhausted who for years watched his son endure agony and torment. Jesus asks the man "How long has he been like this?" "From childhood" he answers. The father continues "But if you can do anything take pity on us and help us."

What Jesus says in response could almost be amusing if not for the seriousness of the situation. I say this because you can almost visualize in your mind's eye Jesus taking a step back, looking at the boy's father when He says, *"If you can?"* I was tempted to put two question marks followed by two exclamation points here! But once again Jesus confirms the power of the mind when He says, "Everything is possible for Him who believes." (Mark 9:22-24)

After the boy, now cleansed and his father leave, Jesus and the apostles have time to talk about what has just happened. "Why aren't we able to cast out demons?" at which Jesus answers "You can only do something like this through prayer and fasting." (Mark 9:27-29, KJV, NKJV)

Fasting is a sacrifice that we can make to enlighten us and done with sincerity brings us closer to God. Throughout the Bible fasting is mentioned regularly. Joel wrote that genuine fasting is of great consequence. (Joel 1:14) Daniel used prayer and fasting as he vicariously took on the sins of his people. (Daniel 9:3-17) Not only was he given a vision of seeing a rebuilt Jerusalem, but Daniel was given the perception that the Messiah would be forthcoming, and all of this was revealed to him by the angel Gabriel. (Daniel 9:24-27)

When Ezra and his followers needed direction, and protection against predators and marauders he turned to God in prayer and fasting knowing He would answer their prayers. (Ezra 9:21-22)

Jesus used the power of fasting combined with prayer. After His own immersion along the banks of the River Jordan He retreated to the wilderness to allow His mind to divinely connect with God. For 40 days Jesus not only came into close communion with God but was tempted by Satan. Jesus knew the supernatural strength that abstaining from food for a period of time would have and he knew that that strength would allow Him to outwit the devil.

Jesus also knew the effect the discipline of fasting could have on others—both to those fasting and the observers.

Jesus and the authorities of Palestine and Judea were continually at odds because of His habit of keeping company with "the wrong people." These were the despised, the ceremonially unclean and the outcasts. He consorted with the collectors, the sinners (judging others is not a 21st century phenomenon) and the unwanted. Most of the time Jesus' anger focused on the hypocritical and the prideful. It was no effort to find the posers on the street corners with their sad and dirty faces to broadcast they were fasting. (Matthew 6:16) The self-righteous annoyed Jesus (a case in point today) which was another reason the powerful hated Him. Jesus gravitated to the broken because it was they - like us - who need His medicine the most.

A regular program of prayer and fasting holds tremendous spiritual power as well as physical benefits. (Isaiah 58:6)

Gaining control of our lives—body, mind and spirit—allows us to draw closer to our Creator. Periodic fasting combined with sincere prayer breaks through barriers and into new beginnings with God. It is knowing what we want, not focusing on what we don't want which makes our petitions to God effective. Pray humbly but as you do, pray for guidance that what you want in your life aligns with God's purpose and will for your life. As you read further, you'll discover ways in which to discern both.

4 |

Effective Petitioning

There are three forms of desire. The first is that which turns into determination—strong determination—we mean to have it and we act accordingly to do so. We pray for guidance and the desire is fulfilled. We performed the necessary actions to accomplish what we needed or wanted to do.

The second type of desire is that which we can't do much about. We just 'hope' it happens. We wait. We are totally reliant on forces outside of ourselves, whether its circumstances or on others for the desire to come about.

The third type of desire is the one where we become totally dependent on the outcome. We attach great significance to the object of our desire and feel if we get or achieve that which we want "everything will be okay." In this type of desire where we attach great consequence our self-talk sounds something like this: "If I'm able to achieve this, my life will be so much better." "If I can't get this, I'm ruined." "Once I do this, I'll show everybody how wrong they were about me." And so it goes with our inner chatter.

Unfortunately, most people pray when they find themselves in this third stage. Totally dependent on the outcome, they are stuck in a quicksand that will do nothing but swallow them up as they struggle to get what they want. The treacherousness of being in this state of mind is the more they struggle the more hopeless their plight becomes. This is where what we don't want, we end up getting! "I want to just relax here at home today undisturbed" and then out of town relatives surprise you with a visit. Probably all day since you wanted the day to unwind.

When we pray for guidance, for wisdom on the object of our desire or the subject we need help with, we become calmer because we are allowing and not depending.

When we look up the definition of dependence in the dictionary, we find it to mean to be influenced or subject to something. It is an emotion, which is a state of feeling. You know by now that what we feel we attract.

Intention on the other hand is where you need a quart of milk and go to the corner store and get it.

The more you "hope" for something the more dependent you become on getting it and when you make something so important it will probably never be received or will be taken away. You pray, you fast, you tithe, you try to live righteously and do everything you can to set up the conditions for a favorable outcome and it just doesn't happen! God needs an open, faith filled, uncluttered mind to work with. If your desire has become obsessive, transformed into dependance or into something akin to hysterically striving to obtain something no matter the cost, you have doubt and fear it will not be fulfilled.

When you are at that point you are emanating fear-based energy and trying to convince yourself the opposite is true. Your prayer must be of letting go and letting God. It's not easy to do and it takes a great amount of faith and trust to release the death-grip on the object of your desire. It's just now where you need to recall Jesus' reassuring words "Do you believe I am able to do this?"

By acknowledging God's authority, you will reduce the significance of the objective, you will eliminate dependance on it thereby reducing the emotion of fear and doubt. You will have allowed God's perfect solution to take place. Handle this as you would go to that corner store for milk—intend but don't become dependent.

"Let go and let God" is not a cute little catch phrase just to use when things get difficult. It is acknowledging His guidance on our lives. When we form a goal of some sort, we form an opinion as to how to go about achieving it. In and of itself forming a well-thought-out plan is relevant. After all you wouldn't drive from Boston to Phoenix by leaving it to chance. And many of our goals are not backed by dependance so no fear is attached to not achieving them. But when something holds great significance to us, we want to decide exactly how we'll reach or achieve it. Don't confuse preparation with being obstinate. When we stubbornly refuse to consider another course, not allowing for mistakes, changes, or corrections we are letting our Ego get in the way. Being prepared is allowing for some deviations or modifications but still knowing where you're headed. "Luck favors the prepared mind" is a saying you've probably heard and while the tenor of the phrase is valid the dependance on just luck is short-sighted.

When we rely on ourselves to know the best way to achieve something we are edging God out of the equation. The author Wayne Dyer spoke about this human tendency of relying on our Ego-Edging God Out. Possible but not preferable.

In prayer, we humble ourselves to Him. We overcome vanity and we put our trust and confidence in God. When we create goals for ourselves that are significant, we create the image of how to go about achieving them. When we ask God to help us, guide us and strengthen us, we are calling upon the omnipotence of the creator of the universe to control and manage the course of events and the path we should take. The human challenge is to avoid thinking we can do better.

When the scenario that we had in our mind begins to change we start to believe that God must have made a mistake, or that He decided not to help us. "This is not going to happen" we think, and our doubt impedes God's ability to help us. As human beings we cannot predict God, nor can we outthink Him. God knows the perfect way for a thing to be done. By faith it is accomplished.

Faith.

The word constantly appears in our spiritual quest and in virtually every motivational manuscript. As defined in the dictionary faith is "firm belief in something for which there is no proof."

In ages past humankind devised ways to prompt and motivate people's minds to believe whatever dogma or creed the king, elders or tribe espoused. Truth however, always prevails.

The Romans were not emotionally or mentally prepared to accept that a Messiah had been born in their midst. When any one group or person resisted their doctrine, they were invariably eliminated whether as a group massacre or an individual crucifixion. Similarly, the Jewish elders were predisposed to reject that born among them was the Son of God. But when an idea, dream or message is originated divinely it will not be stopped. Jesus, despite the Romans, the Tetrarchs, the Sanhedrin's, or the Pharisees was able to use the faith of believers to perform works that defied logic.

Faith is the basic foundation of belief. Without faith life stagnates and becomes nil. We see that Jesus, who effected unimaginable deeds throughout Judea was unable to do so in Nazareth. Why?

Jesus Himself had the answer—unbelief.

I recall a humorous anecdote I heard years ago that lends itself to this point: Approaching Jesus, a leper said, "Lord please heal me." For a moment I want you to imagine if Jesus responded in this way: "You know, we're not having much success in curing leprosy right now." Just think of the results of that comment! The doubt, the fear, the despair that comment would have caused. Do you think the leper would have experienced a healing?

Time and again Jesus pronounced, "Your faith has made you well" "According to your faith let it be to you" "Your faith has saved you" I can't recall Jesus ever saying, "Well, let's give it a try."

Although we know the importance of faith, we are all prone to doubt. It takes extraordinary mental fiber in order to overcome fear. Why is this?

Why do these feelings of doubt and fear permeate our reasoning and fill our souls with confusion?

150,000 years of trying to survive in a hostile world has subtly evolved within us which now allows us the ability to take for granted our reactions to the outside world. The feeling of fear allowed our early human ancestors to live another day.

The Limbic System is where we find our fight or flight response. Within a millisecond our prehistoric ancestors decided whether to run from a predator or stand up and challenge it. The Amygdala (which lies deep within the brain, about eye level) is where our body's alarm system is found. Any fearful scenario or 'scary' noise will activate the neurons in the Amygdala. It has even been said that "screeching sounds"—think someone running their fingernails across a chalkboard—can reawaken a "genetic memory" of an ancient predator in our brain.

Fear is a very real emotion, and it takes tremendous inner strength to overcome that which is unknown. We should not feel guilty for this deep-rooted anxiety but instead accept that these emotions were placed into our chromosomes in order to survive by the Hand of God. Through Him we find the strength to not only deal with fear but accept belief and act on it.

Remember that final exam in High School? You know, the one you had no idea how you could pass? As you read and re-read the meager and scattered notes you could lay your hands on, the words "Please dear

God—let me pass!" may have crossed your mind. Unfortunately, "angel dust" did not miraculously appear as the correct answers on the exam. Filled with fear and doubt (because you never took action to learn) your worst expectations came true! Preparation, whether its an exam or anything worthwhile begins at the moment you make that object a goal in your life.

The importance of faith is beyond dispute but as James pointed out, faith alone is not enough. "Thus also faith by itself, if it does not have works, is dead." (James 2:17). There are certain, definite actions that we need to perform in order to realize what it is that we want to materialize in our lives. As I wrote earlier, there is no need to elbow your way through the crowd, pushing and shoving in order to enjoy your day in the sun. Focusing on what you aim to achieve is certainly a start, but allowing His guidance which is perfection, to overtake our Ego and emotions is necessary.

Get quiet for a few minutes. Think about what it is you are trying to bring about. You may feel a deep and profound sense of contentment—pay attention to that feeling. But if the feeling is one of discomfort or you have an uneasiness about the course of action you've chosen, or even about the objective *listen to that*. You give this all to God. Pay close attention to what you're sensing. If you find yourself trying to reason with yourself, attempting to talk yourself into going forward with something, or find yourself arguing your case to your inner self, you can be sure that you have received your answer.

"If you pray don't worry, but if you worry don't pray" as the saying goes. That sounds like another cutesy cliché but there is truth there, nonetheless. Don't dismiss this theory out of hand. I recall reading an interview with the actor Mel Gibson some years ago and something he said in that conversation has stuck with me since: "To worry is a sin against God. It means you don't trust Him." In 13 words Gibson summarized what it means to trust in God.

One of the most insidious propensities that most of us suffer with is guilt. Harboring the idea that "I am bad and should be punished" not only exposes the fear we harbor internally but a sense of self- loathing and unworthiness. Effective prayer is not easily accomplished when we're in this state of mind. What one finds in this manner of thinking, this feeling of guilt, is being prone to bring on numerous misfortunes.

Guilt brings destruction to anyone who internalizes the feeling. People begin to feel undeserving, depressed and if left unchecked, un-motivated. Satan is at home in the guilt-ridden mind. He reminds us—if we allow him—that we have no right to strive for anything better than what we now are in the middle of or have caused to happen. Additionally, you need to beware of manipulators.

Manipulators are those people who are adept at pulling the strings of others. These people can somehow snare the weak and the vulner-able—which is another reason why you need to be mindful of the impression your posture and body language conveys, as we discussed in the previous chapter.

These schemers try to exert a feeling of guilt over others by put-downs and intimidation. They loudly proclaim their supposed self-worth and usually can be found trying to dominate a conversation by talking over the other person. They are not above crying or using that age-old practice of giving someone "the silent treatment" if all else fails. They are people who are (they believe) 'always right' and have a need to lecture. Not only must you distance yourself from such a person but also need to refuse their attempts at making you feel guilty. You must accept that you owe no-one anything.

As a child of God, you are forgiven. When you accepted Jesus Christ as your Lord and Savior you were washed by His blood on the cross. *You are loved!*

If you are the type of person who is prone to justifying yourself (about anything) you need to stop doing that. "I know I just asked you this but…" "I know you just covered this but…" "I hope you don't get upset that I'm asking this again but…" Stop it! Avoid victimizing yourself at all costs! When you compare yourself to others like this you are allowing them to be superior to you and you are giving them the right to do so! When you free yourself of feeling guilty no-one will self-assert themselves at your expense. Feeling guilty while praying negates effective prayer. And why not? You (think) you don't deserve anything anyway!

Feeling guilty, you tell the world "I'll do what you tell me because I'm worthless anyway." When you live in guilt you agree to be punished, you're fearful, full of doubt and everyone (in your mind) has the right to abuse you in some way.

We all make mistakes. We all, each of us, fall short of the glory of God (Romans 3:23). If you've wronged another—whether yesterday or 25 years ago—ask for forgiveness. Admitting mistakes, taking responsibility, confession, praying for one's sins—all of this helps to heal. Ask for forgiveness only once. No groveling. Genuine remorse. *But ask only once and never more.* The results of removing the feeling of guilt were eloquently put into words by the Russian writer Anton Chekhov: "Drop by drop I am squeezing the slave out of me."

Don't confuse asking for forgiveness with extending forgiveness. Although asking someone to accept your apology only once does not absolve or excuse you from extending forgiveness to another, no matter how much pain, grief and hurt they caused you. Jesus, when asked how many times we should forgive said "seven times seventy." 490 opportunities to lay up treasures in heaven.

To be effective, prayer must be done with a clean heart. Retaining bitterness toward others, wishing misfortune on someone, feeling guilty or lacking gratitude will keep boundaries and walls between you and God. An optimistic outlook, having a positive attitude, maintaining empowering thoughts coupled with prayer, allows God to work His favor in your life.

St. Francis of Assisi wrote "Lord, make me an instrument of your peace!" As essential as putting our intentions before God are, you should always recognize to speak blessings over others. With your words you have the ability to elevate others into their destiny.

Too many of us spend more time complaining and not enough complimenting. How many relationships could go from good to great if instead of finding something wrong, we were to point out something outstanding?

Although there can be a certain comfort in verbally railing against what we perceive to be wrong or unjust, the turbulence it causes within our physical body is detrimental to our health. Robert Sapolsky, professor of neurology at Stanford had this to say about complaining and anxiety, "If you turn on the stress response chronically for purely psychological reasons you increase your risk of adult-onset diabetes and high-blood pressure."

Who among us enjoys a constant stream of negative comments from someone? Who can take pleasures in hearing about every fault, perceived or just? What we say and how we project our opinions has a definite impact on those we associate with.

In 2009 Congressman Emanuel Cleaver of Missouri introduced H. CON. RES. 155 designating the day before Thanksgiving as "Complaint Free Wednesday." It was designed to encourage "each person in the United States to remember that having a positive life begins with having a positive attitude." (Congress shot it down!)

Most of us come into contact with dozens of people daily. The clerk at the store, the nurse at the hospital, the flight attendant, the mechanic, the salesperson and of course our co-workers. Some we pass by for a moment and others are with us for a lifetime, but no-one comes into our lives by accident. Be free with your compliments. When the thought comes up, keep in mind that God placed it there.

Raising someone up with blessings and compliments has a joyous effect on them. Norihro Sadato of the National Institute for Physiological Sciences in Japan did research in 2012, on the effect praise has on us and said, "To the brain, receiving a compliment is as much a social reward as being rewarded with money."

In 2015 Harvard Business School also observed that commending others led people to have "positive changes in their physiology, creative problem solving, performance under pressure and social relationships."

Encourage someone with your words "Thanks for helping me. This store always has the most helpful people" When someone has shown kindness, went out of their way for you, tell them. If it's on behalf of their employer, let the employer know.

Your words of encouragement can heal a hurting heart without knowing it. Satan has been busy telling people they're failures, they'll never be good enough, no one wants them, they're worthless. Your words of promotion and uplifting can inspire someone the rest of their day. The more negativity that is in the world, the greater the need to talk blessings over one another.

Sincerely spoken words have a positive, lasting impact on people. Not only can you turn a person's day around, but you can also change a life. Mark Twain once wrote, "I can live on a good compliment two weeks with nothing else to eat."

Showing gratitude for what others do for us doesn't only brighten their day but glorifies God. As we'll learn in the next chapter being grateful for what others have done for us, for what we ignorantly take for granted and even for the hardships and challenges that sometimes appear in our lives is a door that God has opened into a life of opportunities and blessings for us all.

5 ▌

The Power of Gratitude

Fortunately, each of our thoughts do not materialize in our lives.

The Conscious Mind of a human being is capable of processing hundreds of thoughts a second. The Subconscious Mind will not create all of those thoughts into physical reality because, as these thoughts rush past, little or no feeling is being projected on the clean state of the subconscious.

We accept that our bodies were brought into being by our Creator and part of that creation included the Subconscious Mind.

The subconscious is that place where we *feel* what is most meaningful in our lives. Choice, as it were, is not part of the subconscious. That duty is left to the conscious mind where decisions on multiple topics and a multitude of stimuli are sorted through by importance *and by emotion*. The more emotional the topic, task or decision, the more importance is conveyed to the subconscious. This is why that which you fear or don't want in your life usually appears.

As I began my career in finance at the age of 20, I was introduced to the book "Think and Grow Rich" by Napoleon Hill.

If you've read the book, you'll recall that Hill does not use the word "God" but instead "Infinite Intelligence." Personally, that designation bothered me for some reason. It wasn't until years later that I could understand that He *is* infinitely intelligence and that His name is truly one that cannot be spoken. Spoken with humbleness, reverence and honor is what is significant. The acknowledgement that all that we are, all that we do, and all that we will ever become begins with the acceptance that He is present in our lives. With a grateful heart, the life that God has planned for us is made possible.

Consciously accepting an idea, theory or notion should be based on a foundation of truth and virtue. To be based on something less usually causes grief or disappointment of some sort. When you make it a point to say 'thank you' or express gratitude you are transmitting positive energy. Being grateful for what you have now prepares your spirit to receive greater blessings in the future. It is just not possible to overstate the importance of maintaining a grateful heart. What you consider the least in your life, an extra blanket let's say, can (and should be) be a source of joy and gratitude.

Dissatisfaction combined with resentment are incompatible with attracting God's favor. "I hate this job. The people are petty and mean and my boss has no idea what he's doing." Not only is a promotion unlikely but you will probably be unemployed soon.

Not being satisfied is not the same as being ungrateful. You may have higher goals in your career but still show gratitude for the chance to work. Too many people refuse to take responsibility for the choices they make and one that is very common at the workplace is associating with the complainers and negative thinkers. In an effort to "fit in" (especially if your newly hired) people will listen to these pessimists and suddenly a few weeks go by. To these people, your silence (if you've not already joined the chorus) is taken for agreement. God expects you to do your best wherever you are. Listening, or worse, participating in cynical and discouraging conversations can never bring out the best in you. If you find yourself in this predicament this is a call to action to change your attitude. Now.

Paul wrote in Ephesians 5:20, "Giving thanks always for *All Things* to God the Father" and is inspiring when you realize he was writing that in prison! You'll notice Paul didn't write "some things" or "most things" but *ALL THINGS*!

In our world today, especially in Western society, there seems to be a noticeable lack of gratitude unfortunately. We seem to have taken so much for granted—fresh water, unsurpassed health care, abundant food and a standard of living previous generations could not have imagined. We travel across oceans in hours as opposed to months. We ask a computer for directions, and we can bring up any specialized knowledge the world has ever known in literally the palm of our hand.

Might it be possible that these blessings have bred complacency and a general lack of gratitude on our part? When was the last time that when you sat down in front of your Big Screen T.V. and said, "Thank you Father for this blessing."?

Adversity can bring about two very powerful impulses in people. They may admit they're defeated and crumble like a dried leaf or they rise to the challenge and move forward with confidence and purpose. Winston Churchill comes to mind.

When, in 1940, Europe was under the domination of Hitler's armies, and those armies who thus far had never known defeat, poised twenty-one miles from England's shores, one man—Winston Churchill—rose up in courage and fortitude;

"We shall defend our island, whatever the cost may be, we shall fight on the beaches, we shall fight on the landing grounds, we shall fight in the fields and in the streets, we shall never surrender."3

In life we must go through the tragedy to get to the triumph. To get to the promised land we must go through the wilderness, and you'll need to go through the fight to get to the victory. When you can't go on anymore, when your own strength is exhausted you go to God's strength. Let's go back in time, now over 400 years ago, to a story you've heard many times. But let's look at this story beyond the pies and parades.........

As the Bible became more accessible through the printed word, it became apparent that people were beginning to think about scripture for themselves. There were men who, at that time, began to oppose the religious policy of the reigning monarchy in England and were known as "Puritans"—they wanted to 'purify' the Church of England.

Reformers in the church had been actively encouraging Christians to worship God in a more personal way for a hundred years by the early 1600's.

As the struggle for a personal manner in which to worship God intensified (and became more treasonous in the eyes of the authorities), a minority of Puritans set up a congregation from—but apart—of the Church of England. These were called Separatists.

After spending a decade in Holland, these men and their families returned to England to plan their lives, deciding that the new lands in North America offered their only option to worship God in their own way. William Bradford, one of their ranking members wrote of their group that "they knew they were Pilgrims."

What does this story have to do with gratitude? Actually, quite a bit.

We as Americans have been brought up with the story of the first Thanksgiving since childhood. We hear the names associated with that celebration—Squanto, Bradford, Standish, Winslow—but we seldom grasp, or understand, the significance these people had on the lives we live today. Or the opportunities God puts before us.

Sitting on their hands, praying fervently that everything in their lives would get better was neither going to work nor was such an attitude part of their character.

With a vision for the generations yet to come, and a burning desire to proclaim the word of God, 102 people set sail for a 3-week journey westward to a new world.

Living in a space between the decks 4 ½ feet high in a ship, that until that voyage, had been transporting wine throughout the British Isles, these 'Pilgrims' survived a voyage that eventually became 8 weeks. Setting out in September 1620 was not the most auspicious time to do so. For those who know the sea they know that the North Atlantic is no place to be in the autumn and yet these intrepid Christians ventured into the unknown at just that time.

Believing that God was with them and that nothing happens by accident, they put together a document decreeing their hopes, goals, and ideas for governance - known forever after as the 'Mayflower Compact'. What would eventually become the United States of America could truthfully be said to have been given birth between the decks of that weather-beaten ship.

After landing on the western shore of Cape Cod on the day after Christmas 1620 they faced a future with no shelter, no food, and the possibility of encountering hostile natives. Six or seven of the men could still walk and did what they could to find provisions for the rest, but with two to three feet of snow on the ground and no shelter, their options were limited. Their faith in God allowed them to face their future despite their human frailties. As their strength began to decline, they relied on God's. 4

By March 1621, the women, in order to keep them warm at night, sacrificed themselves by sleeping on top of the children, and most died.

Unlike the adventurers and conquistadors looking for gold and riches these Pilgrims came with their families to find a place to worship God.

The following autumn, as they looked back over the previous months since landing on these remote shores, they decided to celebrate God's blessings by rejoicing together in thanks. The hunters among the surviving men returned with enough birds and shellfish to feed the 50 colonists and invited some 90 Native Americans who brought along venison to add to the table. According to Edward Winslow, one of the 50, the feast lasted three days.

Instead of counting treasure, they counted blessings. Instead of praising accomplishments, they praised God.

Our lives are ones of continuous change. Some changes we embrace. Some we abhor. We must continually maintain the awareness that we are walking in God's presence. God puts motivation in our heart—if we stay in that awareness—to look for His purposes in our life and leads *our will* into submission to *His will* when we're suffering and in pain.

Do you thank God first thing in the morning for another day? Do you thank Him for your eyesight? Your hearing? The ability to breath? Psalms 92 observes how favorable it is to thank the Lord, declaring gratitude for what He does in your life. Thanksgiving, in 1621, was something God wanted His people to do. The Pilgrims, like us, were dependent on God and by giving thanks we—like those who came before us—acknowledge our dependance on Him. "Whoever offers praise glorifies Me; and to him who orders his conduct aright I will show the salvation of God."(Psalms 50:23)

Giving thanks for the food we eat was once as important as the food itself. Dinner was the time when the whole family sat down together to discuss the day's events—and effects—on one another. Whether the family consisted of 2 or more, the acknowledgement that gratitude for God's blessings took predominance at the table, as well as the recognition that Christ was also present, dinner was held to a high standard. No iPhones ringing, no TV intruding, no video games being played just a time to reacquaint, reflect and rejoice.

Acknowledging God's favor on our lives also fills us with awareness for what He brings into our lives.

In his book 'Talking with My Father' the author Ray Stedman related an incident that Dr. H.A. Ironside wrote about concerning the day he went to a cafeteria to eat.

"Taking his tray as he scanned the dining room for a seat, he found all but one seat occupied. Noticing a man in a chair opposite him at the table, he asked if he might sit down. Nodding his head, the man looked up and grunted his approval.

When Dr. Ironside sat down, as was his habit, he bowed his head, silently giving thanks for the food before him. As he lifted his head the man sternly asked, "What's the matter? Something wrong with the food?" "No, it seems all right to me." responded Dr. Ironside. Not yielding at all the man persisted "You got a headache or something?" "No, I feel fine." Ironside answered, "Why do you ask?" "Well, I noticed you bowing down and putting your hand up to your head and closing your eyes. I thought maybe there was something wrong with your head." "No, I was simply returning thanks to God for my food." Replied Dr. Ironside. "Oh, you believe that garbage, do you?" "Don't you ever give thanks?" "Nah, I don't believe in giving thanks for anything, I just start right in." the man sneered, "Ah" cheerfully Dr. Ironside said, "You're just like my dog!" "Huh?" said the man, "My dog never gives thanks either" said Dr. Ironside. "He just starts right in!" and the man had nothing more to say." 5

Henry David Thoreau once wrote, "I am grateful for what I am and have. My thanksgiving is perpetual." Maya Angelou said, "Let gratitude be the pillow upon which you kneel to say your nightly prayer. And let faith be the bridge you build to overcome evil and welcome good."

We fail to admit that God has blessed us. We neglect to thank and praise Him because of the smugness we feel in our accomplishments. When we reach a goal, we not only fail to acknowledge Him but act like we did it ourselves!

Being grateful for your failures and disappointments is not a very common reaction for many people. But it is those defeats and frustrations that cause a person to grow stronger. I sometimes wonder if God allows agonies and irritations in our life so we don't get so arrogant as we might if we would always be triumphant. We would get spoiled, and we would think it's us. "Tragedy is a tool for the living to gain wisdom, not a guide by which to live" wrote Robert Kennedy. Everyone runs into problems but just keep in mind that these too are not permanent.

Too many people persist in looking in the rear-view mirror sighing for "the good old days." Well, I'm here to proclaim and declare—The good old days are ahead of you! When you hear "you'll never" in the future, just remember: the devil is a liar!

Whenever negative thoughts about what you did, what you didn't do, what you should've done, what you could've done appear it's time to begin forgetting those things which are behind and reach to those things which are before you. Lean forward toward the calling God has for your life.

Bitterness about something is usually the result of an unfulfilled dream, unobtained goal or an unanswered prayer. Rarely is a disappointment or defeat looked upon as an opportunity for growth, or for gratitude. Many people blame God, but at times like these they should be praising Him. Yes, God allows events to unfold in our lives but when we experience setbacks, we need to pray for understanding, and for strength. Keep in mind that God is not hurting you. He's weaning you. God is forcing you to look into yourself and to come out of yourself and use the talents you have. People are nourished by adversity. It doesn't seem that way at the time but most of a person's greatest accomplishments were incubated through their greatest trials.

We need to get out of our own way. By that I mean, when you're thinking loss, what you don't like, or don't have you become stuck on a frequency of that exact radiation. Fortunately, changing that radiation is not overly difficult to do.

First, accept your present circumstance or situation as it is. Rid yourself of resentment and dissatisfaction. Pray for perception, to see clearly with an open mind. Realize that there is always something helpful and "good" in every situation. You will never need to go far to find even the smallest things that bring you happiness and joy. Being grateful for what you have now, experiencing love towards everything surrounding you not only makes your life easier, but gives off positive energy. The importance of your actively being grateful for even the smallest blessing can NOT be overstated.

Life is not going to happen without challenges and to count on such an event is unrealistic. Never lose sight of the fact that those challenges promote change which in turn becomes those things for which you are grateful. Start talking—'it's on the way, it's here in me and it's coming about now.' That's positive radiation. Remind yourself that "no weapon formed against me will prosper." (Isaiah 54:17)

If God still says no after you've petitioned, prayed, and plead *"Lord, get me out of here! Get me out of this trouble!"* then know your triumph will come about through your trouble! If God starts it, He'll finish it. Praise Him when you're down! Praise Him when you're in agony! Praise Him when you don't see a way out! Praise Him when the tears are falling so hard that you can't see! Praise Him through hell and high water! This is what it means to be broken and this is where you run out of strength, and you drop down on your knees and let the Holy Spirit take over your life!

But then someone asks, to no—one in particular "What do I have to be grateful for?" You have shelter, a home that keeps you dry and warm. You have food. No longer does a man need to pick up a spear and hope he catches something. You are able to walk and see and hear. Thank Him for the ability to throw a ball, hold a baby and for the muscles that give you the strength to do so. Build a foundation of gratitude for what you have no matter how insignificant you think it is. Just stop for a moment and reflect on where you'd be, or how you'd feel without it.

Countless lives have been changed when gratitude replaces grumbling.

Willie Nelson has had his share of adventures in living. When the IRS was dogging him in the '80's Nelson still gave back. As an organizer of "Farm Aid" he wanted to help those who are some of the most underappreciated people in America—the farmers. Nelson once said, "When I started to count my blessings, my whole life turned around."

Be grateful for those things you throw away. That sounds odd but keep in mind—they had a purpose in your life and now they've served their purpose. This is another way to keep positive energy flowing around you. "Be thankful for what you have" observed Oprah Winfrey "You'll end up having more."

When we do a kindness of some sort it's nice to hear the word "Thank you" and although most of us do for others without expecting a Thank you, a show of gratitude is always appreciated. I heard a story recently, much above where an ordinary "Thank you" would suffice: During an intense fire-fight in Iraq, a Captain noticed one of his men lying wounded on the ground about 50 yards away.

Despite being in a murderous crossfire, the officer ran out to pull the man back to their line, himself being seriously wounded. The enlisted man was treated and eventually recovered. The captain, in his attempt to save one of his own, did not fare as well and being mortally wounded, died shortly after.

Once again at home, recovered from his wounds, the enlisted man received an invitation from his Captain's mother and father to join them for dinner at their home. They felt being next to the man whom their son gave his last full measure of devotion to would, in some way, bring their son back to them if for just a brief moment.

Arriving hours late, the now–recovered veteran stood at their door intoxicated. Inviting him in, they sat down to eat trying to reconcile their son's sacrifice and their heart break with their ill-mannered and rude guest.

After what seemed like a lifetime, their visitor finally left. Collapsing in tears on the couch the Captain's mother looked at her husband in shock and dismay. "Our son is gone. He sacrificed his life for that?!" After a moment she went on through tears and anguish, "He never even said thank you."

In the 21st Century we don't hear much about Hansen's Disease, but Jesus lived at a time when a person was not only avoided but banished for possessing it.

Imagine never being given a smile, never a hug. Never shown sympathy or shown love but instead ridiculed and cursed at. The disease, known by its historical name, is still a word used to mean being shunned—a Leper.

In ancient times a person with Leprosy was obligated to shout out "unclean, unclean" to warn the healthy to keep away. Hair unkempt, faces partially hidden, bodies covered in putrid filthy clothes, hands and feet gone, life as a leper was as near to living hell on earth as possible.

Most people then, as today, tended to look at the afflicted with a feeling of indifference, if not callousness—"That's just the way things are." Jesus however, was not most people. The compassion of Jesus is evident throughout the Gospels and is so once again as He walks into a village somewhere between Galilee and Samaria.

Lepers, ten of them, holler out "Jesus, Master, have mercy on us." With tenderness Jesus advises the Samaritans to show themselves to the priests. Making their way to the temple to do so, they are healed.

Luke doesn't tell us what exactly goes on with the ten once they discover they are cleansed, but we could safely guess there was shouting, laughter, running with excitement—anything that would bring a hearty display of exuberance.

Through all the hysteria one of them pause, looks at the hands that were once twisted, touches the face that moments before was covered by gray death and in astonishment understands what has just happened. Catching up to Jesus the restored pariah falls to Jesus' feet in appreciation and gratitude. We can almost hear the praise that the former vagabond heaps on Jesus. We can imagine the tears falling down his cheeks in thankfulness. Acknowledging him, Jesus said, "Were there not ten cleansed? But where are the nine?" (Luke 17:11-19)

We all want to identify with the one who returned. The one who says thank-you, the one who remembers. But in truth so many of us presume so much, we take so much in stride. In Pastor Joel Osteen's book "Fresh Start" he relates a story he heard about a man driving around a crowded parking lot looking for a space. "He got so frustrated" Pastor Osteen wrote, "that he finally said, "God, if you'll give me a parking spot, I'll go to church every Sunday." Right then" relates Pastor Osteen "immediately, a car backed out of a space, and as he pulled in, he said, "Never mind, God. I just found one." I'm afraid many of us can relate!

How do you rectify ingratitude? What can you do to restore the feeling of being thankful? I write 'restore' because as children our parents taught us to say, 'Thank you'. Each of us carry the internal template of gratitude and depending on the magnitude of the bestowal we not only 'feel' grateful but have the inclination to say so. Then why doesn't everyone? How does a person become thankful?

Begin by praising God. The definition of Praise is "to glorify." The Samaritan experienced the miracle of restoration and "turned back, praising God with a loud voice."

When we lose sight of worshiping and praising God, we easily become self-centered and self-absorbed. Put aside the Ego and be humble. Know that God has a divine decree for your life. A heart full of appreciation brings a peace of mind that becomes a recipient of even more blessings. Be thankful for the smallest things. Be thankful for the 'life lessons' too because without an 'attitude of gratitude' there is a tendency toward becoming desperate. You feel trapped instead of delivered. Enslaved to regret instead of released into God's perfect will in your life.

Being anxious and fretting over things is not the will of God, and by thanking God for the blessings *we do have* removes those anxieties. There are times in our life when we have the least to feel thankful for, but we need to thank Him anyway. "This is not what I want in my life Lord, but I thank you and praise you just the same." Praying a prayer like that will not change God's will but it will change your attitude.

Habakkuk, one of the prophets, lived to see the Babylonians invade Jerusalem and was of the habit of laying his concerns directly to God. "Why doesn't God do something about evil? Why doesn't God do anything to those people who themselves do evil?" Habakkuk's concerns are as valid and timely today as they were 2,600 years ago.

But Habakkuk also knew the way to overcome disappointment, adversity, and apprehension and that was through praise and thanksgiving. He knew that having a positive outlook on life, no matter how bleak things seemed to be, was essential. He was always prepared to show his gratitude.

"Though the fig tree may not blossom, nor fruit be on the vines; Though the labor of the olive may fail, And the fields yield no food; Though the flock may be cut off from the fold, And there be no herd in the stalls –

Yet I will rejoice in the Lord, I will joy in the God of my salvation.”
(Habakkuk 3:17-18)

Giving thanks before you receive is a powerful use of gratitude. You are acknowledging the thing, confirming your trust and believe that you'll receive and implanting that thought in your mind. It's not a hope —it's a fact.

Maintaining an attitude of thankfulness elevates the human mind into a confidence of more to come. Even sharing with others is a form of gratitude. It allows us to feel good about helping someone else and it also acknowledges that there are more blessings on the way to us. Keep this premise in mind when the occasion arises to help, to accommodate or to share with someone. Being grateful, in the final analysis, is a reflection of our character.

Allow me to end this chapter with this poem by Valerie Cox. It's called "The Cookie Thief."

A woman was waiting at an airport one night
With several long hours before her flight.
She hunted for a book in the airport shop
Bought a bag of cookies and found a place to drop.
She was engrossed in her book but happened to see,
that the man beside her as bold as could be
grabbed a cookie or two from the bag between
which she tried to ignore to avoid a scene.
She munched cookies and watched the clock
as this gutsy cookie thief diminished her stock!
She was getting more irritated as the minutes ticked by
thinking "If I wasn't so nice. I'd blacken his eye!"
With each cookie she took he took one too,
and when only one was left she wondered what he'd do.
With a smile on his face and a nervous laugh,
he took the last cookie and broke it in half.

He offered her half as he ate the other.
She snatched it from him and thought "Oh brother,
this guy has some nerve and he's also rude,
Why he didn't even show any gratitude!"
She had never known when she had been so galled
and sighed with relief when her flight was called.
She gathered her belongings and headed to the gate,
refusing to look back at the thieving ingrate.
She boarded the plane and sank in her seat
then sought her book which was almost complete.
As she reached in her baggage she gasped with surprise-
there was her bag of cookies in front of her eyes!

*   "If mine are here" she moaned with despair,*
"Then the other were his and he tried to share."
Too late to apologize she realized with grief,
that she was the rude one, the ingrate, the thief.

What is Inside

What quality does a person have that inspires others to perform and accomplish objectives or goals that seem extraordinary?

What motivates a group of men to run across a battlefield toward a fusillade of gunfire or a team of workers to achieve an assignment that a week before seemed impossible?

It's easy to think "It was their duty" of "if they want to keep their job, they don't have a choice." Those conclusions can't explain why a superior effort was maintained through to the end. It takes more than self-initiative to make a part fit into a device that allows something to operate and it takes more than excitement to take a machine-gun head-on. Without a doubt a person must possess some of these traits but how does someone become motivated, from where does one get the strength to accomplish the difficult, dangerous, or impossible? Only from a person with integrity.

Most people would agree that to respect someone, that someone needs to be a man or a woman of integrity. A person of integrity can lead and motivate because of the opinion of others. Whether they are "liked" or not is immaterial and not a basis for leadership. Some of the most effective leaders in history were in fact, not well liked. One military leader, George Patton, quickly comes to mind. Patton was difficult to get along with, highly opinionated and occasionally confrontational.

Whichever position you held in the US Army—superior, staff or plain dog-face soldier you knew that his personal creed was above reproach. He demanded as much sacrifice from himself as he did from his men—and they knew it! Actually, those soldiers who served under Patton never forgot the character of the man. My mother's brother was one of them. Uncle Angelo spoke often about his time serving in the Third Army during World War II and of his respect for his general. Such is the impact that a man of integrity can make.

"Let another man praise you, and not your own mouth; a stranger, and not your own lips." (Proverbs 27:2)

The most powerful endorsement always comes from another person, not by boasting. That sounds logical enough but how many times have we experienced that person who is their own cheerleading squad? 'Me and I' are their two favorite pronouns. They are not only boorish but obnoxious and as we walk away from that person, whatever opinion we had of them has diminished considerably. Usually, we harbor those vexatious feelings about such people because somewhere down deep we don't trust that they would have our back. Such people are too busy pumping up their importance because, in the end, they feel a lack of self-esteem.

When you are comfortable in, and confident of yourself, you don't feel the need to promote it. You usually don't even give it a thought because you go about your business demanding better of yourself. Being too big to do the little things is never the description of a true leader. They're the ones who put the box on the top shelf when you can't reach or the one pushing your car out of a snowbank. Somewhere they learned that the greatest among us are servants and they truly lead by example.

These people are usually quiet and if their accomplishments become known it's usually through others. Hyperbole and dishonesty are just not part of their make-up. They take the good with the bad knowing that they need to be who they are and be true to themselves.

I'd like to share a story – one that I was made aware of several years ago - with you:

The owner of a large manufacturing firm, Michael Bradley, had been contemplating stepping down as CEO of the company he started many years before. Growing older he knew the time to find a successor had come.

His children were in professional practices of their own and his board of directors held no one who could take the reins of such a large firm.

Calling all the young executives in his company together, Mr. Bradley made an announcement. "The time has come for me to step aside as CEO. I'm getting older and we've all worked too hard to get the company to where it is now for me to hinder the company with a bad decision or two. I've decided to look to one of you as the next CEO." The managers were shocked yet excited as Mr. Bradley continued. "I am giving each of you a seed today. One very special seed. I want you to plant it, water it and we'll get together one year from today. Bring your plants with you so I can judge them. It will help me to decide who'll be the next CEO of our company."

One of Mr. Bradley's managers, Jim, was there that day and like the others received a seed. When he got home, he excitedly told his wife the story.

They went to the nursery to get the best container; a bag of soil and some rich compost, came home and planted the seed. Every day he watered and waited for the seed to sprout.

After a few weeks some of the other managers began to talk about their seeds and the plants that were beginning to grow.

Jim kept vigil over his seed, but no shoot ever appeared. Two months, four months, six months—still nothing.

By now the others were talking about their plants, but feeling like a bonehead, Jim kept quiet. Somehow Jim killed his plant. "Maybe I used the wrong soil." But he kept at it, watering it, setting it out in the sun hoping now for some sort of life.

Finally, a year passed, "There's no way I'm taking an empty pot" Jim said to his wife. "I'm going to buy a small tree." But reminding him that he was always an honest man, Jim's wife encouraged him to bring the empty container and be done with it. Although it was going to be embarrassing, he knew she was right.

When Jim arrived at work, he was amazed at the variety of plants grown by the other executives. They were beautiful and there were all shapes and sizes. As he laid his empty container on the floor, he could hear some of his co-workers laugh. Most just felt sorry for him.

Entering the room, Mr. Bradley looked around and observed "Wow, you all did a great job on your plants. These are beautiful!" He went on "Well, today's the day..." Scanning the room before he went on, he noticed Jim in the back, "What happened to you Jim? Bring your pot here." Feeling like a complete fool, hearing the chuckles from the others he could only hope that this went quickly.

When Jim approached the podium, Mr. Bradley asked everyone to sit down. Asking Jim for an explanation he listened as Jim told him the story.

As he listened and with tears in his eyes, Bradley turned to the group and said, "Ladies and Gentlemen, meet your new CEO!" It took a few moments for Jim to process what was just said. "How could *he* be the new CEO?" the others said to each other.

Mr. Bradley then went on, "One year ago today, I gave everyone in this room a seed. I told you to take the seed, plant it, water it and bring it back to me today. But, I gave you all boiled seeds; they were dead— it wasn't possible for them to grow. All of you, except Jim, brought me flowers, trees and plants. When you found that the seed wouldn't grow, you substituted another seed for the one I gave you. Jim was the only one with the integrity, courage and honesty to bring me a pot with my seed in it."

Quoting from Psalms, Bradley went on, "The steps of a good man are ordered by the Lord" (37:23) and I believe God will continue to show His favor on our company with a man like Jim at the helm. Therefore, I name Jim our next Chief Executive Officer!"

God will always guide, defend, and strengthen those He chooses to lead. He will honor and protect them as well as vindicate them. God shields those people He chooses for leadership. He anoints them and they never need to worry about defending their accomplishments or their lives.

Being a "Christian" leader is not the same definition that the world has of a leader. God's work will never be left undone until those objectives and purposes of that work are achieved. (Matthew 25:23)

Being called into leadership is nothing that should be taken lightly. Whether you are the shift manager of a crew of three or the Chairman of the Board of a Fortune 500 company, your calling into that position was ordained by God.

Unfortunately for many people a leadership position has become an Ego-based accolade to either have authority over others or a pay increase. Usually both. But stepping into a leadership role is serious business. The best action one should do when a supervisory or leadership role is to be undertaken is by prayer, asking God's guidance and for the wisdom to lead.

When asked by God what he wanted in order to rule Israel, Solomon first expressed gratitude for what he had already been given—the throne. But to Solomon, the most important blessing he could ask for God was for wisdom. (1 Kings 3:9) It is interesting to note that because all Solomon wanted from God was an understanding heart to lead His people, he was given so much more. If our plans, our work, is from God, nothing can tear it apart. If it is not anointed by God, not being from Him, no good purpose will be served by keeping the undertaking going. When His purpose is no longer of primary importance, problems - often insurmountable problems - pop up and can lead to disastrous consequences. We need only look back into history to see not only individuals but whole nations come to ruin by abandoning His guidance. The best example of this is God's rejection of Israel. After warning Manasseh, the consequences of disrespecting Him, God eventually turned His face away from Israel, culminating in the destruction of Jerusalem and the exile of the nation of Israel. This is an object lesson not only for us but for our country as well. (II Chronicles 33:10-11)

To be a leader, one must have a foundational basis on which to build. That foundation, like the house destined to stand, must be built on solid rock. What are the ingredients that make up that foundation? Honesty, sincerity, uprightness, righteousness, decency, persistence, a strong moral fiber, and a sense of purpose.

There is a correlation between being a leader and being inspired to be the best you can be. To make the best decisions and to live our lives in such a way that glorifies God we need to first examine our core values and how they relate to our place in the world.

Being a leader does not necessarily mean to lead others in the sense of directing the operations. *It is essential that your inner individuality be in order.* That takes a commitment of time for introspections and to remove any misconception in abilities, talents, proficiencies or resolve. This kind of self-examination (if done honestly) can be unpleasant but productive. More importantly it provides you with a sturdy–and powerful—basis to move ahead in confidence and strength. If you look back on your life experiences, you will recall 'leaders' who never took a personal analysis of their strengths and weaknesses.

All of us have encountered supervisors - or those with control over us who, for want of a better word, were hypocrites. We recall those managers who didn't 'lead' they 'bullied'! These were the people whose ethos was "do as I say, not as I do!" Most people of character and integrity find it difficult to work for or follow such people.

As you consider your qualities, a helpful start—if you're serious about integrity (and you would not be reading this if you weren't) and potential for leadership—would be to ask yourself "What would someone say of me?" I'm not talking about seeking people's approval but an honest and forthright evaluation of what's called "your character"?

John Wooden once said, "Your reputation is what you're perceived to be. Your character is what you are." Character is that distinctive trait which a person possesses. Over your lifetime your actions, decisions and your deeds attest to Wooden's observation. The deepest part of our character is made up of integrity and honor. It is essential in the world we live in today, to hold ourselves to a higher standard than what seems to be going on around us.

Having moral character today has the appearance of being in short supply. Now more than ever it's important to decide what you stand for. There is no compromising when our character is concerned. I could not possibly overstate the absolute necessity to accurately discern what your character is. There may come a time in your life when who you are, what you stand for, and who you've been, will be not only called into question but assailed and assaulted. You will need your faith in God, and in yourself, to be unshakable and resolute.

When does someone begin to compose, or alter, if need be, their character?

One effective way is to study the lives of people whose character are worth emulating. When you study the traits and lives of "people of character" in the past you get a good sense of what it takes to be the same. You'll find these people were not perfect—we only know one who was—but you'll discover how their decisions affected the life they lead and what it took for them to do so. Its instructive to learn what changes they made when they realized they had fallen short in their quest to be better men or women or discovered the faults that needed to be corrected. It wasn't until the death of his son Willie in February 1862 that Abraham Lincoln could personally know the anguish that the families of fallen soldiers during the Civil War were experiencing. It also was the catalyst that began Lincoln's reliance on God.

Be patient with yourself and understand that we all fall short at times. As human beings we struggle constantly to correct habits developed over a lifetime. Building character takes time and frustration can derail the best of intentions. Don't give up!

Setting a course of high standards will put you at odds with the world. You will notice this when your characteristics become nothing like those around you. Trying to avoid displeasing those you associate with or making them uncomfortable will be challenging and cause many good Christians to backslide. Don't allow yourself to fall into that trap. Emerson said, "Whoso would be a man must be a non-conformist."

You can't decide to alter your ethics because of those around you. You can choose who you allow into your inner circle but in most cases not who you work with. You can choose your friends but not your family. To maintain a course in right action takes more courage than is generally credited. To say no to something that goes against your core beliefs is not easy, especially when you are alone in those beliefs. Calling in the Holy Spirit at this point can bring strength into your character. Knowing God is there with you in all things is *very* powerful.

Acting one way at home or with friends and those you love, and another way in public is hypocrisy and sooner or later found out. When Jesus said to let your no mean no and your yes to mean yes, He could also be addressing a man's character. (Matthew 5:37)

It's not at all easy to maintain high standards. You must develop a solid belief in the code of ethics you've chosen to live by. By prayerful contemplation you can navigate the hazards of conforming to the negative habits of others. The Jesus prayer ("Lord Jesus, have mercy on me") is a way to re-center yourself and can help align you divinely.

Humbleness and unpretentious attitudes are important components in a man or woman of character. You do not bring attention to yourself and by so doing neither are you a target of others. Sun—Tzu wrote "The superior man does not give up good conduct because the inferior man rails against him." Your underlying principals will surface naturally on their own. You will be looked on with respect but be forewarned: at times you will be ridiculed but as Shakespeare once wrote "This above all; to thine own self be true."

All of us walk a path. All of us want to be happy, be comfortable financially, enjoy good health, and just generally live in peace. That's what we want, but usually that's not what we get.

Somehow circumstances get in our way.

This is called life.

It seems that something comes up that 'forces' us to compromise something or other that we inwardly hold important, and we know that each action we take—whatever that action is—influences most everything else we experience in our lives. Thankfully most things that are a consequence of something we've done are not so dramatic—"I went to the mailbox but I got wet because it's raining." or "My wife and I went to dinner and we ran into our neighbors." Our lives are a series of ripple effects and if we do nothing to interrupt the actions we create, then our lives effectively become out of control.

How do we control as much of what happens in our lives as possible, control meaning "manage" in this case? It comes down to how we choose to live our personal lives from this very moment forward. Today. Now.

When we speak about character, we're really speaking about a pattern of behavior that resides within each of us, but it is integrity which holds it to the principles which form our character. Solomon wrote that "The righteous man walks in his integrity" and a man's behavior cannot be hidden, not from another person for long and not from God at all (Proverbs 20:7).

The word integrity comes down to us from the Romans. In Latin 'integer' stood for unbroken completeness. Merriam Webster's dictionary defines the word as "firm adherence to a code of moral or artistic value." Integrity is the ability, strength really, to hold steady to what we believe is good, true, honest and incorruptible. It is holding these values even when it has profound effects on you.

I heard a story a few years ago about an attorney in Philadelphia, Mike, who was a rising star in his firm. Going through the accounting records he noticed that the billing practices of the firm included over charging the clients or charging for work not done. Mike had been a few years out of college and was deeply bothered by the discovery. Having strong, core Christian values, Mike spoke to his mentor who suggested to "just let it go. You have a promising future here. Every partner thinks highly of you. It would do you no good to bring this up." Mike's conscious would not allow him to be associated with such practices.

It's easy to talk about doing what's right, it's quite another to live it. Mike left the firm and looking back at it years later he has never regretted it. The feeling of peace combined with his moral strength to do what was right has, in his opinion, allowed God's blessings not only in his private practice but in his life. When making important decisions in his life now he reminds himself of the day he decided to live by his honesty and the inner satisfaction that decision made on his life. Without God in a person's life, more specifically without acknowledging God's presence in our life, the strength we need to hold fast to our moral compass can become compromised.

You are in a large parking lot filled with cars. As you back out of your space you get distracted—just for a moment—and dent the car next to you. No one is around, no one saw you. What do you do? Do you leave your number on the windshield or do you drive away?

Living ethically and morally is a matter of choice to live by them or without them. There is a saying in Chinese "A clean conscious is the greatest armor." There is a price for compromising yourself—self-alienation. You become uneasy and anxious. You worry of being found out. Some people live their lives believing they can separate their ethics depending on the circumstances.

A person hands the cashier a ten-dollar bill and receives change for a twenty. Some people will walk away thinking "If they were stupid enough to not pay attention to what they're doing, it's their fault." They rationalize that it's up to cashier to be conscientious!

Living with a set of morals for a person of character is without compromise. These people know that what guides their conscious is doing what is right, and not a rigid set of rules.

Moliere once said, "It is not only what we do, but what we do not do, for which we are accountable." When you make a decision of importance you must know that your conscious is developed enough to know what is honorable and right and not what others deem to be correct. "What I must do" wrote Emerson "is all that concerns me, not what other people think."

Spending time in the presence of Godly people will bring serenity to most people. Studying the lives of devout and pious men and women can bring us motivation to become better people. Observe the character of those around you. Watch how they talk but carefully observe how they behave. I'm not only talking about morals either.

Examine your association with others because it raises you up or brings you down. It is difficult to live a life of excellence without the association of other like - minded people. Spend time with those people who encourage you, inspire you and motivate you. As a rising tide lifts all boats so too will virtuous, honorable, and faith-filled people elevate you.

7

Know Thyself

It is never—NEVER—too late to remold a life.

Proverbs tells us that a prudent man gives thought to his steps, so it is important to consider where you want to walk. (Proverbs 14:15) When a Christian walks alone, he is unable to gain or draw strength from his fellow brothers and sisters in Christ. Finding a church that has an active Spiritual life helps us to grow in faith and opens our minds to God's words in an extraordinary way that may be difficult to notice on our own. When we have other believers who share in our commitment not only to Jesus Christ but in right living, we are able to develop firm and resolute principals that help us when we need it most. Comforting and improving each other was important in the days and years following Jesus' time on earth. It is what allowed the early believers to propagate and flourish. (II Corinthians 1:4)

Its interesting to note that John D. Rockefeller, who were he alive today would still be the world's wealthiest man, was of the opinion that it was important to become part of a church and to root yourself in Christ. For many years he taught Sunday School.

A bit of sound advice that John D. not only gave but lived was to "avoid ostentation. Watch how you walk, how you look. Go about your business without display or power or money. Be plain and understated. You avoid the gaze of the jealous and the envious, and of the ambitious who want to make a reputation on you." Still a great recommendation 130 years later.

Baltazar Gracian, a 17th Century Spanish author once said, "No man can be master of himself, who does not understand himself." Foundationally it is not possible to achieve greatness, nor to develop into who God wants us to be, without knowing exactly who we are. Although this seems like common sense (after all who knows you better than you?) it is really not as easy as it would seem.

You already know what weakness and shortcomings you have. Maybe its your language you'd like to clean up. Maybe you want to quit smoking.

Maybe you want to stop gossiping. Just know that you need to be patient with yourself. Most habits we are living with have been part of who we are for a long time.

Take the time to discover you. To do that, you'll need to do a disappearing act. To go somewhere for a few minutes or even an hour probably won't help much. If you can drop out of sight for a day or two you could begin your journey of self-analysis and self-exploration. Knowing your strengths and your weaknesses will give you a tremendous advantage in preparing yourself for the rest of your life. It will let you focus on your abilities and how to improve deficiencies and flaws. There is an old Italian saying that addresses this: "He who is an ass and takes himself to be a stag finds his mistake when he comes to leap the ditch!"

Walk with the conviction that you are a leader. Leadership is all about influence. At work you influence those around you. At home you influence your family. You influence people standing in line at your local Division of Motor Vehicles.

Most of us want to be the best that we can be in all areas of our lives. Very few of us want to live a life of mediocrity. In order to do the best, be the best, we need to discipline our lives in such a way that enables us to sharpen the skills God gave us and improve those which we find challenging. Along the way to success there will be found not only satisfaction but a strong sense of accomplishment that you'll find that will carry over to other areas of your life. After you reminded the cashier you gave them a ten, then handing back the change from that twenty you'll know what I mean.

It takes a strong determination of studying - eleven years - to become a physician. With four years of college, four years of Medical School and an average of three years doing residency in a hospital. With pitifully short periods of rest and sleep, it takes a dedication and commitment to helping others as well as strong discipline to become a doctor. To become part of a local police force rookie officers, in addition to a degree in criminal justice, need to learn and retain the complete street layout of his district, town or city. He or she needs to know the blocks, the intersections, bridges—everything that allows that officer to respond in the shortest time possible. That takes discipline.

As you mold yourself into the person you want to become, you need to ask yourself what you'll need to do to become that person. It takes a new approach to living. This only makes sense. If you're thinking remains unchanged, if you do things as you've always done, how can you possibly transform into extraordinary? Napoleon Hill wrote "Self-discipline begins with the mastery of your thoughts. If you don't control what you think, you can't control what you do. Simply, self-discipline enables you to think first and act afterward." Discipline your mind first and your body cannot help but follow.

Most people find encouragement to be somewhat elusive. They try to get it from within and while there's no question there are lots of motivated people in the world, encouragement needs to be given from outside ourselves. Athletes have trainers, salespeople have sales managers and students have teachers. As Christians we have the Bible and its innumerable number of stories. As Christians we turn to God for guidance and although we may not receive the reassurance we need immediately, we eventually secure it. Actually, in many cases it's our own minds or egos that usually block God's guidance. We already have a preconceived idea 'how to' or 'should be' and it takes many of us time to break that barrier down so we're ready to accept His direction and encouragement.

We are unable to see the twists and turns ahead. God sees 'from above.' Football coaches routinely send their assistants to the press box because the view there offers a clear picture of what's on the field and what could lie ahead. In the same way, we rely on Divine guidance by trusting God to give us direction and making Christ our cornerstone of that trust.

Once you've decided what kind of person you want to be, you commit your mind and body to doing what you tell them to do, always keeping the end goal clearly in your mind. There is a quote I'm sure your familiar with "The Lord helps those who help themselves" and not only does this make sense, but it is also true. Your mind must be in a state of belief that *you will accomplish* the intended goal. This allows God to work in your life. It is perhaps interesting to note that although this quote "sounds Biblical" it is not found in scripture! This passage is attributed to the 17th Century Dutch philosopher Baruch Spinoza!

To be an effective leader you should have a history behind you. You should know how the business runs, how the engine operates, how the procedures are handled and what it takes to accomplish the assignment based on past experience. In the centuries before iron ships, it was quite common that the captain of the ship—be it a whaler, warship or mer-chant ship—started out as a cabin boy. Sometimes on that very ship! He knew every inch of the vessel. He knew how to mend a sail, splice a line, scrub a deck and stand a lookout. Knowing your captain had that experience was not only comforting but crucial because your life was now in his hands.

One of the most effective methods of sales training is something known as "role-playing." This entails one person playing the role of prospect and the other being the sales rep. Once the shyness of being "on the spot", usually in front of their peers, wears off there is no better way to prepare to go into the field. Whatever objections to the product can come up, usually does so in these staged events. It gives the sales professional a live-action scenario in which to sharpen their sales skills preparing them for the real thing.

Warriors since antiquity have role-played to prepare for combat. A warrior's life depends on being ready for action. He needs to prepare for a multitude of challenges in order to emerge successfully from a fight. The Samurai's code included the precept "Tomorrow's battle is won during today's practice." Sun Tzu wrote, "Know the enemy and know yourself; in a hundred battles you will never be in peril. When you are ignorant of the enemy but know yourself, your chances of winning or losing are equal. If ignorant both of your enemy and of yourself, you are certain in every battle to be in peril."

These words are worth remembering. In most of our lives we are not fighting for physical survival. But it is always advisable to know your competition and to know what skills or attributes you possess to achieve a successful result. If you are prepared, if you are disciplined enough to gather as much knowledge as is possible you have an above average chance of success. While not selling a car will not put your life in mortal peril, it could affect paying the mortgage on time.

It is not enough to know that your dealership has 120 cars in the lot or that there are twelve cars in the color red in stock. An automotive specialist needs to know engine sizes, gas mileage, passenger capacity, trunk space as well as a host of other details. They also need to know their competitor's products as well and be able to provide the rationale for purchasing their product over the competitions. That specialized knowledge can make the difference between a sale or "we'll think about it."

Preparedness does not always entail a physical object or an achievement that hinges on victory or defeat. In most cases the purpose is to prepare for something we want or are anticipating. Both Isaiah and John the Baptist exhorted Israel to prepare their hearts for Jesus' arrival. In like manner we need to prepare ourselves for abundance, blessings and God's favor. We do this by expecting the most favorable outcome. You've heard the saying "hope for the best, but prepare for the worst?" A more positive statement would be "Prepare for the best but be flexible enough for contingencies." This attitude prepares your mind and body to receive the goodness of the Lord and have the comfort of knowing you'll handle anything that comes your way. When you're concentrating and expecting something, you're attracting it to you.

There are various places to go to in your quest for information, data, and enlightenment. Reading, Training, Studying and Experiencing. It is best to be knowledgeable on a few subjects (at least) but it would be wise to not only become informed about a particular topic or object but become an authority on it. Controlling who you are through knowledge, discipline, prayer, and integrity can bring a life well lived.

Independent thinking is an attribute that has seemed to have been lost in our society. Independent thinking is not something humans are born with it. In prehistory the chances of survival were much better by staying in a group or being part of a tribe. Hunting with a band of other men brought a better chance of success as well as safety. A charging buffalo, wounded and enraged, was lethal one on one with a man. The lessons of survival became ingrained into the DNA of homo sapiens and going along with the crowd is a tendency built into our genes.

Its easy to imagine the pride felt in being the best provider of the tribe. That person was acknowledged by the group. They ate the largest portion of food and were looked to for advice. They were the leaders of the pack. They lived with everyone's admiration. In the 21st Century this is called "living by the good opinion of others."

Most people want to fit in. They want to be liked. Most of us try not to offend others and we try to be open to those in need. As Christians we know that we should help and serve one another. The Bible tells us the story of the Last Supper when the Master became the servant by washing the feet of the apostles, performing a duty reserved for the lowliest slave. Jesus knew that to be a true leader one must be willing to serve those who follow them. (John 13:1-17)

With the best of intentions however we can take what it means to serve, to be humble and accommodating to the extreme. Some of us feel that always overlooking, always allowing, always letting people take advantage of us is living a Christian life. Personally, one of the most powerful statements I've ever heard was from Joyce Meyers, "Being a Christian doesn't mean you need to be a doormat!" This statement had a profound effect on me.

I was one of those people who confused being tolerant of the ignorance of others with being Christian. It took the avalanche of legal woes for me to reflect on the distortion I had in leading—and leading with my chin. It was when I heard Joyce's words above that it all came together for me.

To live an authentic and balanced life, and to be the person God wants you to be, you must address living for other's approval and then take steps to grow past such a feeling. The basis of liking and respecting ourselves and not having to look to others is the realization *and knowing* that you are divinely loved. You are a child of the most high God and He lives within you. (I John 4:16)

Issues need to be confronted in a direct manner. You cannot live in fear of offending others just because you are holding to your values and responsibility. Peer pressure begins at an early age. A friend hands you a cigarette "C'mon everyone is doing it." At a party someone says "Go ahead and take a hit. Everyone is." In college a classmate says "Here's the answer sheet for Tuesday's test. The other guys just copied it." At work you're told "Everyone cuts out 10 minutes early."

Swimming against the current is never easy. Saying no isn't either, but it's what sets the winner apart. If you're an employer, you must set boundaries with the people working for you from the beginning. You've heard it said not to become friends with your employees? I suggest you follow that advice. There's no reason to become a tyrant. Be friendly but not friends!

In the military there is a well-defined line between officers and the men they command. Experience taught the US military that lesson. During the Civil War it was customary for the soldiers in a regiment to elect their own officers. Regiments at that time were divided by states and usually those regiments came from a specific location in that state. As the units were being formed, most especially at the beginning of the war, the more popular and prominent men of the community were elected lieutenants, captains, majors and so on. Usually, these men were friends or acquaintances of each other in civilian life. How difficult it was for a colonel to send those he knew at home into the bloodbath that battles of the Civil War became. The men themselves had trouble following orders they disagreed with due to being overly familiar with the officer giving them. As both Northern and Southern armies became more organized and professional the problem worked itself out but not before experiencing a great deal of growing pains and anguish.

Establish duties and expectations of employees when they're hired, and by doing so clearly, you'll be less likely to have responsibility issues later. Keep in mind that whatever you allow from the start of your business relationship will be something you'll live with for the duration of that relationship. Although this sounds like common sense (and it is) if neglected, or a sub-par performance is accepted, your leadership will always be suspect. Worse than that, it will be noted by the staff. Each day ask God to give you wisdom to lead, to inspire and to make sound decisions.

A moment ago, I spoke about role-playing. As I've written, whether you're a soldier or a salesman, a doctor, or a delivery man, you need to be prepared for what life throws at you. Of course, it won't be possible to be completely ready for everything and anything but there are some techniques that can prepare you and to train your conscious mind to meet the challenges that will come your way.

First seek as much knowledge in as many diverse things as possible as I mentioned earlier. Too many opportunities are lost because of a lack of knowledge. You already know that reading is a single best way to become knowledgeable on a subject in a fairly short time. You've heard that "A man is known by the company he keeps" but his character resounds by the books he reads. Our minds need to be fed as well. We need to be discerning in what we read. When you put good things into your head, good things come out.

When you read a book, an article, narrative, or anecdotes you are experiencing fellowship with the writer. You should devote 30 minutes a day (at a minimum) reading material that has the capability to instruct or inspire you. Keep in mind that fiction is a diversion and needs to be thought as such. But for seeking and gaining knowledge—the purpose I'm talking about—you'll need 'red meat' which will nourish you.

Charles Spurgeon, considered by many to be the greatest British preacher of the late nineteenth century, was quoted to have said, "Master those books you have. Read them thoroughly. Bathe in them until they saturate you... Let them go into your very self. Pursue a good book several times and make notes and analyses of it."

In his book 'Spiritual Leadership' J. Oswald Sanders wrote that a good book needs to be read three times. The first reading, he suggested should be done rapidly and continuously. This enables your mind to overview and connect the book's material with your previous knowledge. The second reading should be done carefully and in a timely manner. You should take notes and you should think on them. The third reading should emulate the first reading. By writing a brief synopsis, a brief summary, you will impress the material into your memory.

Another option worth noting is to 'connect' your reading. For instance, if you're reading the history of World War I you could take up the biography of Woodrow Wilson or General John Pershing along with the poetry of Joyce Kilmer. Concentrating on a certain topic or theme for a period of time will cause you to retain more of the general knowledge of that subject matter also.

To become an effective individual, we need to become more knowledgeable on any number of topics. Knowing how to retain that knowledge that you read is essential. What good would it do to spend hours reading only to be unable to recall that which you've read?

To become reliant on our own capabilities we need to think for ourselves. We live in a socially - obsessed world and it is not easy to remain independent and self-reliant. But this is a goal worth every effort you put into it. The constant exposure to other people's business has become a common occurrence and with it the seeming need of some (I hope not most) to share their personal information as well. Be determined and resolute in becoming self-sufficient and self-supporting. There is an old Nepalese proverb that says, "Depend on others and you will go hungry."

Too many people live paycheck to paycheck and if there's anything that is 180 degrees from being self-reliant this is one. You need to be able to pay bills *and* invest, but if money issues are out of control you need to address those issues ASAP. Being proactive in untangling your debts is a first step to self-reliance. Paul wrote "Make straight paths for your feet" and planning your financial life with careful analysis and consideration adheres to that scripture. (Hebrews 12:13) Take an inventory of what your liabilities and assets are. Write down your monthly expenses and monthly income. Believe it or not many people never have done that. An hour per week should be set aside for this. Don't hesitate (or be embarrassed) to call for help. An accountant can help determine income and outgo and in order to realistically achieve your goals you must eliminate doubt and worry. Having a well-organized outline of your finances will benefit you immensely. More importantly you will not have anxiety—a sense of fear—holding a grip on your emotions.

Learning from wise men is not the same as allowing someone to do your thinking. Consider what they're saying and prayerfully make certain what they impart feels right to you before implementing what they say. Tolstoy said, "One should seek the truth himself while profiting by the directions which have reached us from ancient sages and saints."

If there is one thing in life which there doesn't seem to be a shortage of, its advice. Have you noticed that people give their opinion even though you never asked for it? What I think may be even worse is when you do ask for an opinion and after considering the advice decide not to act on it the person becomes offended! Don't allow people to tell (or bully) you what to do, what to believe, or what you should think about a particular subject.

As I was just beginning my career as a stockbroker one of my mentors would often tell me, "Be careful of drug store lawyers!" Now for those of you too young to fully understand that statement, let me explain: Years ago, before the aisles of groceries, the chips and the piped-in music, drug stores were a place where people received their prescriptions, came to socialize and could very well be the location of your first date. The soda fountain, usually found at the back of the shop, offered a long marble countertop where you could order a milkshake, a 'float' or a sundae. Another common fixture was the local know-it-all who dispensed baseless wisdom and unwanted advice, a veritable brass band or clanging cymbal. This 'lawyer' had an opinion on everything—a self-proclaimed expert on everything!

Although most of these drugstores are now just a memory, the 'drugstore lawyer' still remains. You probably even know one or two!

As you plan your future it cannot be stressed enough to do so in conjunction with prayer. When we become emotionally involved with the outcome, we rarely allow ourselves to vary from the script we envision. We hold that end result with a powerful embrace, convinced we know the best way to get there. The dilemma we face in doing so is the doubt we create in our minds when the script changes somewhat. When our "well thought out plans" are altered in some way, we begin to fear that the goal we're reaching for won't happen. We are going to discuss this problem—and the solution—in considerable detail later in the book, but for now if you find yourself going off your pre-set script—let go and let God.

8

Taking the Less-Travelled Road

On your journey through life, it will seem that everyone knows what you should do.

They never hesitate in telling you what's best for you. Finding your own answers are never something they encourage. They thrive on your believing, obeying really, theirs. Today, right now, stop getting your information from the outside. Go inward where "neither moth nor rust destroys" and where dream-stealers can't come in. (Matthew 6:20)

Jesus spoke about people's behavior throughout Israel. He often used the Pharisees as examples of hypocrisy and double mindedness, pontificating without practicing their own teachings. Jesus also knew that by keeping your eyes open you'd know people by their actions. (Matthew 23:25-28)

Our actions will always broadcast what we internally believe, what we really are like. There is no way to conceal what we hold in our heart.

If your actions or your character are not how you want to be known by, or remembered by, its your right to change them. Our minds control our thoughts and our behavior. When we determine to allow the Holy Spirit to guide us our lives cannot help but change for the better.

Emerson once stated, "A man's action is only a picture book of his creed." Many people allow their emotions to control them. They become offended and decide to get even. Gandhi had addressed this very point when he said, "An eye for an eye makes the whole world blind." Always remember that when we become upset, we allow anger or passion to cloud our judgement.

A belligerent samurai, an old Japanese story goes, once challenged a Zen Master to explain the concept of heaven and hell.

But the Monk replied with scorn, "You're nothing but a lout—I can't waste my time with the likes of you!"

His very honor attacked, the Samurai flew into a rage and pulling his sword from its scabbard, yelled "I could kill you for your impertinence."

"That" the Monk calmly replied, "is hell."

At seeing the truth in what the Master pointed out about the fury that had him in its grip, the Samurai now chagrined, sheathed his sword, and bowed, thanking the Monk for the insight.

"And that" said the Monk "is heaven."

How or what is excellence to you? Have you ever written down what your code of honor is? You are the only person who can write that. Lao Tzu said, "The universal way is not just a matter of speaking wisdom, but one of continual practice."

Talking about living righteously becomes an embarrassment as well as hypocritical if you're not living it. Yet it's important that you're not living to impress others. You're living an honorable life because *you've* made a personal decision that nothing less than excellence will be your measure. When you live a life of uprightness you honor God. Doing your best whether it's at a job or on a task not only brings a sense of satisfaction to us personally but is an affirmation of our love for the Lord.

Despite our caution of living our lives by what other people think, we still need to be mindful of how we live. Whether we look for approval or not (or want it) people will naturally accord us respect, or they won't.

To be respected is different entirely than to be liked. While both can be found simultaneously one is more valuable than the other. Respect, scripture tells us, is coveted if given by God, and crushing if not. (Isaiah 47:3)

Sometimes its tuff to know what is right action and what is wrong action. Complimenting someone for doing a less than satisfactory job is nice but is it proper? Does that encourage mediocrity or encourage someone to continue doing less than their best? But is pointing out what was wrong, or not to yours or your company's standards, the best course?

If you have been or are in this dilemma, what do you do? Unfortunately, it is many human beings' nature to do the least amount of work, with the minimal amount of effort. To allow employees to continue doing substandard work is an encouragement to carry on in the same way. To allow children to 'skate by' sets a pattern of mediocrity their entire adult life.

You must make a decision of what you expect and what you'll accept. Not only for others but for yourself. *For your life.* For some people decision making is a scary thing. When you make a decision, you're drawing a line in the sand. It's a commitment and determination. There are also times that making an instant decision is critical.

Although making decisions based on emotions seldom work out well, there are times when there is no choice but to do so. At a time like that you really have only one option. Be prepared.

Bodhidharma, a 6th Century Buddhist Monk said, "If you're not sure, don't act." and if time is not an adversary this is excellent advice. But what do you rely on, where do you go when a situation requires that you act immediately? *You must go inward.*

When you commit to going inward, into silence, into prayer, you are preparing yourself for making decisions in God's will. Your conscious becomes open to guidance by the Holy Spirit.

Make no mistake—this type of preparation is not the way of the world. Were you to tell someone what you're doing you'd hear "that makes no sense" "your naive" or "you're crazy." As a Christian you operate on a different wavelength. You walk a different path. One where you trust God to direct your steps. A word of advice, caution even: do not attempt this reliance until you know that it is the Holy Spirit leading you and not the Deceiver. *You can only know the difference through constant prayer and dialogue with God.* You must live Isaiah's words "Your ears shall hear a word behind you, saying, "This is the way, walk in it," whenever you turn to the right hand or whenever you turn to the left." (Isaiah 30:21)

There needs to be a steady and current stream running through your subconscious. This stream needs to be pure, powerful, and unyielding. This can be brought to the subconscious by daily practice of prayer and supplications. You must also take physical action when called for. Gaining knowledge on the subject or objective helps to clarify how to proceed. You need to do your part which allows God to step in.

Preparing your inner self takes commitment and patience but worth the effort every time. Robert Crowley summed this thought up when he said, "Survival favors the prepared mind."

Keeping your mind focused on doing what's right, living with integrity, honor, and virtue leads to those very qualities. The direction you inevitably end up taking will ultimately be dictated by what you concentrated on.

Next time you're behind the steering wheel of your car, driving on an expressway let's say, start noticing the yellow line on the side of the road. Before you even realize it, the car will drift toward the line. You instinctively follow what you concentrate on. There needs to be a deep well, a fathomless reservoir of virtue that springs up when you need it most.

When you read words like the one's written above— "there needs to be a deep well, a fathomless reservoir of virtue that springs up when you need it most" you may think "sounds good but how do I go about that?" Like all the theorems set forth in this book, we go to scripture.

The description 'A mighty man of God' easily fit Moses' deputy Joshua. He not only commanded the Hebrew military but was the only person to go with Moses part way up Mt. Sinai. When everyone seemed to be paralyzed with fear it was Joshua, along with Caleb who encouraged the taking of the land God promised to the Israelites. (Numbers 13:30)

It can be said that Joshua was one of a very few personalities in the Bible who usually got everything right. He was an exceptional leader, was totally committed to God and never was disobedient to the Lord. In order to become prosperous and to live a happy, joyous life, God instructed Joshua to meditate on His words day and night. (Joshua 1:8)

Meditation, according to the dictionary, is to engage in contemplation or reflection, to focus one's thought. We'll talk about meditation later but for now it's necessary to know that it can be a strategic part of living an enjoyable, gratifying life that will strengthen who you are as a person and as a Divine child.

Quieting your mind and focusing on silence allows you to hear the still small voice more readily during the day. There is something that happens to a person—call it profound calmness—that settles into them when they take a few minutes a day to meditate.

As I wrote earlier—don't let certain words (in this instance *meditation*) bother you if until now you've only associated the word with New Age jargon.

When you commit yourself to act in accordance with righteousness remember to keep your motives sincere and true. Purity of intention is vital to not only achieve your goals and desires but to do them with Divine blessings. God knows our hearts. What may be confusing to us is very clear to Him.

Avoid basing your objectives and goals on how it will seem to other people. Base your objectives on what is right. As a person of honor your objectives are bound to cause reactions both bad and good. Allow others to believe what they want. This is easier to read than to put into practice as most of us want approval for our actions. I know these words sound like common sense, but I can attest "I've been there." Throughout the years, and especially during those years I faced accusations about my business and my honor, I was able to take the greatest comfort, gratification—and the courage to go on, knowing that God knew the truth and knew what was in my heart.

Have a clear vision on why you do what you do. Without that vision to guide you it becomes difficult to stay motivated. Knowing the goal helps keep you focused. Pay special attention to the details. Concentrate on how you perform the work to achieve your objective. You can practice doing just this. Strength training is not just for exercising - it can also apply to performance of any deeds.

You sweep the floor. You see some hard-to-reach spots. Do you make certain to sweep those spots? Do you tell yourself "Who'll ever notice?"? You cut the lawn but as you're putting the mower away you notice a spot you missed. Do you go back to complete the job? Not only is there a sense of satisfaction in doing a job the right way but you're training your mind to only be satisfied with excellence.

Personally, I have never mastered the 'art' of multitasking. Somehow our society has made doing many things at once praiseworthy, but it is anything but admirable. It just is not the best way to get things done. The Zen proverb says "When walking, walk. When eating, eat."

If excellence is your objective (as it should always be), focus on the task at hand. Confucius said, "By nature, men are nearly alike; by practice, they get to be wide apart." If your objective is to become everything you consider perfect and worthy start from where you are today and begin to transform your behavior and conduct. As Lao Tzu observed, "A journey of a thousand miles begins with one single step."

Train your mind to do the smallest task with perfection. Train your mind by starting out with easy duties to be done and doing them thoroughly. Train your mind to leave no task undone. Train your mind as you would train your muscles, that is by starting out with 'light weights' and gradually the more difficult will become achievable. Never settle for mediocrity or ordinary.

Train your mind to be faithful in *all things*. Additionally, get into the habit of being thankful for the realized goal—even though it has not physically appeared yet!

Predicating success on being thankful before the goal or objective has been reached may seem a bit unusual but is extremely powerful. It is a practice that, if it becomes a habit, will see the incredible become reality. Remember—faith must accompany that for which you are expressing gratitude. Saying meaningless 'thank you's' with a mind full of doubt will be a waste of time.

It is important to experience calmness which is why prayer and meditation need to be included in the petition. When your mind is calm and faith-filled you are likely to discern the best course of action and give over to absolute belief that which your showing gratitude for. In reality you are showing respect to God and his laws.

Respect is a word that can be used in many ways and with many meanings—"I respect him because he always keeps his word." "He never shows any respect" What do we mean when we use the word?

The dictionary defines respect as "high or special regard: Esteem" By keeping His commandments we know God will not only multiply our family but give His respect to us.   (I John 2:3-5)

There are many ways to show respect—holding a door for a lady, taking your hat off in someone's home, staying silent during church service. There are different categories of respect: To a thing, or to another person, to the Lord. When referring to another human being there is only two places that respect comes from and that is from the heart and mind.

I have always been of the opinion that respect is earned, not given.

You can show a respectful attitude to your boss, but if your personal opinion of them is not high, that attitude is usually not heartfelt.

Who do you respect? Take a minute and think about how that person (or persons) earned your respect. Now think of someone you must show respect (a respectful attitude) towards but is not coming from your heart. Can you feel the difference?

The actor Bruce Lee observed, "Knowledge will give you power, but character respect." if you find yourself in a position of not respecting the person who holds authority you must answer to, you should move on. Whether it be a committee you serve on or the job you've always wanted—move on. If your commitment is to be the best you can be, you can make no compromise. This is easier said than to put into practice. The challenge becomes more difficult because continuing to tolerate someone you have no respect for you begin to dislike yourself. You question yourself. You may even go so far as to loath yourself for being "weak". This is tuff stuff no doubt. Plan your exit strategy. Don't make rash moves. And above all—have faith that the Creator of the Universe has you in the palm of his hand.

Psalms 91:11-12, declares, "For He shall give His angels charge over you, to keep you in all your ways. In their hands, they shall bear you up, lest you dash your foot against a stone."

There are times when you are not able to walk away from people you do not hold in high regards. Keep in mind that treating someone in a respectful manner is in no way hypocritical even if they don't deserve your respect or admiration. It is a statement to who you are to be able to not only know the difference but actually speaks to your character by being respectful.

In 1951 President Harry Truman relieved General Douglas Mac-Arthur from command during the Korean War. MacArthur, who had led American and Allied forces in the Pacific during World War II, had a long and successful military career and was popular with the American public. When Truman announced his decision, the nation was shocked, but Truman held fast to his judgement. Harry Truman knew MacArthur did not respect him personally and he could tolerate that. But Truman would not put up with MacArthur not treating the office of the Presidency in a disrespectful manner.

If you find yourself being treated disrespectfully, they are rude to you, ridicule you, then you have no obligation to treat them with tolerance. Going further with this idea however, by tolerating this person's boorishness for any length of time not only demeans you but your silence invites further abuse! This is where your own sense of who you are, your self-respect, needs to be front and center. If you are troubled that as a Christian you need "to be the better person" and allow this behavior to continue, to rise above the hurt, then you are misinterpreting scripture. ***NO—ONE SHOULD ALLOW THEMSELVES TO BE DEMEANED.*** Jesus instructed his disciples to deal with disrespect by leaving only dust to those whose rudeness defined them. (Luke 10:10-11)

Live your life in such a manner to be respected, but by the same token don't become preoccupied with what others think. Let your light shine as a testament of who you are as a child of God. Set your standards and principles high and commit to achieving them. Allow for mistakes and missteps and never be too hard on yourself if you fall short. Simply pick yourself up and keep moving forward.

Respecting another person can only be accomplished by observing that person—how they behave, who they associate with, if they keep their word, if they walk the walk. To achieve this, you must know how to recognize these characteristics. This is called discernment. Discernment is essentially the ability to intuitively perceive the nature of a person, as well as situations.

Insight is the capacity to read people's motives and learn what their objectives are.

The Bible speaks about "the still small voice" that resides in each one of us. It is a voice that you must learn to differentiate from the constant mind chatter and that will take effort to accomplish. (I Kings 18:20-40, 19:12) In order to quiet the mind, you will need to enter into silence, and meditation is an excellent method to do so. Our direct connection to God is through our spirit. You'll hear people say "My heart is telling me..." And this voice should not be ignored. The more attention you give to the still small voice, the easier it will become to tell the difference between noise and something profound. The voice of the Holy Spirit is sweet and never harmful. This voice will never use dangerous words nor will ever speak hatred or harmful statements. (John 14:17, 14:26)

This sacred voice will allow you to feel a 'nudge' but as mentioned above you'll be able to discern this sound with practice and dedication.

If you have to talk yourself into something—when your 'gut' is saying the opposite—that's your soul directing you to the right path.

In our everyday interaction with people, we'll come to understand that most of the time a person's motivations and true objectives are hidden. This is not to imply that we should be constantly suspicious of everyone, but we do need rely on our ability to read between the lines by using logic, rational thinking and intuition. There are books on the market dedicated to help you learn techniques in being able to discern what a person's unspoken intentions and purposes are. We spoke about body language earlier, but it would be wise to explore and learn more of how a person's unspoken indicators can reveal what is in their heart.

We already possess a measure of perception in our DNA, passed down from our early ancestors. This somewhat dormant ability is centered in our Reflexive System. The Reflexive System uses sensory and emotional signals as shortcuts and observes all the stimuli around us. Whether its people passing us by, a couple holding hands, or the sound of a jet, our Reflexive System will blend each sight and sound into a tangible interpretation as much as possible.

As humans we are genetically predisposed to spotting anything out of the ordinary. The same impulses that our prehistoric ancestors experienced are immediately activated when anything "doesn't seem right". It is what they felt when the thick growth of plants and grass began to part as it headed in their direction. It is the system that kept them alive to allow the human race to grow.

The Zen Buddhist priest Dogen instructed, "Don't follow the advice of others; rather learn to listen to the voice within yourself." It's quite amazing to realize that truth surpasses ethnicities as well as borders!

9

Becoming an Overcomer

What are you willing to do to achieve your goals?

What is it that would be worth expending the last ounce of strength and resolve you possess? Are you prepared to "March into hell for a heavenly cause"? [6] In order to realize a goal you must give it your complete focus and be determined to do so. You commit yourself to success. If you are in sales, do you spend the extra 20 minutes to make certain your appointment book is filled for the week? If you own a gift shop, do you stay an hour longer after closing to clean, organize, and restock the shelves? If you are an accountant, do you prepare your clients return in a timely manner? There needs to be a sense of persistency, as well as commitment to be able to endure problems and distractions. To endure means to withstand hardships and adversity.

Life presents obstacles as well as opportunities. It can cause insensitivity, yet it also provides insight into how to overcome setbacks. Recently I read a narrative of a presentation given by the Chief Justice of the US Supreme Court to a group of ninth-grade graduates in the spring of 2017. The Chief Justice's son was among the graduates and was intended to be low-key. However modest the intention, the words he spoke are both profound and timeless. Justice John Roberts told his audience that commencement speakers typically will "wish you good luck and extend good wishes to you. I will not do that, and I'll tell you why."

"From time to time in the years to come, I hope you will be treated unfairly, so that you will come to know the value of justice."

"I hope that you will suffer betrayal, because that will teach you the importance of loyalty."

"Sorry to say, but I hope you will be lonely from time to time so that you don't take friends for granted.

"I wish you bad luck, again, from time to time so that you will be conscious of the role of chance in life and understand that your success is not completely deserved and that the failures of others is not completely deserved either."

"And when you lose, as you will from time to time, I hope every now and then your opponent will gloat over your failure. It is a way for you to understand the importance of sportsmanship."

"I hope you'll be ignored so that you know the importance of listening to others, and I hope you will have just enough pain to learn compassion."

"Whether I wish these things or not, they're going to happen. And whether you benefit from them or not will depend upon your ability to see the message in your misfortunes."

Life demands that we either persevere under stress or we cower and retreat under pressure. The outcome of one path taken is inspiring to do so again in the future when it comes up again while the other allows a person to become depressed and to be continually taken advantage of. Endurance is a quality that allows you to catapult toward what you aspire to do or to be.

Endurance combined with living in the will of God is the stronger force in the unseen universe. As Paul wrote "If God is for us who can be against us?" (Romans 8:31)

You've heard the oft quoted "When the going gets tuff, the tuff get going" and although the phrase has become trite it is meaningful. You'll never get far or accomplish much by quitting when things become difficult.

All of us have periods in our lives where everything goes wrong. It can seem that, like the fly in the spider web, the more we struggle the more difficult the chance of success becomes. We hear the great Deceiver saying "Just forget it. It's never going to work out. You'll make a fool of yourself. You can't do this. It's too hard, just give up and try some other time."

Each one of us experience setbacks and failures. Whether they are temporary or not is really up to us. At times these reverses are shared by a whole group of us. It has even happened to herd of Buffalo.....

When the odds are against you and everything's awful,
and nothing is going your way,
And everyone's saying, "it's out of the question,"
for clearly it isn't you day.
Just remember what happened in Buffalo
when the Oilers came into town.
They were making a rout of it. The Bills were just out of it.
By thirty-two points they were down.
When a lot of your friends have just written you off,
abandoning you to your fate,
And they say "there's no point" even trying to win,
that for you it is "simply too late,"
Just remember how Buffalo pulled it together
when their team was so far behind.
It took such heart and soul to climb out of that hole,
that I tell you it boggles the mind!
How both offense and defense refused to accept
that the game and the season were over.

Though everyone said they were buried and dead,
the Bills simply wouldn't roll over.
When everyone tells you "you might as well quit,"
that you simply don't have what you need,
Think of somebody like back-up quarterback Reich,
and a pass-catcher named Andre Reed.
LESSON ONE in that wildcard playoff they played
is IT'S ALWAYS IMPORTANT TO TRY!
No matter how hopeless your own situation,
you never, no never say die!
LESSON TWO is the lesson the Oilers learned on a day
they were doing so well.
People said "You just know it, there's no way
to blow it."
The truth is THERE'S NO WAY TO TELL!
When the breaks are all yours and you're riding so high that victory's
coming real soon,
Remember what happened to Houston,
to the Oilers and Warren Moon.
Whether they're booing or cheering you now,
and whether you're cold or hot,
You've got to keep trying and doing your best,
and giving it all you've got.
For the contest's not over until it's all over,
and in life it's almost the same.
Until it's all over, in mud or in clover,
you've got to keep playing your game."[7]

Napoleon Hill once said "Patience, persistence, and perspiration make an unbeatable combination for success." In his monumental work 'Think and Grow Rich' Hill wrote about succumbing to temporary defeat:

R.U. Darby related the story of his uncle to Hill who was then taking notes and about to write on motivation.

Darby recounted how he and his uncle, after toiling with pick and shovel for what seemed like forever, discovered gold. Realizing they needed more than just muscle and sweat, they returned home, raised the money to purchase the necessary machinery and equipment and returned to Colorado where they began to fill rail cars with the precious metal.

Soon after however, the vein of gold ore disappeared. Try as they might the were not able to locate the continuous vein. Dispirited and depressed they finally gave up and selling their equipment for pennies on the dollar to the local trashman, returned home to Maryland.

This junkman was no ordinary salvage dealer however. He recruited a mining engineer who, after a little calculating realized that Darby and his uncle failed to adjust their search by taking fault lines into account.

Armed with this knowledge, the trashman used the costly machinery —of which he paid a few hundred dollars—to extract millions of dollars of gold! Darby however went on to become one of the most successful insurance salesmen in the country because of the lesson he learned from the experience—NEVER GIVE UP! Unfortunately, when him and his uncle lost heart and gave up, they did so because they were not informed, prepared or knowledgeable. Had they specific information and understanding—what Hill refers to as "specialized knowledge"— they would have been inspired to press forward. You see Darby and his uncle gave up, abandoned hope, and quit—three feet from where they stopped drilling!

Author Max Lucado in his book 'Facing the Giants' wrote that we should "imitate David. Never give up. One prayer might not be enough. You may get knocked down a time or two—but don't quit. Keep loading the rocks. Keep swinging the sling."

Although a vital part of endurance is fortitude and tenacity it is equally vital to be informed and gain as much knowledge of your undertaking as possible.

Each of us makes mistakes and all of us fall short, but we are measured by our ability to carry on despite the failure. In order to benefit from the fall, we must learn from it. When we were children, we were told not to touch a hot stove. Whether we heeded the warning or not did not prevent our cooking on that stove when we were older.

As we go about our daily lives, we should keep open the possibility of not doing something completely mistake free—again we need to give ourselves a break. This is not however an excuse to underperform. In Corinthians Paul spoke about things being done decently and in order.

(I Corinthians 14:40) Always strive to do your best, but if your plan to achieve your objective falls short, don't give up—just create a new plan!

You've heard that fire hardens steel, and our character is like that. Persisting through a trial or an adversity builds your character. You become emboldened and confident from moving up and over temporary failure. I say temporary because by overcoming the defeat you are not dwelling on the defeat but benefiting from the memory of your moving past it. It is anything but easy to survive a prolonged hardship, when instead of a few moments of misfortune, you get years of sorrow and grief. The true test of a person's makeup is being able to turn that difficulty or misfortune into something positive.

The foundation of endurance is survival (which is an achievement in and of itself) but complete triumph is achieving the objective.

Survival in a non-lethal setting is not the justification for "anything goes" where the use of unethical means is acceptable. However, if our physical safety or that of our family is in mortal danger 'anything goes' is rational.

Endurance comes in many forms and our connection to God, the strength of that underlying connection, is where we gain the wisdom to determine our actions. Endurance also includes the moral turpitude to stand for truth and for justice. It is to be willing to stand against evil in a proactive way. It is volunteering at a soup kitchen, and it is manning a forward position, rifle at the ready in a battle-zone.

Although we all wish that everything in life would be smooth sailing, we know that storms cross our bow now and then. It's how we respond to those storms that composes our character. Virgil once said, "Come what may, all bad fortune is to be conquered by endurance." It is within us to respond in strength to whatever life throws at us. Whether it's a football game or a firefight, a sorrow or a setback, it's our response—and more importantly our attitude—that defines who we really are.

When you refuse to take no for an answer. When you refuse to quit. When you are prepared to go up against what seems to be impossible and endure the pain and sacrifice that comes along with your quest, you are also demonstrating courage.

Courage shows itself in many ways, but there is a difference in being brave and being foolhardy. Wisdom is what allows us to know the difference. Solomon wrote about wisdom and being wise over 120 times in Proverbs alone. As a child of the Most High perhaps asking for wisdom may be our most intelligent request. Using wisdom to endure what seems impossible allows us to know what should be feared and should not be feared. Without knowing the difference our actions could not be classified as courageous. A person could not know if they are acting out of courage or ignorance of understanding the danger.

Throughout history courage has been defined in different ways. Straight out we could define courage as being brave. But being brave doesn't mean to lack fear. Indeed, fear is a natural emotion, and a brave man feels that as well as the coward. Courage is the quality of being brave despite the natural inclination to feel fear and being able to overcome that fear.

Referring again to our distant past, our ancient forebears were able to withstand the harsh conditions of the prehistoric world through the Amygdala which I referred to earlier. The Amygdala releases cortisol into our bloodstream. A stress hormone, cortisol helps our bodies respond to emergencies. Our Reflexive System where the Amygdala is located, will usually shove our analytical reasoning to the side and a problem, risk or an upset of some sort will magnify other things.

Our brains and how it processes and retains all the stimuli that passes by us is nothing if not a manifestation of a miracle. At 2% of our total body weight, and weighing about 3 lbs., the brain consumes 20% of our oxygen intake and the calories burned. The brain is composed of two sides called "hemispheres" with each hemisphere playing unique complex activities unique just to it.

The *Reflexive* brain, that found in the right hemisphere, is an important part of our emotional system. What's known as the *Reflective* brain is primarily found on the left hemisphere. It is known as the analytical part of our brain. We will explore these systems in more depth as we move forward.

Our decisions - how we act and re-act—are often made by our feelings and once we put our feelings into risk or fear, we magnify risk or fear greatly.

You may recall accounts of soldiers, emergency workers or an average person who said that when they performed an act we deem courageous, they did so by instantly reacting. The reason for this is because the Amygdala releases fear signals and we act instantly without input from our Reflective (analytical) system where it would begin to weigh options and attempt to use logic before taking actions of any kind. When the event has passed, when you say to yourself (or others) "I acted out of instinct" you're not far off. It is at that point you'll experience tremors and emotional instability (usually temporary). This is due to the neurons located in the Amygdala firing in unison for hours afterward. Additionally, another area of the brain known as the Hippocampus, located near the Amygdala, will replay the episode over and over cranking up the fear, upset and anxiety.

When we take a moment to think about and consider the amazing miracle that our brains truly are, we cannot help but be overwhelmed by the unimaginable power and love of our Creator.

Mark Twain observed that "Courage is resistance to fear, mastery of fear—not absence of fear." This was evident on a Tuesday morning in September 2001 when hundreds of firefighters, policemen, and first responders ran into two burning buildings in lower Manhattan to rescue total strangers.

In writing about the Peloponnesian Wars of 431-404 BC Thucydides, the Greek historian wrote "The bravest are surely those who have the clearest vision of what is before them, glory and danger alike, and, notwithstanding, go out to face it."

Most of us are familiar with the story of the 300 Spartans. Although it was the Spartan custom to train a boy from the age of 7 in the art of war, courage is not learned, and fear is not banished despite many years of training.

In the year 480 BC King Xerxes 1st of Persia (known in the Bible as Ahasuerus) about the time he was demanding that his wife Queen Vashti disrobe for his nobles to gawk at, was preparing to invade Greece. Attacking with his army by land, and navy in the waters below Athens, Xerxes had at his disposal upwards of a million men. [8]

Travelling from the north of Greece, the Persian Army were stopped at a pass 50 feet wide at a place called Thermopylae. With Leonidas 1st

their king, 300 Spartan soldiers held off what most scholar believe were over a half million Persians for two days.

The courage shown by so few against so many has been remembered by freedom—loving people for twenty-five centuries. Calling up every fragment of audacity, resoluteness, and courage possible, they delayed the Persian Army long enough for the Greeks to prepare for battle at the island of Salamis where the Persian invaders were defeated.

If a man doesn't know who or what he is facing, bravery is not in the equation, only ignorance. The Spartans knew what they were facing but they also knew themselves. They prepared in their bodies, in their minds and in their spirits. They fully understood what was at stake if they allowed fear to overcome their judgement. Fortunately, most of us will never be called upon to battle thousands but never forget that everything you want in life is on the other side of fear.

10

Only the Brave

There is a time and place to allow our emotions to guide us but facing the giants in our life is usually not the place.

Being foolhardy in your pursuit of whatever objective you're striving towards is not a wise course of action. Being compulsive—not preparing—is acting without thinking and although you will undoubtedly face times when you'll react through instinct it would be in your best interest to be foundationally fortified spiritually. To be prepared in spirit is wise. "Only the wise are brave" wrote Francesco Guicciardini, "Others are either temerarious or foolhardy, thus, we can say that every brave man is wise, but not that every wise man is brave."

David had been pursued by King Saul for so long, he hardly remembered what a peaceful night felt like. Time and again David absorbed the abuse, the cutting remarks, and the jealousy of Saul not only out of respect for Saul's position as King but more importantly because Saul was anointed by the Lord. Saul's insecurities led him to believe David intended to kill him and take the throne of Israel for himself. David however harbored no such plan.

Although he had been sanctified by the prophet Samuel to one day be King, David chose to allow God to work through him for His own purpose. Finding Saul alone in a cave, David cut a piece of cloth from

Saul's robe without Saul knowing it. David knew that to walk away from confrontation is not weakness but strength. (I Samuel Chapters 18-31)

Refusing a personal confrontation is an action that can be a demonstration of self-confidence. Courage has a lot to do with what's going on inside of us.

C.S. Lewis said, "Courage is not simply one of the virtues, but the form of every virtue at the testing point." No matter the provocations —always live up to your standards. It takes courage to walk through the valley of the shadow of death, and it takes courage to live to your standards and your personal code of honor, especially if you are faced with a moral decision.

Most of us will never be called upon to sacrifice our lives for our beliefs and principles yet history is replete with those who have - another reason to study the lives of those whose example can affect us even today. The people we choose as role models should be of the highest virtues but keep in mind that building good character can only come from you. Not from them.

Focus your mind on what is right in the present moment. With wisdom comes the ability to consider all possible consequences, alternatives, and decisions. As Jesus said, "be wise as serpents and harmless as doves." (Matthew 10:16)

When Jesus suggested that the apostles be "harmless as doves" He was not only talking about being peaceful but being virtuous.

Being a leader, one who commands the total respect and admiration of those under him, takes more than issuing commands and expecting others to follow them. Certainly, respect of the position, even fear, will cause others to follow the orders of that leader. But people are more likely to want to be led by someone who they know possesses moral excellence and whose actions and thinking are based on honesty and ethics.

Although you may work or associate with a 'peer' you probably have followed advice now and then from that person if you think of them as virtuous. People may look at you that way.

Perhaps up until now you've allowed negative, pessimistic, or cynical thinking to occupy your mind. But if you begin to develop your positive traits, you'll bring about so many changes in your life that you'll barely have time to appreciate them. It takes work to develop virtues and with time it becomes a large part of your character. Keep in mind that when a person defines character in another it is based on a reasonably consistent set of traits. As in anything worthwhile, you'll need to allow yourself the freedom of time to absorb into your life the lasting principles of virtue.

Baltazar Gracian the Spanish writer described virtue, beautifully summarizing the quality this way, "For virtue is the bond of all the perfections, and the heart of all life's satisfactions. It makes a man sensible, alert, far-seeing, understanding, wise, courageous, considerate, upright, joyous, welcomed, truthful, and a universal idol.... Virtue is the son of our lesser world, the shy over which is a good conscious. It is so beautiful, that it finds favor of God and of man. There is nothing lovely without virtue...for virtue is the essence of wisdom, and all else is folly; capacity and greatness must be measured in terms of virtue... Virtue alone is sufficient unto itself, and it only, makes a man worth loving in life and in depth, worth remembering."

Although Gracian lived hundreds of years ago, the qualities of virtue are as significant and essential today as they were in the past. Be selective in who you associate with. The wrong people will not only talk you out of your dreams and destiny but will interrupt your journey toward moral excellence.

This recommendation applies to any age, but I think applies most especially to young adults.

After spending years in middle school and high school trying to "fit in" it isn't easy changing behaviors. After making every effort to 'be one of the guys' it became part of many teenagers and young adult's personality to hang with the more popular kids. You may have compromised yourself (your soul knew and even told you at first) by associating with people who were less than honorable. But in an attempt to get along you went along. It became a habit. As you now embark on the journey called life its time to form new habits. Make new goals. Make new friends. I am not saying it will be easy or even pleasant. Starting anew never is. Every new birth is painful. The people who 'knew you when' (and sometimes this includes family) will challenge you, even ridicule you. You are about to experience an unfortunate human tendency—judging others. They will define you by your past and because of it will feel they can determine your future. *Don't accept that!* You could end up missing what God has planned for you if you do. No matter your age its time to give up the wrong people to make room for the right ones to appear. Get together with people of faith so you will step into your destiny.

By this point you've probably realized that in order to lead a life of exception and righteousness your personal creed and core values need to be well—defined and intact within your heart. These values must be genuine and above reproach.

As I've written before—you need to give yourself a break. Don't be overly critical of yourself if you fall short of the objectives you've planned for yourself. Beware of the Deceiver's negativity. Put your focus on the Redeemer and not on the Repressor.

Its important to allow for mistakes and shortfalls while going into anything worthwhile because you won't become discouraged and give up completely. If your heart is right, and your goal is true you will succeed. Don't sabotage yourself however with griping, complaining, and talking failure. God cannot work through a spirit of pessimism. God knows our hearts and in the end that is what matters more.

Being sincere in who you are, what you stand for and what defines you among mankind is how you will be known and remembered.

Sincerity according to the dictionary "is the quality or state of being sincere: honesty of mind: freedom of hypocrisy."

Most people find sincerity to be a difficult quality to incorporate and maintain in their lives. This stems not so much as wanting to deceive or be dishonest but to just get along with other people. Wanting to be part of a group, being welcomed, and accepted, is not only an objective of young adults who I mentioned previously.

To avoid a scene or a confrontation some people will nod (or mumble) an agreement although they may not agree inwardly (the Presidential election of 2016 is a great example). Where does common sense and honesty come together for the common good? Avoiding confrontation is not being insincere but agreeing to do something or say something you don't believe in, is.

It is important to be honest with everyone you encounter, but you should not feel obligated to share every thought or your private feelings with them. You should use discretion and wisdom when sharing your life and your views with others. Don't confuse sincerity with being an open book.

Its to your benefit to keep your private business, private. Paul wrote that we should conduct "ourselves in the world in simplicity and godly sincerity." and to show a pattern of good works, to not go from good to bad, to be sincere in all we do. (II Corinthians 1:12, Titus 2:7)

Self-confidence is really the foundation of sincerity. Although honesty and sincerity go hand in hand, honesty has more impact on being truthful, being fair and having moral uprightness. Wanting the approval of others, many people will acquiesce to those with a strong personality or who they see as a superior. Be objective in knowing what (and who) is and isn't sincere in your life.

As time goes by, you'll notice the changes within yourself as you work on improving who you are. When you fall short, you'll notice it immediately, where before you never paid attention (it was part of who you were) the inner voice, the Holy Spirit, will lead your consciousness to recognizing the misstep. Celebrate you when that happens. Changes —positive changes—are taking place!

You'll also begin to notice that being insincere is uncomfortable. Its work because you must put on an act. "The most exhausting thing in life, I have discovered" observed Anne Morrow Lindbergh "is being insincere."

Prepare for a full assault by Satan as you begin the process of turning your life around. "You're a phony." "What happens when they find you out?" "You're wasting your time, who do you think you are?" These are just a few examples of what you'll hear. The words may be different, but the objective is the same— "You're never going to improve." Rejoice when you begin hearing these assaults! This confirms that you're reconstructing yourself and remolding yourself into who God means you to be!

Insincerity is obvious to most of us. Maybe it's a person's body language that gives it away. Their facial muscles, the phony smile, the eyes. Maybe its just nothing more than a feeling but in any event, it doesn't take long to spot a fake.

Years ago, there was a sit-com on television called "Leave it to Beaver." One of the characters on the show, Eddie Haskell, was known for his over-the-top compliments, especially to Mrs. Cleaver, Beaver's mother. "What a beautiful dress you're wearing." "My Mrs. Cleaver, you look lovely today!" Everyone knew Eddie was a phony and to be called an 'Eddie Haskell' back then was anything but a compliment!

Francois Delaroche Foucaud taught that, "Sincerity is an openness of heart that is found in very few people. What we usually see is only an artful disguise people put on to win the confidence of others." Sadly, this truth is found often.

Be confident that when you commit yourself to become the best you can be, you will be joined by the Holy Spirit. Think about and meditate on who you want to become, who you want to be and what contribution you want to make to the world. There is an old Shinto proverb that I've found both profound and encouraging "Sincerity is the single virtue that binds the Divine and man in one."

We spoke earlier about how you appear to others—your posture, your handshake and so on but how we talk to others is another evaluation that people immediately make about us. Its through our speech that others know our thoughts and feelings. After the initial introduction, our actions then begin to affect how a person decides who we are, what our character really is.

Throughout this book I've quoted gifted writers, essayists, politicians, spiritual leaders, and philosophers. We have a basic knowledge and know a bit more about those men and women who appear in the Bible. We know the life of Jesus the best due to the gospels but by and large we'll never be able to hear how the other personalities quoted spoke. We'll never know what caused them to express the maxims we hold in esteem today or what occurrences in their life formed the observations that caused their declarations. We are only able to conclude their brilliance by the words they left us that enrich our lives each time we read them.

Words have meaning and for this reason it is essential that you maintain control of what you say and how you say it. As you probably know by now, how you say things carries as much meaning as what you say.

The wise take time to think about what they want to say. They know the impact those words may have. Nagarjuna, the Buddhist philosopher said, "Those who speak with discretion are respected by mankind." Also keep in mind that people overhear you.

Intentional or not, people take in what others say. During the second World War a popular phrase was "Loose lips sink ships." Whether it was talk about troop movements, sailing schedules or any number of war-related activities, words had the power to cost lives. Your discussions are probably not as consequential as that, but chances are someone will not only form opinions but relevance and meaning from what you say. Speaking of opinions don't feel obligated to always give yours!

Even when you're relaxing with your family or friends be mindful of what you say. Although this may sound practical, I mention this because even in a comfortable and informal setting things you may have said can be mis-construed or even used against you! This is not meant to create paranoia but just as advice to always be aware of what you say and how much you say. We've all said things we wish we could take back and that usually results from spur-of-the moment, unthought-out comments. Practice using discretion. Think before you talk. Remember —Silence is Golden!

Francesco Guicciardini, observed that, "unless you are forced by necessity, be careful in your conversations never to say anything which if repeated, might displease others. For often at times and in ways you could never foresee, those words may do great harm. In this matter, I warn you, be very careful. Even prudent men go wrong here, and it is difficult not to."

In our world today we have the opportunity to interact with people across the globe in live time. Many businesses maintain offices, factories, or a presence of some kind internationally. Not only what and how you say something can carry different interpretations, but body language and gestures do also.

Keep in mind that how you say something reveals your true feelings. In Paul's second letter to Timothy, written around the year 65 AD, he reminded followers not to "strive about words to no profit" which would hurt those who heard them. (II Timothy 2:14)

When you're making your point about something it is good advice to A) Know what you're talking about B) Know who you're taking to and C) Use gentle words backed by facts that can be verified. The foolish not only make the listener uncomfortable but irritated also!

11

The Pursuit of Our Desires

Most people, particularly in a business setting, are looking "to get."

They hope to impress their superiors. They hope for recognition, a promotion or a raise. Some people are just happy to be noticed hanging out with management to impress their peers. Instead of looking how to get, make the commitment to give!

People want to realize their significance: I am loved. I am admired. I am beautiful/ handsome. I am respected. I am valued and so on. Satisfy those desires in another and immediately you become significant—to them! Now this is not to encourage you to be deceitful. To compliment or falsely praise others to promote yourself is dishonest and consequences follow. But to genuinely pick out qualities you admire in another is engaging.

When you find someone is socializing with you, you will become aware that they are interested in the attention you show to them. Talk about what is of interest to them. Keep in mind the following: In everyday life, as we interact with others the important thing is not how interesting you happen to be, rather how suitable you are, or could become, as a relationship with that person.

As you're talking with them, this person is evaluating—both consciously and subconsciously—how well you fit into their idea of associating with you.

Remember my talking about adding significance to someone? If someone feels that you give them significance, they will shut their eyes to your flaws and forgive any weaknesses you have.

Most of us want to be liked. This is not the hang-up of being hung-up on people's approval. Wanting to be liked is natural. I have never heard of anyone whose goal was to be disliked in life. We just need to be who we are—who we really are. Putting on an act lasts just so long. If you're concerned that you lack certain "endearing" characteristics, this is the time to identify them and improve on them.

Be sincere when talking with someone, whether its discussing their problems, their children or grandchildren or anything that is the topic of your conversation.

Each of us want to be loved as well as be liked. Although we don't expect love from each person we come in contact with, we thrive as pure personalities knowing there are people that love us. Conversely this is why being rejected by someone we love hurts so deeply. Rejection it is said, is one of the most painful experiences a human being can endure.

The Bible talks about love in one way or another over 540 times! How many of us simply love?

Usually when we love someone else, we expect love in return. We want to possess their love and we depend on that love. Can you simply love without hoping for love in return? Frankly speaking that kind of love is very rare, yet this is the kind of love God has for us.

There are so many cliches concerning love that abound throughout our lives. Innumerable songs have been written about it, people want to possess it (and become possessive of it) and talk about it.

A stand-alone book could be written (and many have been already) about the subject so we won't spend a lot of time here, but for our purposes I want us to consider taking a different, actually more difficult, approach to loving.

Most of us love in the following way: "If you love me, I'll love you." "If you really loved me, you would buy me that ring." "I can only love you if you agree with me on this." You get the point. Who can you say that you love unconditionally and unequivocally? Most of us would say our children. Probably our parents. Our spouse? What we value most in our lives—love—usually entails controlling and holding onto the feelings of another person. Loving without stipulations is scarce. Loving without expecting reciprocal feelings is rarer still. Why am I using this brief interlude concerning love in writing about achieving goals? The reason is as uncomplicated as it is remarkable—it is learning to control your emotions. It also involves detachment—which you will need, as you'll see before you finish this book—in order to achieve what you desire. It is about becoming both aware and dispassionate and the wisdom to know the difference.

We pursue so much during our lives: money, happiness, a beautiful home, a nice car, a loving and loyal companion. It seems however as we live our lives our pursuits don't always bring us the desired objective or outcome. Why is that? We spend an inordinate amount of time chasing dreams but are those dreams, whatever they may be, worth chasing? Deciding what is right can only be accomplished by knowing what results are possible and understanding the consequences. This is what's known as thinking things through.

It is our ability to reason and our inner degree of wisdom which sets us apart from other animals. It is understanding the difference of alternatives.

Wisdom is a word that we hear a lot about and desire to have in abundance, Rumi the Sufi poet wrote, "Wisdom is not in words, it is in understanding."

To acquire wisdom requires dedication and prayer (James 1:5).

Although the world's view of wisdom usually means doing the right thing, Christians view it a bit more deeply. Wisdom to believers means viewing things from God's perspective.

There are three steps allowing us to walk with wisdom: 1) Live life skillfully 2) Add to your learning 3) Live life fearfully. If you don't fear God, you will never be successful in achieving wisdom. It is assured that you can acquire wisdom by meditating on God's word, and by observing God works.

One of the biggest challenges we have in living wisely is living foolishly. We sometimes make foolish decisions, plain and simple. We sometimes do stupid things. We live in a world that can be shameful, prideful, and vain. We try to navigate our way through the debris and floating wreckage but trying to do so without a relationship with God will ultimately fail. Acquiring wisdom is a gift that God gives to the righteous, "For God gives wisdom and knowledge and joy to a man who is good in His sight (Ecclesiastes 2:26, New American Standard Bible) Notice Solomon writes "good in God's sight" not in people's sight. Trying to 'go with the crowd' using our EGO, edges God out.

You and God need to be on great terms. It takes a constant dialogue with God. This doesn't mean that you need a constant discourse, mouthing every word, but a communion of Spirit. Asking God every morning through prayer "Give me wisdom for this day Lord" allows God to speak to your heart. Soon without even realizing it you will observe God's work in your life. He will develop you and prepare you to take hold of the life He has planned for you. Proverbs says, "The way of a fool is right in his own eyes, but he who heeds counsel is wise." Heed God's counsel. (Proverbs 12:15)

Too many people tinker and trifle with God. Adam and Eve sought to deceive God in the garden. When the people were corrupt before the Lord, and filled with violence, the waters overtook them. When ten righteous men couldn't be found, flames leveled Sodom and Gomorrah. Pharaoh's smile disappeared after 10 plagues. Ananias and his wife Sapphira's deception caused them to be dragged out feet first.

When we hear the word 'fear' we naturally think of the feeling of dread or fright, but it would be erroneous to apply that definition to God.

The meaning of "to fear the Lord" is *to show profound reverence and awe toward Him*. How many of us looked at the Bible, especially Proverbs and with a wave of the hand said, "I got this!"? We live in a world that is no longer 'fast paced'. We now live in an immediate world. Within seconds we are made aware of an event that happened anywhere on earth. It is easy to get distracted to what not only is important but to ignore the teachings and instructions that give our lives true meaning. Technology and all of the options and choices that it has brought forth has in many cases reduced some people's dependance on God. A recent survey found that the average amount of times a person touches or accesses their cellphone is in excess of 2,600 daily! When people put diversions between them and their relationship with God their lives become vacant. Sadly, as this process takes place, they don't even realize it. Fortunately, we are never too far gone for God to break the fall. God never loses His focus on His children so even if up until now you've not been as attentive and observant as you believe you could have, start now because God is not through with you.

In your pursuit of wisdom be receptive to learning from what you read and from whom you meet. Learn from experiences—not only in your life but from others. Understanding that which you read and from observing what you see is what makes that knowledge useful. To understand is to perceive, comprehend and know the nature and significance of something. Then it's being able to use that knowledge to your benefit.

Experience as it's said, is the best teacher and while certainly that is a valid statement you don't need to know everything—just to possess the wisdom to access someone else's experience. You don't need the experience of repairing furnaces to fix your furnace. You simply call an expert who has that experience to fix it. Your wisdom dictates your actions.

Leonardo da Vinci wrote, "Wisdom is the daughter of experience... Shun the teachings of those speculators whose arguments are not confirmed by experience."

Fighter pilots learn combat tactics before they themselves see combat, by combat—experienced pilots. It would be unwise to learn from another novice. *As long as learning wisdom from another is based on the experiences of that person we can internalize and make it our wisdom, or we take that knowledge and create our own experiences.*"Learn the words of wisdom uttered by the wise and apply them in your own life" wrote Kahil Gibran author of 'The Prophet' "Live them—but do not make a show of reciting them, for he who repeats what he does not understand is no better than an ass that is loaded with books."

Pursuing wisdom takes dedication and commitment, and prayer. You'll first need to determine what wisdom means to you. You'll find that reflection and evaluating your past—your habits, your daily routine, interaction with others and so on—will be invaluable in your quest. Ecclesiastes tells us to decide - "I applied my heart to know, to search and seek out wisdom and the reason of things" (Ecclesiastes 7:25-26) Baltasar Gracian wrote that "Self-reflection is the school of wisdom" then went on to say "With men of understanding, wisdom counts for everything."

There are books within the Bible that are known as "Books of Wisdom"—Proverbs, Ecclesiastes and Job.

Who exactly wrote Job is unknown, but scholars believe it to be one of the oldest stories in the Bible, written perhaps 2,000 before Jesus' birth. Solomon has been credited as the primary author of Proverbs and Ecclesiastes about 3,000 years ago. The Catholic Bible includes The Book of Wisdom written approximately 100 years before the Nativity.9

There's no one who can measure your strengths and weaknesses as well as you can. After contemplation you might consider writing them down. I know this sounds like work but if this is a serious pursuit, there is no better way to focus than to see something in writing.

If you've decided that gaining wisdom is important to your personal growth, I would invite you to begin reading from the Book of Proverbs.

There are 31 chapters in Proverbs—one for each day of the month. Read one chapter every day. If you are reading this on the 12th of the month, begin with Chapter 12. If today is the 22nd begin with Chapter 22. Spend time thinking on and absorbing the words. Meditate on the meanings behind the words.

Be realistic. Don't expect immediate results. When we plant a seed we water it, nurture it with fertilizer, keeping it weed-free. The seed takes time to grow. Patience is required. Keep nourishing your mind with scripture and bold expectancy. Prepare your field for the impending harvest of edified wisdom.

You're probably familiar with the saying "nature abhors a vacuum." When there are differences in temperature, they become compensated by heat exchange. A drop in atmospheric pressure is balanced out by the wind. Anywhere in nature there is imbalance, forces appear to create balance. Absolute balance, however, has never been observed! Absolute balance would mean that absolutely nothing is going on and we know that there is never nothing going on!

Life—death, day—night, high-tide / low-tide. Nature on its own demonstrated contrasts but human beings do what they can to remove, or at least minimize disparity. Although the laws of nature are sometimes thought—at least by man—not to affect us, in reality they do, hence the similarity between nature and man's proclivity toward eliminating imbalance.

In life, harmony is keeping the three main components of being human—body, mind, and spirit—in balance. We know that devoting an excessive amount of energy on any one of these segments to the exclusion of the others creates abnormalities—what we sometimes refer to as 'Quirks'. Spending 6 hours in a gym on a daily basis and neglecting spiritual fulfillment is not achieving balance. Continual and uninterrupted meditation may be called for if you are a Yogi in the Himalayas but not practical if you have a family to provide for. We need to work to ensure that nothing we focus on becomes obsessive.

Balance is about organizing our life in such a way that we can spend time developing each part to the fullest.

It's common for some of us to take skills, hobbies, exercise, and other interests to the extreme but it seems that the single most common example is the person who is a workaholic. He (or she) focuses all their time and energy on their work. Sometimes its used as an escape but working all the time at the expense of their family life is not very wise. Despite the success (if one could call it that) at work, they find their marriage falling apart, their relationship with their children suffering—sometimes permanently. That is a life out of balance. Ironically were you to ask the workaholic why they are spending so much time working, they'll say "To benefit my family!"

Despite achieving outstanding results at their job, the balancing forces of nature will result in the direct opposite of what they intended —in this case losing those they love!

You've seen people who worked themselves to exhaustion. They get sick or depressed. They end up with a chronic fatigue syndrome—all of which will put an end to any thought of doing their job efficiently—

another example of the balancing forces of nature at work. We'll have more to say later about balancing forces but for now let's go on.

Epicurus observed that we should, "Be Moderate in order to taste the joys of life in abundance." When he spoke about being moderate Epicurus meant to intentionally limit ourselves and not go to extremes. This doesn't mean to devote less quality of whatever we do, just not to be obsessed. Whatever we do we should do impeccably. We need however, to know how to relax and to know when the benefits of waiting on God's timing, through His guidance by prayer, serves both His purposes and ours.

There are times where putting your complete focus and energy into a project or task is necessary. There is, without question, a sense of satisfaction—profound satisfaction—into something and observing its success.

In 1961 President John F. Kennedy proposed that, "Before this decade is out, of landing a man on the Moon and returning him safely to the Earth." On July 20th, 1969, Neil Armstrong became the first man to step onto the lunar surface.

A few days earlier, on July 16th the spaceflight known as Apollo 11 was launched by a SATURN V rocket from the Kennedy Space Center in Florida. The 'Space Race' as it eventually became known, actually began on October 4th, 1957, when the Soviet Union launched SPUTNIK I, the first artificial satellite to orbit the Earth. The United States made a total commitment to achieve superiority in space employing thousands of Americans to achieve that goal. The US and its civilian space agency NASA (National Aeronautics and Space Administration) illustrated completely the passage "Whatever the mind of man can conceive, and believe, it can achieve."

We should always avoid living a routine life, monotony being a sedative to our desire to achieve. W. Somerset Maugham once wrote,

"Excess on occasion is exhilarating. It prevents moderation from acquiring the deadening effect of habit." This should be by choice, however. Not by habit.

Leading a dull and boring life, never enjoying a vacation, constantly obsessing about work, never taking in fresh air with a walk in the woods is not the way God intended us to live, "Life is like riding a bicycle. To keep your balance, you must keep moving." observed Einstein. Be vigilant against living your life in hyper-drive, conversely as likewise that becomes unbalanced as well as unhealthy. Set your aim somewhere between these two extremes.

As we've discussed, nature constantly balances things out. If a man continually lives in a rut, if illness strikes, the opportunity for excitement and fretting about Emergency Rooms, Intensive Care Units, doctors, hospitals, IV's and medication will come about. Likewise, the hyperactive man experiences a slow down with Emergency Rooms, Intensive Care Units, doctors, hospitals, IV's and medication, The secret of living a balanced life is to maintain a stable life of work and play.

For those who don't know how to relax they really don't know how to work either. Actually, it is possible, make that probable, that by *not working extremely* hard you'll manage to get more done! Why, you ask? Because you are keeping your awareness open to anything that comes up. You are detached from obsession and calmly dealing with whatever needs to be done. The important point however is to always act irreproachably in whatever you do. There will be times when putting your heart and soul, as well as complete focus, into something will be necessary as we've seen, but otherwise great results usually result from maintaining a level of stability in all you do.

Beware of comparing or contrasting yourself to something or someone. When things are done in comparison the balancing forces begin equalizing. By that I mean you can expect to see something pulled apart or uniting them. Either things will get into a common agreement with each other—come together in not always positive ways, or confrontational. This result is usually from putting too much importance on something. If we tend to idealize something (or someone) balance will eventually be restored when we discover or see the whole picture.

All of us have experienced this feeling— "I know if I only have (fill in the blank) my life will be so much better, easier, happier, etc." You've overestimated and idealized, possibly romanticized the object or person only to eventually watch the halo fall off or be disappointed by it in some way. Moses cautioned us against idolization exhorting us that only God deserves our extreme devotion. (Exodus 32:1-24)

When you cease experiencing or causing extremes, no excessive creations are present. There are no 'empty spots' for the balancing forces to fall into. This all seems a bit complicated and maybe has never been something you've been cognizant of until now, but if you think back to those times you over-revered anything you'd recall that something seemed to prevent either the attainment or your attachment to it, or to them. For now, its important to remember to be discerning and disciplined, to keep everything in proportion. Neglect nothing but always be the best you can be without sacrificing other areas of your life to do so.

12 █

Doing Unto Others

Thirty-five years had passed since Jesus left the tomb when Peter decided to write two letters to the Christian community.

In his first letter he spoke about suffering for the sake of Jesus. He equated trials, problems and tribulations as noble acts so long as we surrendered those sufferings to Jesus. Shortly before his own execution Peter warned of false teachers within the early church to avoid being misled. Peter advised that one should adhere to the Christian qualities of faith and virtue. (II Peter 1:5-7) Of knowledge and godliness. Of patience and love. Only by combining these qualities with understanding scripture could the disciples avoid deceptions. Two thousand years later the assignment is still as compelling.

Showing love usually involves showing kindness and Peter wrote that brotherly compassion provided the opportunity to receive God's favor. The ability to express and confer these qualities is what separates us as human beings from other species. You seldom hear of a Zebra going to the aid of one of its kind as it's being attacked by a lion (where the attitude is 'better you than me') but you have read of someone running into a burning building to rescue a stranger.

We are blessed in that we have a military, though personally unknown to us, who jeopardize their lives for us, so we don't have to.

Training endlessly for years, these men and women dedicate themselves to keeping us safe. Who could put their own life in danger without compassion, kindness, and love for others? They could not.

Kindness is an internal conviction toward others to ease their burden in some way. It is not possible to gage what a small random act of kindness can do for someone - and what it can do for you. I recall a day, years ago now, when, as I was putting the key into the ignition, I happened to glance over toward the car next to me. I had just put a few groceries in the back seat, but I couldn't help but notice the look on the elderly lady's face next to me—confused, panicked and near tears. Getting out of my car I walked over and asked if everything was alright. "No" she said "I lost my keys. I can't find them." As tears welled in her eyes she said, "I don't know if I dropped them in the store." Before I retraced her steps backwards, I thought I'd look through the car first. And there under the seat is where I found them.

As I handed the keys to her, she said, "I sat here and prayed for a guardian angel to help me, and you appeared. Thank you so much. God bless you." As I watched her pull away, it was me that sat there and cried. Someone, a person I would never see again, gave me a gift of kind words at a time when she could not possibly know how much they would mean to me. You see, this incident took place shortly after my legal ordeal began. Everywhere I was being vilified. The epithets being thrown my way were coarse, unmerciful and so hurtful. Those tender and warmhearted words had imparted a sense of peace and comfort at a time that was anything but. That blessed lady did more for me that day then she will ever know this side of eternity.

Each of us is responsible for our own actions and how we've decided to live. The standards we set for ourselves can be contaminated by the rudeness and selfishness of others. There are people who will always be self-centered and ungracious. They will do and say things that we will find hurtful and offensive, but this cannot excuse us from living by the standards we've chosen for ourselves. To show kindness and benevolence to people that have treated us without regard to our feelings is nothing if not a test of our own faith.

As the years march past, you've probably lived the adage where some will take kindness for weakness. Unfortunately, there are people whose consciouses are dead because they've never listened to the Holy Spirit, or so many years have passed since they have that living in spiritual dormancy is normal. These are people who's first thought before they show any kindness is "What's in it for me?" People cut you off in traffic or allow a door to crash in your face. When the conscious becomes lifeless it doesn't talk any longer. People refuse to hear the alarm early on and when you continue to disobey God, you cannot hear Him anymore.

Paul spoke about maintaining faith and a good conscious because he knew that a constant relationship with God restrains us from doing what's wrong. He encouraged the disciples to program their conscious mind with the word of God. (Ephesians 6:10-20)

Accept God's word as the basis of your life and when you pray ask the Lord for direction. *Being helpful, being kind and being humble does not mean that He wants you to be a speed bump!* Be true to who YOU are. Don't bend your convictions to conform with someone else's but be aware of that inner voice that will guide you through questions and conflicts.

Henry Wadsworth Longfellow wrote "The little I have seen of this world teaches me to look upon the errors of others in sorrow, not in anger." That is the essence of kindness of spirit. We also hope for kindness, compassion, and understanding to be given to us. Whether we are at the pinnacle of our life and career or at a challenge and crossroad in our lives, we welcome, crave and cherish really, the goodness and thoughtfulness of others. This does not mean living by the good opinion of others but living in such a way that brings out not only the best in us but brings out the best in others.

Francis was the life of the party. His friends knew that and when the word went out that Franny was hosting another soiree each of them knew a fun time would be had by all. His father was a very wealthy man, and all his young life Fran knew only the finest. What he wanted most however was to be a hero on the battlefield but after his first battle he ended up a captive in the enemy's prison.

It took nearly a year for his father to arrange his release but while there something happened to Francis that he never saw coming - God - who began His work on him (it happens) and his life, as they say, was never the same.

After his release Francis began to hear the voice of Jesus telling him to repair the Christian Church and live a life of poverty. His life and his words have touched the spirit of millions of his followers since his death in 1226 and today St. Francis is known for his humbleness and unbounded benevolence. Known as 'The Prayer of St. Francis' these words strike at the very core of what being a Christian means:

Lord, make me an instrument of your peace!
Where there is hatred—let me sow love
Where there is injury—pardon
Where there is doubt—faith
Where there is despair—hope
Where there is darkness—light
Where there is sadness—joy
O Divine Master, grant that I may not so much seek
To be consoled—as to console
To be understood—as to understand
To be loved—as to love for

it is in giving that we receive
it is in pardoning that we are pardoned and it is in dying that we are
born to eternal life....

According to a study done by the Center for Compassion and Altruism Research and Education at Stanford, when patients receive focused attention from medical staff and also kindness, they tend to have less pain, decreased anxiety and shorter hospital stays. The study also found that by showing empathy and kindness the doctors and nurses feel more involved with the patient and they experience exhaustion less frequently. Kindness really does go both ways.

In their book 'On Kindness' authors Barbara Taylor and Adam Phillips explain "The self without sympathetic attachments is either a fiction or a lunatic" while Henry James wrote, "Three things in human life are important. The first is to be kind. The second is to be kind. And the third is to be kind."

Kind words can carry major consequences. Daniel Lubetzky, the founder of 'Peace Works' relates a story about his grandfather.

During the Nazi occupation of Lithuania, Lubetzky's grandfather was about to be executed when the janitor in his apartment building intervened. "I let you live" said the janitor "because you would talk to me like a decent person."

Having a major impact not only on the fact that he is here today because of the ripple effect since those dark years, Lubetzky, who is also the founder of 'Kind Healthy Snacks' says, "Every day I recognize the power of kindness to change our world, I've never been so convinced that kindness is the essential antidote to the divisions and disconnection we're seeing in the world."

Kindness is as immutable today as it was when our hunter—gatherer ancestors banded together knowing that when one member of the tribe suffers, they all were at risk. Compassion is hardwired into us. We need to remember that caring about each other is what equalizes us, binds us together and is what makes us fully human.

"Forgive us our trespasses, as we forgive those who trespass against us…" Each time we pray those words from the Lord's Prayer we re-inforce our petition to God to forgive us by the same absolute measure we give to others.

Over and over, we are confronted with the certainty and reality that words have meaning. We accept that each time we say "I can't" we don't, and to ask to be excused the same way we excuse, is prophesying our future—in this life or the next.

It is accepted that most people learn better and retain more by imagery than by other methods. Learning by instruction and teaching tends to allow people to lose memory of the lesson. Jesus was able to paint stories with His words. Called parables, they were a way for Him to illustrate a moral truth of a simple tale.

Jesus explained what it meant to be treated as we treat others in His parable to Peter and the disciples. Owing ten thousand talents (a talent being the equivalent of $1,000) a servant begs his master for leniency in repaying the debt he owes him. Prostrating himself before his Lord he tearfully pleads his cause and being a compassionate man, his master forgives the debt. With eyes still red from crying the pardoned servant meets up with a fellow servant who owes him a hundred denarii (a few dollars). Taking the man by the throat he throws him into prison until he pays the debt. Eventually the king learns of the servant's treachery and using the same measure in which the servant used, hands him over to be tortured. "So my heavenly Father" explained Jesus "also will do to you if each of you, from his heart, does not forgive his brother his trespasses. (Matthew 18:21-35)

Forgiveness is a word that can mean different things to different people. It can be easy to forgive someone if they're late for dinner, but not so easy if you've been waiting for them for a few hours. How can you forgive when you or your family directly suffer because of the actions of others?

During my career I had the opportunity to meet people from different backgrounds and experiences. Many of them shared memories of events that shaped their lives. I had several clients who were Holocaust survivors. Recalling their stories, I am still aware of the profound impact they had on me then, and even now. I remember sitting there, trying to absorb and discern what they endured decades earlier "How is it possible to forgive what they went through?" I thought. Yet they were able to do so in order to live.

Years ago, when my son Guy was still in Middle school, I decided to sponsor a few of these clients to go to the school and speak to the students to share their memories and how it was to "live" through those terrible days.

Breaking the silence toward the end of their presentation, one little girl raised her hand and asked if they hated the people who did this to them. One of the men, Bill, answered "I don't hate anyone. I forgave Hitler long ago. To have retained hate would have given him power over my life and that I was unwilling to do." Bill chose to see his torturers with different eyes. "The one who pursues revenge should dig two graves" recounts a Chinese proverb.

Corrie ten Boom and her family became involved in the Resistance efforts in the Netherlands during the Second World War. Along with her sister Betsie and her father Casper, Corrie decided to hide Jews in their home in Haarlem. As Christians, their conscientious' would not allow them to stand idly by, feeling that persecuting the Jews was an affront to God.

In 1944, a few years after they began their defiance of the Nazis, they were arrested and imprisoned. In September of that year Corrie and Betsie were sent to the Concentration Camp at Ravensbruck in Germany where Betsie died that December. A few days after her sister died Corrie was, incredibly, released. In a camp, people were just not "released"—at least not in a physical sense—but due to a "clerical error" that is exactly what happened.

Corrie, who died in 1983, devoted the remainder of her life in spreading the message of God's Mercy and grace.

After the war she returned to Germany to declare Christ's love for a broken world. In Corrie's own words, she recalled the following:

"It was 1947 and I'd come from Holland to defeated Germany with the message that God forgives. It was the truth that they needed most to hear in that bitter, bombed-out land, and I gave them my favorite mental picture. Maybe because the sea is never far from a Hollander's mind, I liked to think that that's where forgiven sins were thrown."

"When we confess our sins" I said, "God casts them into the deepest ocean, gone forever, and even though I cannot find a scripture for it, I believe God then places a sign out there that says 'NO FISHING ALLOWED'."

"The solemn faces stared back at me, not quite daring to believe. And that's when I saw him working his way forward against the others. One moment I saw the overcoat and the brown hat; the next, a blue uniform and a cap with skull and crossbones. It came back with a rush, the huge room with its harsh overhead lights, the pathetic pile of dresses and shoes in the center of the floor, the shame of walking naked past this man. I could see my sister's frail form ahead of me, ribs sharp beneath the parchment

skin. *"Betsie, how thin you were!"* That place was Ravensbruck, and the man who was making his way forward had been a guard—one of the most cruel guards.

"Now he was in front of me, hand thrust out: "A fine message, Fraulein! How good it is to know that, as you say, all our sins are at the bottom of the sea!"

"And I, who had spoken so glibly of forgiveness fumbled in my pocketbook rather than take that hand. He would not remember me of course, how could he remember one prisoner among those thousands of women?

"But I remembered him. I was face-to-face with one of my captors and my blood seemed to freeze.

"You mentioned Revensbruck in your talk" he was saying. "I was a guard there." No, he did not remember me. "But since that time" he went on, "I have become a Christian. I know that God has forgiven me for the cruel things I did there, but I would like to hear it from your lips as well, Fraulein." again the hand came out, "will you forgive me?"

"And I stood there, I whose sins had again and again been forgiven and could not forget Betsie had died in that place. Could he erase her slow terrible death simply for the asking? It could have been seconds that he stood there hand held out, but to me it seemed hours as I wrestled with the most difficult thing I had ever had to do.

"For I had to do it. I knew that. The message that God forgives has a prior condition: that we forgive those who have injured us. "If you do not forgive men their trespasses" Jesus says, "Neither will your Father in heaven forgive your trespasses." And still I stood there with the coldness clutching my heart.

"But forgiveness is not an emotion. I knew that too. Forgiveness is an act of the will, and the will can function regardless of the temperature of the heart. "Jesus help me!" I prayed silently. I can lift my hand. I can do that much. You supply the feeling.

"And so woodenly, mechanically, I thrust out my hand into the one stretched out to me. And as I did, an incredible thing took place. The current started in my shoulders, raced down my arm, sprang into our

joined hands. And then this healing warmth seemed to flood my whole being, bringing tears to my eyes.

"I forgive you, brother!" I cried. "With all my heart!" For a long moment we grasped each other's hands, the former guard, and the former prisoner. I had never known God's love so intensely, as I did then. But even then, I realized it was not my love. I had tried and did not have the power. It was the power of the Holy Spirit."

Corrie ten Boom went on to touch millions of lives, a living testament of one who'd literally been through Hell on Earth and what God can do when you ask for His guidance.

Let's not kid ourselves—its not easy to forgive. Most of us can get past the small transgressions and annoyance that can occur daily. Someone darts into the parking space you've been waiting for. Someone promised they'd come through and didn't. These are irritations that are soon forgotten in a busy life.

What I'm talking about is a loved one's betrayal. The one you loved so much they took your breath away who walked out on you. Or the lies told about you that damage not only your reputation but leave a lasting impact on your life. Perhaps its deceitfulness on a nuclear level that devastated your very soul. It takes more than courage to forgive those torments. It takes God's love working in your life. It's taking your eyes off the hurt and looking at Christ instead. It's making a choice to handle the pain through benevolence.

We need to rely on our awareness that God is our vindicator and any consequences given to the offender are done through His perfect justice. You can hate what the person did to you without cursing them. You move on without excusing the behavior, knowing that forgiving is not excusing.

I believe that there is a misconception that God wants us to "forgive and forget." Moving on is not forgetting. It is accepting the experience as it happened and enhancing our character with a further capacity to endure. After the resurrection Jesus kept visible the scars from the nails, the puncture in His chest. Jesus did not want anyone to forget what He'd been through or who He was.

Remembering His crucifixion and by showing His wounds did not diminish His capacity to forgive nor did it require that He forget. Although there will be times where forgetting is appropriate, Christian forgiveness does not call to forget.

Remembering hurt in a toxic manner increases the likelihood of poisoning the present and contaminating the future, however. There seems to be, deep within most humans a propensity to exact revenge. Or at least to 'get even.'

It seems that the 21st century has set up a perfect storm of vituperation through social media that causes most of us to want to defend and explain. Whether its cyber bullying, being branded as promiscuous, personal attacks or false accusations, we feel the need to respond and justify.

Certainly, we are called to protect our name, especially when untrue or misleading stories are written or told about us. But to try to hit back only elevates the drama. As difficult as it is to walk away there comes a time when you let go and let God become your vindicator. Jesus taught us to never lose our focus on God. "Who when He was reviled, did not revile in return, when He suffered, He did not threaten, but committed Himself to Him who judges righteously." (I Peter 2:23)

Most religious doctrines also encourage their followers to extend forgiveness to those who've offended or transgressed them in some way.

When reflecting on Buddhism and Hinduism for instance, one finds parallel lines of thought on the type of forgiveness Jesus taught. "Hurt not others with that which pains thyself," said the Buddha. "Him I call a Brahmana from whom anger and hatred, pride and hypocrisy, have dropped like a mustard seed from the point of a needle." he said. Likewise with Hinduism - Krishna states: "A man should not hate any living creature. Let him be friendly and compassionate to all. He must free himself from the delusion of 'I and mine'. He must accept pleasure and pain with an equal tranquility. He must be forgiving, ever contented, self-controlled, united with me in his meditation."

To harbor revenge or anger to another ultimately affects us. Not only is our peace taken from us, but our physical body suffers as well. Anger creates stress. Stress causes the release of cortisol which is discharged by the adrenal gland located on the kidneys. Research has shown that the release of these hormones is responsible for heart problems, high blood pressure and stroke as well as a host of other ailments. Every human being will experience upset and upheaval from time to time but exposure to sustained agitation and anger is indisputably hazardous to your health.10

Before I end this section on forgiveness, I want to acknowledge that I know there are some individuals that are just too difficult to forgive. Their betrayals, their violations, their hurts are just too deep, too overpowering to forgive. Like Corrie ten Boom relates of her encounter with her former tormentor, we reach out to Jesus. For His strength and through His strength. We acknowledge that we just can't do it alone.

Like most everything in our lives worthwhile, there is a degree of work, dedication, and persistence that we must put forth in order to accomplish what it is we want. To forgive an excruciating and unbearable hurt takes determined resolve. It is possible to do. This is about *YOUR* freedom. Make no mistake about that. Herewith are the steps to allow the Holy Spirit to work in you.

1. Ask God to forgive you, personally for everything you have harbored toward this person and in the situation.
2. Ask God to forgive them for everything they harbored toward you and in the situation.
3. Write out a "note of forgiveness" stating that you have been forgiven by God and now you are forgiving them completely and will be praying for their peace going forward.
4. Now, forgive them by reading the note out loud, allowing your emotions to be released and restored.
5. Say a prayer of healing, goodness, and peace into their life.
6. Thank God for the gift of this forgiveness.
7. Receive your 'forgiveness' as it is now achieved.

This proposal is not predicated in your actually sending them the note, reading it to them or even them accepting it! This is about your freedom from unforgiveness. Their ultimate freedom from unforgiveness must come from God and their personal actions in acceptance of it or not. Continue to call down healing, goodness, and peace into their life even if they continue to ratchet up the rhetoric within their yet unforgiving life. Then, continue moving forward, being thankful daily for your new-found and steadily growing peace.

Finally, I would like to leave you with this recognition of pardoning written by Mark Twain:

"Forgiveness is the fragrance that the violet sheds on the heel that has crushed it."

13

The Lord's Law of Finance

To lead a balanced life, we need a means of providing the necessities —and the enjoyments—that make us actualized human beings.

At one time our ancestors used salt to purchase things and provide for themselves. Sheep, goats, oxen, camels, and horses were also determined to judge a man's wealth. Today it's money. Whether it's dollars, Euros, Pounds or Yens, currency needs to move through our lives.

Money however, without a purpose, is useless. Perhaps no one taught you how God views money until now: He created it. He owns it. God owns the dollars, the gold, and the silver (Haggai 2:8).

Money is divinely spiritual and in order to have it you need a divine connection. We all know people whose lives revolve around money and riches. These people hoard it, are miserly with it and think they don't have enough. This is not to denigrate money but to put it into perspective and what money really is. For those who align with God, He'll put you into prosperity at the right time. He'll place you in the right business. He'll lead you to the right people. When your heart is right you bring in money without losing your soul. Proverbs tells us that the realization of the righteous is their riches. (Proverbs 8:18) A righteous man will never fear his wealth because he knows the methods he used to gather it. He doesn't look over his shoulder with fear of getting entangled with legalities. He knows with a total belief that God will always provide for him. He also knows that it is God's money and being divinely provided for, he knows that it is necessary to honor Him before all else.

God plainly tells His people that He requires the first fruits of our labor! (Proverbs 3:9) We as a people need to learn not to love money and the only way to do that is by giving money. The system of God is already established—you either work it or you don't. We need a Divine connection and being a part of the fellowship of a church brings our thoughts to something greater than ourselves. You need to be guided to a church, if you are not currently, so you can give to the church. Your attitude is the key. You need to know what you're doing, why you're doing it and for whom you're doing it.

There is no other way to say this—*you must love God, trust God, and crave God to do His will in your life in order to give Him your first fruits without reservations.* This is a tall order for many in our very materialistic world. It also means that you must overcome an attitude of lack, of having a fear of never having enough. Giving to God first allows Him to work in a mind that TOTALLY BELIEVES in abundance and due to that belief BECOMES FACT! Do you recall the widow whom Jesus observed offering God her last two mites? Despite knowing it was all she had in the world she was compelled to give from her heart. Could anyone possibly doubt that she didn't trust God to provide? (Luke 21:2-4) 11

Throughout this book you will have read how, with a positive attitude, with maintaining the feeling of achieving the goal or objective now, that you will achieve what you desire. While that is true, *it can only happen if you trust God.* Simply put, God is unable to empower you, and your dreams, without faith. You must do your part in the natural so God will do the supernatural.

Too many people are broke because they think they can go it alone. They don't need an unseen presence interfering with their logic, views, decisions, or perceptions. I recall someone once saying to me (when I counseled them to seek God's guidance) "God doesn't pay the bills!" which I suppose was their way to excuse their behavior.

Scripture tells us that Solomon was the world's wealthiest man, but wisdom and understanding were more important to Solomon than riches. It was because of this lack of greed that God gave Solomon riches and honor beyond any man before or since. His reputation spread over many nations including Sheba, whose queen traveled to Jerusalem to see the king and find out for herself if what was said about Solomon was true. Although she brought gifts of spices, jewelry, and gold to give to him, when she left not only did Solomon give her what she desired and asked but "Much more than she brought to the king." (II Chronicles 9:12) Solomon knew that not only was everything he had owned by God but by giving back, more would be given to him.

We have become so used to making money the illustration of our success that to give any of it up challenges both our reasoning and understanding. As we'll explore later, operating from a sense of lack—real or imagined—invites even further experiences of lack. Conversely operating from a spirit of giving, knowing God gives so much more, causes an avalanche of abundance in every area of our life including money.

God funds your bank account to fund His purposes. We need the Holy Spirit to help guide our finances. The Holy Spirit will control what we have if we allow him to do so.

Giving and receiving, two action verbs that are synonymous with our financial lives and convey the natural laws of God's limitless and generous blessings to us. If you hope to experience abundance in your life—give with an open heart.

Paul wrote "He who sows sparingly will also reap sparingly, and he who sows bountifully will also reap bountifully" (II Corinthians 9:6). This is a profound statement. It deserves to be read again. It deserves to be written and put on your mirror so when you're getting ready for the day you read it!

Continuing, Paul wrote in the next verse "So let each one give as he purposes in his heart, not grudgingly or of necessity; for God loves a cheerful giver. And God is able to make all grace abound toward you, that you, always having all sufficiency in all things may have an abundance for every good work." (9:7-8) Here, somewhere between the years 55 and 57 God, through Paul's hand, promises us that we can not only have enough to survive but AN ABUNDANCE if we happily give to Him.

When Paul wrote these words, he was addressing a congregation in turmoil and confusion. The believers in Corinth were involved in immoral activities and anger raged among them. Lawsuits were being filed against each other and a general feeling of hopelessness was permeating the church. The ability of Paul, by his very personality, to bring diverse temperaments and individual purposes into alignment with the purpose of adhering to Jesus' teaching in itself is testament of God's guidance affecting us as humans. Here, at the birth of Christianity, we are sent the perception of how to achieve abundance in our lives today.

How many of us reach into our pockets reluctantly to buy a flower for the disabled? Or we grudgingly drop a few coins in the kettle during the holidays, so we don't look cheap? Maybe we put a dollar in our offering at church because "we have to give *something*". Any of these are hardly cheerfully giving. When you dispense resentment, you can't be surprised when resentment returns to you.

Tithing money, charitable giving, or helping someone in need does not involve being foolish with your finances. As a steward of your church, it is entirely appropriate to interview your pastor or priest asking where your support is going and what it is to be used for.

Trust in God's strength to help you determine where your money will best work for Him. Certainly, your church first but there are so many worthy causes that positively help others. Money should be our servant, but it is also God's servant as well. Unfortunately, as a society we have made money an idol, a god to be worshipped. How then should we view money with accuracy and correct reasoning? *By studying scripture, going to church, putting Him first in everything we do and fully immersing ourselves in godliness.* To accomplish this is a process. Be patient with yourself. Start your morning with a simple prayer—"Thank you Lord for this day, thank you for working your will in my life." Sometime before you go to sleep read a chapter from Proverbs as I mentioned earlier.

Men of God are always blessed because the power of the universe is behind them. Tithing is a principal God established to measure our belief. Our belief in Him to trust Him and our belief in knowing that we will always experience abundance.

Tithing is first mentioned in Genesis when Moses tells how Abram gave 10% to the priest Melchizedek. Moses wrote again about tithing in Leviticus and the divine importance that God puts on it.

Giving involves trust. You trust that the person you're giving to knows how to take care of it wisely. You trust the church will use it for God's purpose. You trust that the charity will really help people. Giving to God involves trusting that He will provide even more.

I recall a story someone told me not long ago about how, while attending a church function, his wife asked, "What do we have in our bank account?" Since they were on Mission work overseas, he said, "Not much, $150.00 is all" "Give it to me!" she exclaimed. Arguing that this was all they had for the next few weeks, he reluctantly handed it over. Staring in disbelief he watched his wife tithe the total amount to the church. Later just before they left the event, this gentleman was approached by a virtual stranger who said, "I was led to give you this, please accept it." He looked to see a check for $300!

God supplies seeds to the Sower and He multiplies to the Giver. (II Corinthians 9:10) Connecting to God's ministry will always keep us supplied. As Christians, we don't work on the world's system any longer—"There's not enough." "There's no way." "It's impossible." God gives to us and helps us to do His work through our abilities. Wisdom is knowing not to ignore the work He wants us to perform. We ignore His call (as so many of us do) at our own peril. When you prove yourself, God gives you more. He takes from those who don't know how to handle money and directs it to those who do. (Matthew 13:12)

Becoming prosperous, living in abundance, accumulating wealth, and living comfortably is a process and every time you receive good fortune God is watching to see if you recognize that it's Him who prospers you.

How we act with money reveals our wisdom—or lack of it. We are familiar with the term "A fool and his money soon part" and we know this to be true when millions of us are in debt and have very little prospects of ever becoming debt-free. It's not only individuals who are foundering in liabilities but nations also. As I'm proofing this chapter the national debt of the United States has surpassed 31 trillion dollars! Could there be any connection between a nation that has abandoned its Christian roots, barred its children from acknowledging God as they start their school day, banned any municipal display of the Savior's birth in public, and attempt to erase the memory of God's place in our lives, with the very real possibility of catastrophic financial collapse?

As a young man starting out in a career in finances, it was my responsibility to set appointments with potential clients, usually in their homes (it was a different time!). I recall one of those appointments when, after locating the address, I entered a stairwell that recked of dampness and 'unique' scents. Had it not been mid-day I may have changed my mind before walking up the steps. "If anyone has money to invest" I recall thinking "Why would they live *here*?"

Knocking on the door I was greeted by a couple even younger than me. The apartment was warm and inviting, the opposite of what I expected after working my way up those musty stairs. With a baby in their arms and another that was obviously due to arrive soon, they laid out their financial hopes and objectives. Surprisingly they were financially comfortable but had chosen to live frugally in order to save for a home of their own. He was working full time while studying to be a pharmacist while she stayed home with their child.

As I went over their finances, I was a bit taken back when they told me that they tithed 10% of their income to their church! "Living in a place like this?" I remember thinking. I am still inspired by their devotion these many years later. After reviewing their goals and objectives it was just not possible to develop an investment plan for them given their income and expenses. As I reviewed their assets and liabilities, I was fascinated that they devoted their first fruits to God. Such was their faith that instead of trendy clothes, a night on the town, or an upscale apartment they put God first.

Although I lost track of this godly couple so long ago, I would not be surprised to learn that he now owns his own pharmacy, that they live in a beautiful home and that their lives have known peace. The kind of peace only God can provide. When joy radiates from a man or woman of God, nothing can hide the radiance.

When God spoke to Moses, He was telling Moses in effect that money is His, the Lord's, first. To not honor the Lord with our first fruits is to rob God himself! "Bring all the tithes into the storehouse, that there may be food in My house, try me now on this, if I will not open for you the windows of heaven and pour out for you such blessing that there will not be room enough to receive it.' (Malachi 3:10) So it was written. So let it be done!

Throughout the preceding pages I have written about qualities and attitudes needed to be predominant in our personalities in order to prepare our individual nature for acceptance of God's blessings. Simply put—if you feel unworthy due to your beliefs and actions, you interfere with God's destiny for you. Possessing moral strength does more than make you feel good about yourself. It creates an intellectual consent of receiving God's favor. Without the strength of a stable support structure, whatever is depending on that strength will collapse. So, it is with living an enlightened and meaningful life that creates the opportunity for abundance.

There are a great number of books that help inspire and motivate us to become that which we want to be and accomplish what we want to accomplish. Many of these books have caused a great many people to become jaded to ever getting what they want out of life. We try suggestions that seem to have worked for others, but don't for us. We follow formulas that have us think that if we emulate them, we'll achieve what we're striving for. We read about secrets, and paths, shortcuts and alternative approaches and come up empty. We think that if we keep repeating the same mantra over and over "I am rich, I am happy, I am successful" that somehow we become rich, happy and successful.

In the second half of this book, I will put forth proposals that you may not have thought of, read of, or heard of before. These ideas, if done with virtue and righteousness *can become fact.* Keep an open mind. Don't create barriers that can—and will—prevent you from having, and becoming, all that God has in store for you. I say this with complete confidence because, as you'll see, the framework, the method, the process, and the guidance are already in place. Verified unequivocally. They are found in God's own words......

14

Inspired in Word and Deed

You may be a person who reads the Bible daily. You know scripture and verse and know where to look for a passage to guide you. On the other hand, you may be someone who rarely, if ever picks up a Bible. Or you may be somewhere in between the two.

In looking to scripture for instruction it would be wise to contemplate the history of and impact that the Bible has had on humanity for the past 2,000 years. How nations once mighty and now humble and once humble and now mighty have been affected by it. It also is a story about us as individuals. The quiet we hold to ourselves that is known only to us and God.

Theologians have pondered the words that now make up the Bible for over 30 centuries and it's safe to say these discussions will continue for as long as humankind exists.

For hundreds of years only a handful of men were privileged to know and review the words of scripture. Writing under candlelight, Monks throughout Europe's numerous monasteries crafted beautifully illustrated Bibles by hand, writing each word and verse in Latin.

By the Middle Ages, a shift in man's consciousness swept across the European continent. Men of faith began the quest for greater access to God's Holy words, and as men sometimes do, began to mobilize opposition to prevent others that same access. It was generally accepted that only the religious hierarchy be allowed to read the Sacred Writings, then interpret those writings to, what was then known as, the 'Vulgar Masses' - the common people.

Events in the Middle East contributed to the realization of how truly fragile the Holy Writings were. These were the original manuscripts written by the authors of the Bible. There was genuine concern that these documents would disappear forever.

In 1453 Constantinople fell to the armies of Islam. Miraculously scholars were able to gather up the precious Greek manuscripts of the Bible and flee to the West. The Bible had already been circulating throughout Europe by then, but these *original* documents were priceless and were in very real danger of being destroyed.

St. Jerome began a revision of the Bible around 383 AD using Hebrew and Greek texts and Latin translations for the Old Testament, and Greek and Latin texts for the New. The process took Jerome over 20 years to accomplish. The first complete English translation was finished in the 1380s by the priest John Wycliffe.

The more one looks at the history of the Bible, the more astonishing it is that it survived as we know it at all. No one could overstate the very real possibility that it could have vanished all together. Can this thought be even imagined?

Over thousands of years God has placed in men of righteousness the responsibility of guardianship of His words. Ezra was one such Chaperon.

By 608 BC Israel had turned its back on God, putting aside the spiritual tenants that had made it a great nation. It was in that year that Babylon ransacked Jerusalem, carrying off tens of thousands back to Babylon.

In 538 BC, seventy years later, Persia conquered the Babylonian Empire. Persia's King, Cyrus, encouraged the Judeans to return home, also supporting and inducing them to rebuild the temple which the Babylonians destroyed.

Eighty years had passed since the return to Jerusalem when the Persians decided to send Ezra to Israel, appointing him to restore order to the city and throughout Judea. Ezra's first act was to appoint godly men to the positions of magistrates and justices. Having rank, privilege and great power, Ezra compiled the Pentateuch. The Pentateuch consisted of the first 5 books of the Bible—Genesis, Exodus, Leviticus, Numbers and Deuteronomy—the compilation known also as the Jewish Torah. Ezra rescued what was very nearly lost.

Eventually as the centuries after Jesus' birth passed, the Bible began to be translated into various languages. Around 700AD Aldhelm, Bishop of Sherborne, England translated the Book of Psalms. The historian Bede, fearing that the local priests had little or no knowledge of Latin, translated the Bible into Anglo-Saxon. On his deathbed in 735 Bede was found to still be working on the translation of John's gospel.

The challenge for the translators came from the fact that the sacred writings had originally been written in several languages. Jesus and the disciples spoke Aramaic. Hebrew was the language for much of the Old Testament, however Ezra and Daniel were written in Aramaic. In the mid 200's BC a group of scholars living in Alexandria, Egypt translated The Law (as the first 5 books of the Bible are known) into Greek. At the time of Jesus' birth Aramaic, Greek, Syriac (an Aramaic dialect) and Latin were the chief languages spoken in Judea.

By the middle of the 15th century, Johannes Gutenberg had advanced the use of the printing press (which had been conceived by the use of a wine press) and produced what became known as the Gutenberg Bible in 1456.

The 16th century saw an upheaval in the Catholic Church, which until that time was "The" Church, that still reverberates throughout the Christian world.

In 1522, Martin Luther translated the Bible into German. Luther, who had already become troubled by a number of practices within the Church, not the least of which included the selling of what were known as 'indulgences'. Indulgences were sold on the basis of guaranteeing the buyer that they would not suffer damnation at death. Although never intending to break with the Church when he posted his "95 Theses" in 1517, Luther was formally expelled from the Catholic Church in 1521. This action not only had profound effects on the Church itself, but began a transition, a movement really, to a more individualized association with God's written words.

In England at about this time. a new generation of religious philosophers appeared.

William Tyndale was just a young priest when he arrived at the walled city of London in 1523.

Born in 1494, Tyndale was of the mind that everyone deserved the opportunity to read Scriptures and endorsed the ideas that the Bible be translated into English so the poorest farmhand could know the word of God. This, at the time, was not only a heretical concept but a dangerous—and possibly life-threatening-opinion. For example, in 1519 one woman and six men were burned in Coventry for teaching their children the Lord's Prayer, the 10 commandments and the Apostles Creed in English. Also at this time a 9-year-old boy in Norfolk was burned at the stake for owning a scrap of paper with the Lord's prayer in English. A New Testament in English could be bought for a load of hay—if you dared to do so. The Constitution of Oxford proclaimed that it was forbidden to read the Bible in English without a Bishop's license!

At this point of time, English was the language of the commoners. French was spoken in the royal court while Latin was the language of the church and the Law. The Great Hall, located in the Manor Houses and larger homes was the center of information. Sitting around the great oak table, the nobles and wealthy were able to debate, reason, think about and talk over the topics and concerns of the day. It was at one such gathering where a confrontation occurred between an arrogant friar and Tyndale took place.

The friar, it seems, endorsed the idea that the Pope's mandate should over-rule Christ's teachings, also adding the opinion that commoners should not have the privilege of reading the Bible. Outraged, Tyndale proclaimed "If God spare my life 'ere many years, I will cause a boy that driveth a plough shall know more of the Scriptures than thou dost..."

Tyndale commenced his own translation of the New Testament from the original Greek and later he rewrote the Old Testament from the original Hebrew. He changed words from the Catholic Bible to create, in his opinion, effect. For example, the word *penance* became *repentance. Charity* became *love. Confession* became *acknowledgment. Grace* to *favor. Priest* was re-written as *Senior* or *Elder. Church* became *Congregation.*

Politics and religion were very tightly entwined during this period as they had been for hundreds, if not thousands, of years. It was believed that Kings were appointed Divinely (especially by the King!) and it was accepted that their mandates were endowed by God. In 1534 King Henry VIII of England severed the English church from Rome over the issue of his divorce from Catherine of Aragon in order to marry Anne Boleyn. Henry christened this new Christian denomination the Church of England, declaring himself (and future English Monarchs) head of the church. In time these changes in Britain would have profound and enormous implications in what would be called "The New World".

Despite numerous threats against his doctrines and his life, Tyndale continued to preach that everyone should be able to read and meditate on Scripture until agents of the crown tracked him down and killed him.

For his refusal to endorse the separation of Catherine and Henry's divorce, Sir Thomas More, the Chancellor of England, was beheaded in 1535. Sir Thomas could simply have yielded to Henry's demands, but such was his ecclesiastical convictions that he could not, opting to yield to his conscious and convictions instead.

Throughout the remainder of the 16th Century beheadings, burnings, strangulations, and hangings were carried out in the name of God, perverting His Holy Scripture.

The word of God reads: "We know that all things work together for good to those who love God, to those who are the called according to His purpose." (Romans 8:28) It could be argued that the religious excesses in Britain and throughout Europe would directly result in the founding of America.

The influence of Scripture, especially in the Western world, can never be overstated. The Bible affected the social, political, and religious structure of Europe and ultimately to the lands across the Atlantic. It is simply not possible to understand Modern Western thinking and mentality without taking into account, and understanding, the Bible.

As we'll see in the following chapters, the Bible clearly validated the ability, given Divinely, for us to live a full and enjoyable life. To accept this realty—and it is reality—you need a working understanding of the message brought forth in the Bible as well as the significance that this book, which so many today take for granted, had on those who risked everything to transcribe those words and preserve the implication it would have on all of mankind. The principles of life, liberty and the pursuit of happiness are just as important today as they were upon the founding of the United States and are the ideals found in Holy Scripture.

There are those who would have us believe that the Bible is a suggestion at best and a fantasy at worst. These are the same people who have done their best to Edge God out of our lives. As you'll read in a moment, there are forces at work in our own land that would have us believe that God has no place in our lives. Before we go there, allow me to relate the following true exchange which took place at a university. The topic discussed was 'Does Evil Exist?"

The university professor challenged his students with this question: "Did God create everything that exists?' A student bravely replied, "Yes, He did!" "God created everything?" the professor asked. "Yes" the student replied. The professor then said "If God created everything, then God created evil. Since evil exists, and according to the principal that our works define who we are then God created evil." The student became quiet before such an answer. The professor was quite pleased with himself and began boasting to his students that he had proven once again that the Christian faith was a myth. At this point another student raised his hand and said, "Can I ask you a question Professor?" "Of course," replied the educator. Standing up the pupil asked, "Professor, does cold exist?" "What kind of question is this? Of course, it exists. Haven't you ever been cold?" The other students snickered at the young man's question. The young collegian replied "In fact sir, cold does not exist according to the laws of physics. What we consider cold is in reality, the absence of heat. Every object is susceptible to study when it has or transmits, energy. Absolute zero (-460 degrees) is the total absence of heat. All matter becomes inert and incapable of reaction at that temperature. Cold does not exist. We have created this word to describe how we feel if we have no heat."

The student continued, "Professor, does darkness exist?" The Academic responded, "Of course it does." The student replied, "Once again you are wrong, Sir. Darkness does not exist either. Darkness is in reality the absence of light. Light we can study, but not darkness. In fact, we can use Newton's prism to break white light into many colors and study the various wavelengths of each color. You cannot measure darkness. A simple ray of light can break into a world of darkness and illuminate it. How can you know how dark a certain space is? You measure it by the amount of light present. Isn't this correct? Darkness is simply a term used by man to describe what happens when there is no light present." Finally the young man asked, "Sir, does evil exist?" Now uncertain, the Professor responded "Of course, as I already said. We see it every day. It is in the daily example of man's inhumanity to man. It is in the multitude of crime and violence everywhere in the world. These manifestations are nothing else but evil." To this the student replied, "Evil does not exist. Evil is simply the absence of God. It is just like darkness and cold, a word that man created to describe the absence of God. God did not create evil. Evil is not like faith, or love which exists just as does light and heat. Evil is the result of what happens when man does not have God's love present in his heart. It's like the cold that comes when there is no heat or the darkness that comes about when there's no light." Chagrined and embarrassed, the professor sat down, as did the young man—Albert Einstein 12

In certain circles today there is an attempt to invalidate the words, values, and morals found in the Bible. It has become "fashionable" for some to believe we can go it alone. This same crowd will have you believe that the Founding Fathers were agnostics, deists, and atheists.[13] Although people such as Franklin and Jefferson were not themselves genuine believers and followers of Jesus Christ, they understood on another, higher level that without Christianity there could simply not be a basis for a free and just nation. For this reason, they promoted the principles of Christianity.

In 1782 Congress endorsed the printing of the Bible and were quoted as saying *"A neat edition of the Holy Scripture for the use of our schools."* Interestingly Bibles were actually placed in schools in the American colonies in 1647. They remained in the nation's schools until the courts disallowed them in 1963. The fabrication that the Founding Fathers didn't want Bibles in schools was among the reasons given to remove them, but one need only to go back to the 1782 edition to refute that statement. The fact is that NOT ONLY DID CONGRESS ENDORSE THE BIBLE FOR USE IN SCHOOLS BUT THEY HAD THEM PRINTED AND HAD THEM DISTRIBUTED! They knew that the Bible would produce the necessary character needed to bring about the goodness and virtue of those who would one day lead the country. The Founding Fathers were very aware that without Christianity there would be no basis for a righteous nation. which is why they promoted Christian values and principles.

There have also been authors who have attempted to portray the framers of our country as godless men, but the evidence to the contrary can be found in the writing and pronouncements of these very same men. *Of the 56 signers of the Declaration of Independence, 29 held seminary degrees!*

Standing on the steps of Federal Hall in New York City, George Washington spoke for a people united in their belief in Divine blessings and guidance. On this early spring day, April 30th, 1789, Washington gave the country's first inaugural address. 14 Among the word he used that day were these: "The propitious smiles of Heaven can never be expected on a nation that disregards the eternal rules of order and right which Heaven itself hath ordained." Washington, like most of his contemporaries, knew that God would always protect, guide, prosper and favor America with unending blessings if her people upheld His standards.

Washington also knew history. He knew that when Israel turned away from God, disregarded His eternal truth and departed from His unchanging ways, God withdrew His protection and blessing. Washington implored his countryman to never deviate from His ways, fearing that another group of people, magnificently blessed with His favor, could lose that favor through disobedience.

So here we are now, hundreds of years old as a nation. We—all of us—need to look back on the history of these states that became united twice—once in 1776 and again in 1865 with the end of the Civil War. Where we are going is up to us as its citizens, as individuals, and as brothers and sisters in Christ. We must learn from our mistakes, build on our successes, and be faithful to our one, true Creator.

Glancing backwards does not mean dwelling in the past, however. As a boat leaves a wake behind it, we can only control and determine where we go forward. Where we are headed.

You can choose to complain how unfair life is or you can take command of your thoughts and allow yourself to manage your future. If you think you can, you will. If you think you can't, you won't. It really is that simple. The Bible confirms this fact.

The rest of this book will be devoted to use, simply and efficiently, the truths that God allows us to be what we want to be. This is called free will.

If you *think* misery and unhappiness, you can be assured of misery and unhappiness. If you *talk* misery and unhappiness, you'll experience the same plus an added bonus of no-one wanting to associate with you - unless they are the same way because as you know - misery loves company.

But perhaps, you are looking for effective suggestions and approaches to living a life of favor, to actualize the life that God has planned for you. That's why, apparently, you've read this far. ***You have the foundations now. You are ready to construct your victory.***

One more thing: Overlooking 69 square miles which comprises the District of Columbia, the Washington monument stands as a tribute to our first President of the United States. From atop, a visitor to this magnificent granite and marble structure can take in the awe-inspiring panoramic view of the city. From that vantage point one can easily see its division into four major segments where, by plan of the designer Pierre Charles L'Enfant, or Divine Intervention, a perfect cross is imposed upon the landscape.[15]

Perched on the cap atop the monument, 555 feet high, are two words written in Latin. Defining the love and gratitude of a grateful people, the words comprise just four syllables and only seven letters but represent the national soul: LAUS DEO. Very simply...."Praise be to God"

15

Building Belief

As the boat tilts to starboard another wave catches her broadside pushing her mast into the water. With storm sails set all the men can do is pray that the caulking on their wooden boat doesn't spring and send them all to the bottom........

Although the depth on this body of water can reach over 140 feet, the average depth is a mere 80 feet which causes the waves to crest at over ten feet. The underwater turbulence dragging along the bottom results in breaking waves which then results in the boat becoming part of the wave's curl. The boat now is not only in danger of being flipped end over end but being shoved backwards allowing the waves to directly break over and on it. Shouting, crying, and screaming they think of their families, their lives and how they wish they were anywhere but here. As the wind shrieks through the rigging, walls of greenish brown water drench the apostles.

For millennia the Sea of Galilee has been known for its violent storms. Four of the men—Peter and his brother Andrew and the brothers John and James—have been working as fishermen on these waters for years and have never taken her storms lightly. Technically speaking the tempests in the Sea of Galilee are caused by the steep hills on all sides. The cooler air masses from the mountains that surround the lake's basin collide with the regions warm air. Funneling through the east-west oriented valleys of the Galilean hill country, the winds come rushing down from the western hillside of the lake.

The most violent storms on the Sea of Galilee however are caused by the fierce winds which blow off the Golan Heights from the east.

Although they've just been through another storm a few weeks ago, Jesus who was asleep then had at least been with them. Fearing for their lives they woke Him up and watched in astonishment as He calmed the winds and the waves with a reprimand.

But now they're alone and this gale is even worse.

It is now about 3 a.m.—the fourth watch of the night—when they see Him. (Matthew 14:24-27)[16] Despite being witnesses to water becoming wine, lepers being healed and numerous other unimagined experiences, the disciples are certain they are hallucinating as Jesus strides across the violent water toward them.

Peter, already showing the qualities and characteristics of leadership that will distinguish him among the twelve, yells out to Jesus, "Lord, if it's really you, tell me to come to you and I will." "Come on" says Jesus.

Instantly forgetting where he is, what is going on around him, Peter leaps out of the boat and begins walking towards his friend.

Suddenly logic returns to Peter's awareness as the water churns and boils around him, "I can't do this" he thinks, and immediately he disappears below the waves. Reaching out Jesus grabs hold of Peter asking him what happened to his faith? Why did he allow doubt to overtake him? (Matthew 14:25-31)

The definition of the word doubt is: uncertainty of belief. Like Peter, we all share the emotions of fear, doubt, and unbelief. Our brains are wired in such a way that to stay safe we learn over a lifetime to avoid risky behavior which has its beginning in thought.

It is the left side of our brain—the Reflective system which we referred to previously—where we analyze risk and reward. Specifically, the Limbic system is where the fight-flight responses come from. Very simply put, the very first reaction we humans have is to play it safe and when some type of unnerving experience shows up, we immediately transfer our thoughts to the Reflexive, right side, of our brain shoving analytical reasoning to the side. One problem, one upset, one risk magnifies everything else.

In order to achieve anything we consider worthwhile we need to believe that we can and many of us become stalled at belief. We must first accept that doubt, unbelief, uncertainty etc. are normal. Banish the thought that you can't do, achieve, get, or receive anything that you want - *so long as it aligns with God's perfect plan for your life.*
We must first understand the basis from where these thoughts originated, accept that God gives us free will, and determine what goals are important enough to us to pursue. We have Divinely-inspired masters throughout history to guide us on our path toward success by studying their lives and how they overcame challenges and adversities. It is by understanding those qualities that make us human, also makes it possible to achieve, through God's words, that which we strive for.

There have been a great many books written over the years explaining how goals are reached, success is achieved, wealth is obtained, a better life is created, prosperity is attracted and so on. Unfortunately, some people have misinterpreted and have misconstrued what has been written concerning money, goals, wealth, and achievement.

For some people a feeling of guilt accompanies their quest for attainment. Distortion of scripture can be partially responsible—"Money is the root of all evil" "You cannot serve God and money" "Blessed are the poor" and "It's easier for a camel to pass through the eye of a needle than for a rich man to get to heaven" are just a few examples. However, these verses are sometimes misapplied if not misquoted. For instance, in his first letter to Timothy. Paul actually wrote "For the Love of Money is a root of all kinds of evil..." (I Timothy 6:10) When someone idolizes money in and of itself they are violating one of God's mandates of placing idols in front of Him.

Believing that money causes problems, there are some who believe that poverty or lack is somehow commendable, or godlier. It's not. There's nothing celestial by having the gas turned off. There is nothing pious about eating mac and cheese ten days in a row. There's nothing virtuous in sending your eight-year-old to school with shoes that are coming apart.

We all know people who have a contorted view of money—both fear-based and confused. For instance, when a survey of 800 people having a net worth of $500,000 or more was conducted several years ago 19% of those surveyed said "having enough money is a constant worry in my life". Even more striking was that 33% of Americans, with a net worth of at least $10 million also felt that "Having money is a constant worry in my life!" If you were to ask people you know how they could improve their lives, what do you think their answer would be?

Money is not the culprit. Money is simply a medium that should flow in and through our lives without fear yet even reading this sentence may seem preposterous, such is our view of money.

It is what we do with money, who we help, whose lives we improve that sets us apart from self-centeredness and self-indulgence.

Being successful to some is having a beautiful home, driving an expensive car, going on exotic vacations or generally having the money to do or buy most anything they want. We know that a certain amount of peace of mind and comfort comes from knowing that we are financially comfortable. But as the statistics above suggest, having money doesn't necessarily bring contentment. Too many think "if I had money I'd never have to worry again" however when you take note of the lives of lottery winners, who've suddenly realized massive wealth, you understand that money in and of itself does not bring happiness. In many cases it has brought pain and misfortune.

Why is this? Why does this happen? Simply put—if you are not mentally, emotionally, and spiritually prepared for the stewardship of wealth it will become a curse exceeding any misery imaginable.

Sadly, we have heard of entertainers who have gone through millions of dollars in the false belief that money equates happiness. When we have money, we (seem) to have lots of "friends". The rapper MC Hammer went through tens of millions of dollars entertaining and helping friends only to discover there weren't any around when he ran out of money. The boxer Mike Tyson, after experiencing tremendous success in the ring and massive wealth had to eventually start over from scratch.

Personally, I recall the many "friends" I had when money was not a problem. Being blessed over my years as a stockbroker I had achieved what many (including me back then) considered success. When the music stopped after the government froze my assets in 2008 and then became a target of the US Attorney, there suddenly weren't many 'friends' around anymore. It was never more obvious then when, a few months later, as I was lying in a hospital recovering from a heart attack that I realized there weren't but a few (very few) get-well cards or flowers.

This is a good time to pause and consider the following: are you prepared for massive financial blessings? "Of course!" you might say. Although success and happiness include so much more than money, only the foolish (or the rich but we've already seen how many of them feel) say money isn't important. Money however, is only one small ingredient, one small part of success.

Money needs to flow freely, without stress, in and out of our lives. Unfortunately, many people are actually afraid of money. They may have been conditioned to believe that money brings too much strife into people's lives. They may have heard parents argue or even split up because of it. Through time they may have come to believe it really is evil. If this might be you, ask yourself this question—"Would God have allowed something significant and essential in my life to be evil?" The answer is obviously no.

You do however need to consider what money, abundance, and wealth mean to you. You also need to think about the following—what would substantial wealth denote in your life? Would you be comfortable with your wealth around your family, your friends? Or would you feel uneasy, even embarrassed around them? Would they feel annoyed or ill at ease around you? Would you feel guilty or awkward? If your objectives in life include being financially secure, to never be in a financial position of lack, then you must consider and seriously examine your beliefs and perspectives about money. *I cannot stress this enough!*

Would you know how to manage wealth, how to invest portions of it? In fact, your current financial condition—whether significant or sparse—is a result of not only how you view money but how you feel about it.

This will make more sense later, but you must think over, seriously think over, what money means to you. Only after you fully contemplate your attitude toward, opinion of and relation to money can you create an intelligent financial course of action.

To achieve prosperity, we need to regroup and take charge of our lives. Not just talking about it (we've all been there and done that) but by committing to changing our thinking, readjusting our mindset, discerning the reasons for the goals we have and refocusing where our priorities lie.

Foundations. Rebuilding ourselves from the ground up.

Through each chapter for the rest of this book, we will do just that. Inch by inch, nail by nail. Brick by brick.

16

How We View Things

Jesus did not just say things.

When He spoke, His words were captivating, disorienting, perplexing, transformative and unforgettable. Over and over through the gospels we see the power that His teachings had on His contemporaries. Whether it was a poor widow or a Pharisee, a tax collector, or a crowd on the hillside. Jesus spoke to the inner being of the listener.

Jesus never sowed doubt. He invited people to reexamine and reawaken to God's glory, God's gifts, and God's unending bounty.

Repeatedly Jesus continued to ask – "Do you believe?" to those he would help. One instance that I keep coming back to is that moment where Peter attempts to climb out of the boat. I believe that this is one of the most profound confirmations of Jesus' importance, reliance actually, toward faith – "And immediately Jesus stretched out His hand and caught him, and said to him, **"O you of little faith, why did you doubt?"** (Matthew 14:25-31)

Jesus stood in amazement (one out of two times in the Gospels) when a foreigner, an occupier in Judea says to Him, "Only speak a word and my servant will be healed." Turning to the Roman officer Jesus said, "as you've believed, so let it be done for you." (Matthew 8:5-13)

What constituted faith in Palestine at the time? Actually, it is what faith was and is still today—"The substance of things hoped for, the evidence of things not seen", according to Paul. (Hebrews 11:1)

But the word "evidence" is central to Paul's definition of faith. It is interesting that he uses that particular word—Evidence.

According to the dictionary, the meaning of evidence is "An outward sign. Proof" but how can that be if faith is nothing more than a thought? How can you get 'proof' from a mere thought? The answer is that thoughts are things! There is a direct connection, as you'll see, between thoughts and choice, where the one must precede the other.

We are free to choose whatever path we want. But only an omniscient Being can ever allow such a privilege.

Our God is a God of unconditional love. This type of love is a feeling without the right of ownership. It is love in the truest form. God loves us without trying to be loved back. Although He wants our love, He puts no conditions on us such as "If you love me, I'll love you." "If you do this, then I'll do that." It is God's grace that allows us to live our lives as we choose, and our choices are endless.

The word 'endless' is not an adjective used to make a point. It is a word meant to make a statement. The number of choices, of variations available to you in your life, are endless. You can choose. Whatever you choose you will get! No more, no less. You can master your course of events by doing one very simple thing—making a choice.

"That's not the way it is!" you say? "No one can just do or get whatever they want by simply making a choice!" Adolf Hitler made a choice. Mother Theresa made a choice. Osama Bin Laden made a choice, Billy Graham made a choice, Charles Manson made a choice, Pope John Paul II made a choice. Their choices included self-centeredness and malevolence or kindness and the Holy Spirit. Hatred or love. What do you choose?

"The integrity of the upright will guide them, but the perversity of the unfaithful will destroy them." (Proverbs 11:3) It is our choice to walk on the path—whichever path we decide upon—with God directing our steps or to walk alone in darkness. What do you choose?

How we decide to view reality depends on the point at which we originate the thought or idea. We view things with our conscious mind, yet we are like a man walking through a dense forest at night—wherever he points his light becomes his reality. However, the entire forest is available to walk through. In this case our wanderer has chosen his particular path, yet he is free to turn to the left, or right and illuminate - pick a new path.

Often life seems unfair. Maybe "often" is the wrong word. For some 'often' means every so often, for others very rarely and too many others all the time. Again, it's the reality you view it as. When you are preoccupied with the problems in your life, problems keep appearing in your life. Thinking about all the things you don't want to experience habitually brings them about in your life! There exists a radical way of thinking—thought energy takes on physical form and scripture verifies this. In the King James Version of the Bible, it is written: "For as he thinketh in his heart, so is he." (Proverbs 23:7)

I have mentioned this passage previously and I will refer to it again. Absorbing this message into your subconscious, like watering your garden, allows the seed to grow. Write this verse down and put it on your mirror so you're continually reminded that God allows you to *choose* what quality of life you desire.

As you contemplate where you want to be in life, look around to those people you know. Most lead their lives in ignorance of God's word, heedless of the ability He gives them to direct their lives as they choose. Yet in that ignorance, they do exactly what they want, then loudly, sometimes tearfully, blame God for bringing adversity and disappointments on to them. Without a conscious thought of His divine presence (until there's a reversal) they live their lives as though they were on a permanent bumper car—never knowing where they're headed, getting bounced from one problem to the next.

How does someone get off the merry-go-round when it – life - is going so fast that it seems out of control? *Refuse to fight against the way your life is.*

The more you battle the misfortunes, the more misfortunes show up. The more energy you put toward the annoyance they're causing you, the harder they remain fastened to you. In order to have these problems vanish, choose another possible alternative! Pivot away from the way things seem to be and replace it with a completely different thought! For instance, you're thinking of changing jobs but you can only think of the disruptions it will cause. Not knowing anyone at the new company, feeling uncomfortable for a while, worried about not fitting in - "what if I end up not liking it there?" etc. Instead focus on the excitement of a new opportunity, experiencing a fresh start.

Think on the gratifying aspects of the move.

If, however you find yourself needing to talk yourself into or out of a course of action heed that feeling. When you're sure the Holy Spirit is leading you in a specific way, don't get in the way with negative thoughts.

Don't take up arms against pessimistic or negative thoughts. The more you fight destructive thoughts, the more energy you give them. In football a defensive lineman's job is to disrupt the offense's game plan on a particular play. Quickness, agility, and skill are needed to accomplish this. They need to get past the offensive blockers to achieve the goal. They see ahead, their focus is the goal not the obstacle—in this case the offensive blockers. Focusing on battling the offensive lineman takes them out of their game, away from the objective. It takes precious time to try to win that battle and it also takes energy—in this case muscular endurance—to fight the obstacle.

In life its not always easy to avoid problems. Sometimes they just find you. Keep in mind that we're dealing with other people who also have their own agenda. What do we do? How do we navigate through moments like these? *Create an empty space!*

Allow me to digress for a moment here to illustrate a point. Many of us in the Western world tend to avoid studying the Asian way of living and thinking. Some of us are led to believe that by doing so we might be drawn into practicing Eastern religions. Bowing, monks chanting and meditating and the incense burning. Most Westerners get their first impression of Asian culture from television and movies. In fact, most Eastern religions began as philosophies, not a way to worship and have strong philosophical foundations. Today most Eastern religious thought is deeply woven into the fabric of Asian culture but as a Westerner and a Christian it is important to understand that you do not need to treat these philosophies as religious in order study and apply their principles.

Reading the 'Tao te Ching', 'The Art of War' or 'Go Rin No Sho' (a Book of Five Rings) will not expose you to demonic possession nor will you commit heresy by studying Eastern thought and where appropriate applying its wisdom in your life. We'll look at the applications of Asian thought in a moment, but let's return to an avenue on how to avoid difficulties and predicaments.

When provocations come up refrain from reacting to them. It sounds simple, seems impossible, yet by applying sound insight into the situation it can be done.

Aikido is an ancient Japanese martial art that is a study of grace and beauty. It is the art of falling through into empty space. Aikido uses the force of the attacker to direct him away: the assailant is taken by the arm and "guided" along by the defender (as if the defender is sending him on his way) at which point the attacker is released by the defender, who has used no force whatsoever. The antagonist is sent flying in the direction he was aiming. The idea, the secret really, is that the defender has not fought against the attack—he uses the energy of the attacker to walk him on his way and then lets go of him. The total energy of the attack or provocation in this instance—falls into empty space. There is nothing for the attacker to grab onto and consequently he falls on his face!

Pushing back, arguing, fighting and in general resisting something takes a lot of energy and more times than not is pointless. Actually, we see this paradigm in nature when we observe how flowing water picks the path of least resistance. Closer to home we see the effectiveness of non-resistance when we ask our children to clean their rooms. Rarely do they say no or argue. Usually, the request is received with a resounding "okay!" Mom or dad received the answer they were looking for, missy or junior offered no resistance to the request and life, for the moment, goes on (completing the task is another story!) and an immediate confrontation is avoided.

Take notice the next time you come across an annoying or negative situation and react with irritation, disappointment, dissatisfaction, or any other negative emotion. You'll become aware how the situation that brought about those emotions will immediately become worse. When that happens, react in a different way—or don't react at all. "The discretion of a man makes him slow to anger, and his glory is to overlook a transgression." (Proverbs 19:11) Play a mind-game with yourself: don't react as you would have in the past. Each time you react with indifference or change the way you view the annoyance you become psychologically stronger. Like any exercise you'll become more proficient with practice and what once was foreign becomes second nature. In addition, each time you successfully overcome the temptation to lose self-control you become mentally (and emotionally) powerful knowing that you overcame the temptation to react negatively the previous time. Your attitude toward the situation will dictate your reaction every time! See any problems as an opportunity presented to you as for your greater good instead of a stroke of bad luck or misfortune.

Your subconscious mind is where inspiration makes itself known. It is where divine guidance resides which is a further incentive to steadfastly maintain constant communion with God.

It's important to remind you once more—what you are undertaking here is *not* how the world goes about obtaining objectives. The secular world will simply—and assuredly—say: "You're nuts!" The materialistic world is accustomed to fighting and struggling for what they want. They will grasp their goal by the throat and attempt to reach the objective by any means possible. Sharing your thoughts freely is not recommended at this point. At least not yet. "Well done." is better than "Well said." Let your actions speak for themselves. Keep your own counsel. The only thing you need to keep constantly in mind is that for the God of the universe NOTHING IS IMPOSSIBLE! You do not owe, nor are you compelled to, explain. defend or rationalize anything you do righteously, to anyone. By doing so you open up your belief to the negative influences of others.

Let go, relax, cast away any worry, fear, and anxiety that you're feeling regarding the situation. If the answer doesn't appear right away don't panic—it will appear.

All of this sounds simple and easy as well as idealistic but living in the temporal world, facing frequent challenges is, well, challenging. Peter wrote about casting our cares to God and when illusions and misconceptions are peeled away this is the best course of action. (I Peter 5:7) There is great strength of faith when we acknowledge our inability to handle a problem or issue of some sort which necessitates a strong, consistent, divine relationship.

How often do you check the oil in your car? How about the fuel? Do you check the air pressure in your tires? You'll probably say 'often' to these questions.

How often do you check your emotions?

How often do you gauge your feelings about things? Have you ever paid attention to how you sound to others? Do you notice how you talk to yourself?

Take a day (plan it in advance) and completely commit to observing yourself. It would be most helpful as well as impactful if you write these findings down.

What have you learned by doing the exercise above? What surprised you? Disappointed you?

Too many people look at the glass and say it's half-empty. We think about our job—"This place stinks. I'm not making enough here. My boss is too demanding and no matter what I do, how hard I work, I am never appreciated."

How about your home? "This house is so old. The bedrooms are small, the basement looks like a dungeon." Your car: "This piece of junk. Everything is shot. It needs new tires and even the air conditioner doesn't work right!"

Complaining can become a practice and is a desperate habit that *must* be overcome if your goals are to be accomplished. Most people have forgotten those long-ago days when they were children when everything was fun, when life offered only the best. It seemed that every event had a happy ending. Although our house was old it was comfortable, we had a warm bed to sleep in. No matter how hard the rain we stayed dry and despite the fact the bedroom was small it was ours. Instead, we've traded hope for the future with disdain for the present.

Radiating negative energy, you become a magnet for attracting other situations you don't want. For people like this "Murphy's Law"—with the axiom 'whatever can go wrong, will'—becomes their mantra.

As I was absorbing life lessons in prison, I was assigned a "bunkie" who could have been Chairman of the Board at the Pessimist's Club. Every day was a challenge in dealing with Paulie's attitude. "Hey Paulie, it's going to be in the '70s this week!" "Yea" he answered, "but its gonna rain every day!" Another day, in discussing his case, he said, "Everything was being worked out with the prosecutor and my lawyer went and died on me!" Paulie, who most everyone mistook for the little Monopoly Man, was assigned to the "Greenhouse"—the farm in prison, to work. I said, "I worked there for a while. It was nice." "The bugs are always in my face. It's too hot. I hate it there!" was his answer. Paulie honored my request to change to another cube after a few weeks.

We've all experienced someone like Paulie—negative, pessimistic and anything but inspiring. Once again—how do you sound to others?

No matter the present situation you find yourself in, you can usually find something good in it. Even the very smallest things in life can bring, or be a source of, joy. If you think about it, joy usually is accompanied by gratitude—being thankful to be in the moment to experience delight.

Sadly, as we grow older our lives become cluttered with pressures many of which we bring onto ourselves. We seem to wake up one day and wonder why we forgot to have fun. We take ourselves, our work, our career, even our families so indifferently that we don't recognize our own selves anymore.

No one began their working years with the thought in mind, "I plan on working so hard that the only pleasure I receive is from my work."

Chances are good that the objective was to provide comforts for their family but frequently they become obsessed with their work and idolize the position. The dictionary defines 'Idol' as "an object of passionate devotion". This does not mean to not do your very best at work. Indeed, do everything impeccably, just don't lose sight of the fact you are working to live and not living to work!

Believing in yourself will require talking to yourself. As we know, words have meaning, and thoughts really do turn into things. The caveat however is talking powerful words into yourself. It is important that you know – and believe – *that you deserve the beautiful things in life*. Be open to the blessings that God is happy to give you.

Choose to be what you desire. Choose to be empowered through God's own words. Choose to not allow anyone to steal your joy. Believe on a consistent basis that good things are coming your way no matter how the present circumstances may seem because *with God all things are possible.*

17

Staying the Course

Joy is never likely to appear in our lives when all we do is stay focused on the negative.

Our minds need to be open to what can be accomplished, how we can help others and where our actions can be the most effective. The poet Edna St. Vincent Millay wrote, "O world, I cannot hold thee close enough!" This was a lady who knew how to experience joy and that by looking for joy, it would be found.

Jesus spoke about having, receiving, or bringing joy over a dozen times in the Bible. Sadly, there are some people who feel that enjoying life is un-Christian. To these believers dancing, singing, playing an instrument, even laughing is an affront to God. You've heard people say, "I'm having too much fun" or "This seems so good, it must be wrong!" How sad. Is it any wonder that some followers develop various types of psychosis? Or things never seem 'to go their way'? It cannot be any other way. We attract what we think into our lives.

"Then our mouth was filled with laughter, and our tongue with singing." (Psalms 126:2) God allows us to find and experience happiness and laughter. Paul spoke about how the consequences of living with the Holy Spirit inside us would be "love, joy, peace, longsuffering, kindness, goodness and faithfulness." (Galatians 5:22-23) The psychologist Abraham Maslow conducted a study some years ago to discover how people were affected by joyful occurrences in their lives. He found that a great many people felt "Moments of great awe; moments of the most intense happiness or even rapture, ecstasy or bliss." There is one constant in the universe, and it is always present in every sublime, joyous experience—LOVE.

As I stated earlier, gratitude is usually within the encounter, but love is always present. It is as if the curtain gets pulled back, time becomes non-existent, earthly cares are forgotten and genuine euphoria envelopes us. God is love and it is in those moments of pure happiness that we feel His presence intensely. As we are God's created beings, it is natural that we share this most precious characteristic with Him. Additionally, our emotions, our feelings, our minds, and all that we hold most pure within us would reflect God.

Each of us 'get caught up' in our lives. There are appointments, deadlines, obligations, commitments, and responsibilities that seem to not only monopolize our time but sometimes overwhelm us. When this happens remember that God provides refuge and peace, "Be still and know that I am God." (Psalms 46:10) It is essential that now and then you break free of the heavy loads you carry and listen for His voice.......When the rain suddenly ends, as the drops of water reflect off each blade of grass, as a sliver of light shines from the clouds and a rainbow begins arching across a leaden sky—that's God speaking to you.

As you stand on a beach, feeling a glowing sense of oneness with the water, the sky, and the air—that's God speaking to you.

On a solitary mountaintop, gazing out over a star—saturated sky, the only sound your breath, a feeling of Divine connection—that's God speaking to you.

The dictionary describes joy as an "exultation of spirit" and what truly are we, if not spirit made in God's image? Could it be that those moments of joy we experience are intended to impart the example of how we are meant to live? Keeping a divinely rooted foundation will allow you to recover from obstacles and dilemmas because you know that setbacks are really set-ups for achieving your goals. Keep your eye on the objective. On the end. Be resolute, tenacious, and steadfast. Steve Jobs observed "I'm convinced that about half of what separates the successful entrepreneurs from the unsuccessful ones is pure perseverance."

Allow yourself to become preoccupied with thoughts of what you wish for your life. What we focus on and what we become fixated on is what becomes part of our lives. Negative thinking is a powerful mental activity. For most people negative thinking is much easier than being optimistic. There are a few reasons for this. First, thinking failure, loss, nonsuccess, and futility are powerful images that cause regret and fear—two very potent emotions. Another reason is that being wary—negative thinking's cousin—is hard-wired in our brains as you'll see. For now, just accept the premise that thinking negative is natural. You'll need reason, as well as logical thought-out approaches to deal with negative thinking and you'll get them before you finish this book.

Fortunately, pleasant experiences, realized achievements and positive outcomes also imbed themselves in our subconscious mind. These are where we will put our focus. It will always profit you to take control of your thoughts. Thomas J. Jackson, better known as "Stonewall" Jackson, arguably one of the greatest military commanders in American history once said, "Never take counsel of your fears." He knew that by doing so, one scary thought would lead to another more frightening and terrifying one. Henry Ford said, "Obstacles are those frightful things you see when you take your eyes off your goal."

It's natural to see new, unfortunate events follow any negative reaction that you have to something. Observe the truth of the preceding sentence the next time you forget to maintain conscious control of your thoughts. Expressing constant displeasure and dissatisfaction will put focus on your problems and you radiate that which you're trying to avoid which in turn guarantees your experiencing more of it.

Bringing optimistic outlooks into your life will invariably bring conspicuous opportunities as well as exceptional opportunities. That may sound like a bold statement, but it can't be any other way. "Why?" you ask? Because when your focused mind is on favorable circumstances you notice opportunities, nuances really, that are subtle. When you're acting with negative emotions, you're placing obstructions in your perceptions instead of auspicious expectancy. Look for the good that surrounds you, grasp out for even the tiniest bit of joy and revel in it. "Nobody does that!" you say? Exactly! You are not everybody. You are drawing prosperity, blessings, and success into your life—on purpose!

Remember- express gratitude for every happiness and you'll find yourself experiencing even more to be happy about. You can equalize the not-so-good things in your life by thanking God for the opportunity to grow as well as the ability to gauge how far you've come.

How does someone begin the journey toward readjusting their attitude from complaint to comfort? By relationship prayer. Dialogue prayer. Acknowledgment prayer. Thanking prayer.

Most people pray when they're in a jam. They're desperate and when you're desperate you've already bought into doubt and defeat. God doesn't work through a doubt-filled mind. Yes, He can do anything, but He allows us to find ourselves too. "I can't, I'll never, I won't ever" are statements packed not only with emotion but conviction. When you are about to speak defeat, declare by faith, "I am surrounded by God's favor!" instead.

Another method for calling in favor is by occupying your mind with uplifting outside sources. Motivational and inspirational works enrich our lives by focusing on positive achievements experienced by others, or by examples that we can make part of our lives. This type of diet nourishes our souls. Stimulating our minds in such ways can do nothing but bolster and raise our spirits, inspiring us to achieve beyond our self-determined limits. Absorbing the lessons learned through these efforts imparts the confidence to rise higher and become stronger with each successive attempt. Pay attention to each and every success no matter how insignificant you may think of them. They are solid rock-hard steps toward the destiny God mandated for you.

As you begin your journey toward accepting God's favor it is important to tend your garden. By giving your garden water and fertilizer (right thoughts) you are encouraging growth. You maintain your garden daily making sure that pests and bugs (negative thinking) don't take control and damage the plants. You keep the weeds from taking root so they (pessimistic people) don't over-run what you've worked hard to plant and grow. "Yeah, I know all this and I agree with you," you might say, "but I've known Tom all of my life, It's just the way he is but he's a great guy. I can't just cut him off!"

If you've made a commitment to redefine and refashion your life—something only you yourself can answer—you must limit the time you spend with those people who have kept, you from being your best. Staying stagnant, remaining in the space you've always been, assures you of a life of mediocrity at best. If you're not moving forward, you're incapable of becoming who God intended you to be.

Usually you'll discover that pessimism, cynicism, and despondency are present when faith is lacking. Think on this for a moment. When you're feeling hopeless is it because you have faith in a positive outcome or is it because you just don't see how it—whatever "it" happened to be—could work out? Faith needs to be present for God to provide His blessing.

Earlier I mentioned the amusingly improbable example about the leper who could not be healed. Although meant to be humorous, the fable illustrates the requirement that faith must be present for wonderous results to happen.

Mark relates an interesting and instructive story of Jesus' visit to Nazareth during His three-year ministry.......

It had been a while since Jesus had been home, and being a small village everyone knew one another—in other words they remembered Jesus "when". When He ran through the alleys and lanes to play. When He gathered water for His mother. When He helped His father Joseph in his carpentry shop. But now, all these years later they stood in astonishment as they listened to the words emanating from this young man.

Surely, they must have heard at least some of the stories circulating around Judea about the little boy they remembered.

"Where did this wisdom come from?" they asked after hearing Jesus speak in the temple. "Isn't this Mary's son? Aren't James and Joseph, Judas and Simon His brothers? And this is the same man whose sisters live here in the village? (Mark 6:4-6) As you read Mark's words you can almost feel the resentment, maybe even jealousy radiating from the scripture - *'This is the guy? No way! Who does He think He is coming here and talking to us like this?'* Reading Mark's words, you get the feeling the Najoreans would like to run Him out of town.

But it is Jesus Himself who understands what is taking place in Nazareth. Observing what the lack of faith causes, Mark writes "Now he could do no mighty work there... and He marveled because of their unbelief." Such is the power of faith—of the lack of it—that the Son of God walks away shaking His head in amazement, able to leave just a very few who believed, restored to health.

This account is highly symbolic in that Jesus, who not only is aware of His authority and command, but of His compassion is unable to overcome hardened hearts and attitudes that habitually see the dark side of things!

Please – read the previous few paragraphs again. Above I wrote, *"God doesn't work through a doubt-filled mind. Yes, He can do anything, but He allows us to find ourselves too."* You will recall from the Introduction where I wrote *".....however there are instances where a speaker or an author tries to create a theology that they like. I once read a quote that said, "Whenever possible, let Scripture interpret Scripture."* There will be those who will say, "Yes, that's what is written in Mark, but what it means is....." No. Don't buy into that! As I have observed – "Whenever possible, let Scripture interpret Scripture." We read very plainly in Mark's verses, as well as Matthew, Luke and John, what outcomes the power of faith and belief – or the lack of it – will do!

Have you ever noticed how people tend to repeatedly talk about their bad experiences but quickly forget about anything good they've encountered, rarely mentioning a happy event or occurrence? The reason of course is that good news rarely arouses passion in human beings.

Bad news has drama. It has a "potential threat" quality—"this could happen to me!"—and usually arouses a "negative outcome" response. Is it any surprise that the evening news doesn't cover promotion, fulfillment, happiness, or blessings? As the old newspaper adage states "bad news sells".

It's essential to savor all the good news you hear. Talk about that. Find joy in that. Roll good news—from wherever it came from—over in your mind. Visualize that you're the recipient or participant of it. This is not looking at the world through rose-colored glasses (although what's the matter with that?) but enjoying success in and for others.

In the NIV translation Proverbs 11:25 says "He who refreshes others will himself be refreshed." To refresh is to exhilarate, to delight, to be glad for. You know there are people who crave success, wealth, loving relationships, happiness, good fortune, favor, blessings and all the good that life has to offer. Too often you hear people, who spend considerable time longing for, even visualizing for, these divine occurrences grumble and express contempt for those who've received them! Essentially these jealous and envious donkeys are cursing the very circumstances they covet! How can someone expect favor with such an attitude? If this might be you begin replacing resentments with reverence.

Keep in mind that even reversals and misfortunes can make you stronger, provide lessons you could not possibly receive elsewhere and can help you gain experience. Failures only become them if you quit, and if you let them haunt you constantly. Remember what Thomas Edison once said regarding his attempts to invent the lightbulb: "I have not failed. I've just found ten thousand ways that don't work."

Get into the habit of reacting positively to events in your life. Having a relationship with God, conversing as with a trusted friend will move your life into a direction you'll hardly believe. What you once looked at with fear and worry, you'll now feel protected and guided, knowing that "The Lord guards the lives of His faithful." (Psalms 97:10)

Earlier we spoke about forgiveness. When we've caused another distress in some way we need to own up, apologize and move forward with a greater understanding of how our actions affect others. As I wrote— ask for forgiveness and be sincere in the request but ask only once and never more.

Don't allow people to subjugate you with guilt. There are those whose agenda's purposes are served by making others feel guilty, insignificant, unimportant, and good-for-nothing. Left unchecked you begin to buy into those descriptions and soon you find yourself living down to those expectations. Unless you take action, now, immediately, to begin mastering your self-realization you could face a lifetime of despair and misery.

Be wary of self-condemnation. Confidence begins to form in childhood but can be increased and strengthened in adulthood by paying attention to small wins and not being quick to overlook accomplishments. Avoid questioning yourself with words like "Do I really deserve this?" Abstain from self-exiling yourself. By that I mean sitting in the back of the room for instance. Or taking the farthest seat away from the meeting leader at a conference table.

Refrain from fighting with yourself over any flaws, weaknesses, shortcomings or lack of skill or talent in some area. This type of recrimination does you no good.

To sit and complain how bad everything is and how life has been unfair to you, is not only destructive and selfish but an affront to God. How do you turn misery and misfortune (no matter how long you've experienced it) into contentment and joy?

Know that each setback and negative event holds a positive meaning and view what you consider negative to be a positive step toward your goal!

Human beings, who plan their life script, seldom are happy when things aren't proceeding along those plans. You ask for favor, for guidance, praying for His mighty hand in your quest, then give up when things are not proceeding according to *your* plan! That's plain crazy!

As your dialogue prayer becomes stronger, you'll feel the urge to get out of the way and you'll feel led to let go of the reins in your white-knuckled hands and allow God to control events. This does not mean to not work your plan, nor does it mean to become dormant or inactive. You must do your part. What this means is to be aware of subtle whispers of guidance that is put on your heart and go with that.

Our attitudes toward events also has a physical effect as well as mental and emotional. The ethicist and physician Henry K. Beecher conducted a study in 1956 on how pain was interpreted and processed on veterans and civilians. These interpretations—their attitude in other words—can shape the way people experienced trauma and pain.

Beecher's research found that veterans rated their pain less intensely than the civilians did even though the wounds were comparable! 83% of the civilians requested narcotics to manage their pain while only 32% of veterans opted to do likewise!

What was interesting was his discovery that the difference did not depend on the severity of the injury but on how these individuals experienced them.

Beecher found that veterans tended to wear their injuries as a badge of honor and patriotism while civilians were more likely to see their injuries as unfortunate events that happened to them.

Based on Beecher's study it was found that the more we interpret events as the outcome of something we did as opposed to something done to us, the better our attitude and recovery!

Attitude is your means to a solution as well as achievement or disappointment. You either believe or you don't. I once heard the story of two farmers. Both prayed for rain as they surveyed their fields. Day after day, week after week they implored Him for a downpour but only one of the farmers plowed his field, prepared his ground, and planted his crops. Which of them do you think had belief?

Carry yourself with the attitude of expectancy. Wash your face. Comb your hair. Put on your best clothes, perfume, or cologne. Be ready for blessings. Be ready for anointing. Be ready for good fortune. Act like you are and you will be.

If your girlfriends find fault with your new attitude, find new girlfriends. If your buddies start making fun of you, mocking and taunting you then they're not friends. Anyone who doesn't have your best interests at heart is at best a mere acquaintance and should be given very limited time as well as being trusted with anything concerning your personal background.

Learn the gift of goodbye.

18

Don't Let Your History Hinder Your Destiny

As you devote more and more time to improving your inner self, you'll noticed a change, you won't seem to "fit in" anymore.

The wrong kind of people will give you the wrong kind of encouragement. You need to get yourself feeling worthy because God is about to move in your life. It's similar to the example above with some lottery winners—they're not ready for that type of fortunate event. It may not only be their inability to manage that kind of money but the feeling that they don't feel worthy. You need a radical change in your spirit. Where at one time the ordinary was sufficient, extraordinary is now common.

Begin your day by asking for God's favor: "Thank you Lord for giving me this day. Guide me, bless me and fill me with your favor." Don't be like the grump who says, "Oh god it's morning!" Instead you'll say "Praise God, it's morning!" The old hymn "This is the day (that the Lord has made!)" is no longer just a song but your mantra. When God gives any man wealth and possessions, and enables him to enjoy them, to accept his lot and be happy in his work—this is a gift of His. This person seldom reflects on the days of his life because God keeps him occupied with gladness of heart.

Expecting dreams to come to pass, good breaks to happen, the right doors to open and health to be restored demonstrates faith. It attests to belief. It's what allows God to work in your life. "I know Guy, but I pray, I expect good things, I stay positive as much as I can but nothing seems to happen. I feel so stymied with it all!"

Frustration is such a treacherous emotion isn't it? We want what we want, and we want it now! The longer something takes to arrive the more doubt clouds our mind. As the doubt increases, worry takes hold. Then the castle gate is stormed and in pours unbelief, lack, unhappiness, loss, failure, and the visualization of what life will be like now without the goal, objective, or intention. But at its basis, frustration is not keeping faith. The antidote to this is to keep a strong relationship with God. The more solid that connection is to Him the calmer you'll be. You rely on His word and His will. This is going to take time if you've not developed that dependance yet, but *it will* come about. Stay focused and stay committed. You'll see.

Although your past may be littered with a thousand disappointments, don't let your history hinder your destiny! Don't get in God's way. Don't let worry and bitterness take over your life. Get fired up because you have a destiny to realize. Become a vessel of God's glory—shining, gleaming, and brilliant!

Our thoughts have a powerful and direct effect on our reality. The best example of this is how our worst fears tend to come true. While there may be times where the Holy Spirit inspired a premonition in us, dwelling on worst case scenarios and outcomes is a very destructive thing to do. Declare the authority of Jesus Christ to overcome obstacles, eliminate worry, conquer fear, and call down victory. There is NOTHING in this universe that can stand against God. Speak success and remove doubt. Believe. Allow our Most High God to fight your battles and give you peace. When you pray ask the Lord to send His angels as a hedge of protection around you. Declare health, declare blessings, declare favor. Speak these declarations out loud. As you know by now - words have meaning and words have power.

Avoid condemning yourself, putting yourself down. Although we spoke about this earlier, it cannot be overstated! Ask yourself empowering questions. Too often we self-talk phrases like "Why did I have to be so stupid?" Instead rephrase that comment " I'm glad that I learned such a valuable lesson!" Rather than "I can never do anything right." replace it with "I am blessed and guided in all I do."

As dangerous as denouncing and demeaning ourselves can be, judging, despairing, and looking down on others is equally pernicious. How do people judge? I mean on the base level? First, they need to quickly create a point of reference from which to judge. Usually, this point is themselves. If the other person is bad or worse—the better the arbiter must be. There are some people whose self-esteem is so lofty that they scorn the weaknesses of others. They condemn the achievements of others, or they inflate the flaws that they observe in other people. This is a person who needs constant ego - feeding and usually their ego leaves little space for true and happy relationships. They swim in their own vanity and tend to drown others with their sense of superiority.

Arrogance brings resentment as well as displays of supremacy and exasperation and the person who possesses and exhibits these "qualities" can inevitably look forward to misery. History is full of such people.......

Herod Agrippa was another of the family who left their mark on the life of Jesus and the apostles. Each of his predecessors possessed murderous traits as well as conceit. Herod himself had the apostle James killed and had Peter thrown into prison with plans to execute him. He had the guards who stood watch over Peter killed after it was discovered that Peter had somehow escaped. Vain, pompous, and arrogant, Herod immersed himself in self-importance as his subjects shouted out his praises—"The voice of a god and not of a man!" (Acts 12:22).

Usually we discover that people, who like Herod have a driving need to be praised, are the most insecure. Anytime a person feels the need to feel "almighty" you can be assured that eventually they'll be knocked from their pedestal. The challenge of course is to not gloat over or be happy about someone's reversals, not rejoicing when they fail or feel gladness in your heart if they do. (Proverbs 25:21-22)

Each one of us have virtues but never neglect to work to overcome your flaws. Sometimes we try to overcome our imperfections by hiding them, becoming withdrawn, lashing out, or becoming defiant. These methods are not only useless but annoying and uncomfortable to those around us. To compensate for your blemishes—enhance the gifts and talents that God gave you!

Being self-confident overcomes a physical flaw. Charm overcomes a lack of beauty. Avoid imitating others, however. Imitating here means to become a parody of someone famous. For example, walking around in a black cape imitating the manner and speech of a French Count will not only make you look ridiculous but is embarrassing, the example of helping others as Mother Teresa did is a treasure. See the difference?

Each of us have a natural desire to want things but attaching a great amount of importance to something or on someone creates a dependancy. When your life "depends" on a particular outcome you're in danger of obsessing over it, which in turn causes a form of idolatry. Although this may seem absurd, it happens more often than you realize.

For example, you just bought new furniture. You'd saved and planned for the day you'd bring it all home. You customized it. You brought the fabric patterns home and matched the wallpaper, the curtains, the carpet. You've pictured how it would look in your living room. But the moment the furniture is delivered you're terrified of any scratch on the wood or spot appearing on the cloth. In a word - you 'adore' this beautiful furniture. As a result of being overly concerned - in other words dependent on it - you'll soon spill coffee on it! Or a guest does it for you.

This scenario plays out in various ways and with various objects on people. Cars, boats, clothes. We've all experienced this "phenomenon", but it really isn't a phenomenon. It's putting up a false idol in your life.

The remedy to this is to stop worshiping the object of your desire and treat it as anything ordinary. This does not mean to be indifferent towards or unconcerned about your objective or intention but to cease making an idol of it.

Let's take this viewpoint a step further. When we desire something so much, we begin to depend on getting it. You become almost psychotic, neglecting any inner guidance. You become convinced that this is the only thing in the world that can make you happy and you try to convince yourself that you'll obtain it.

I'd like to pause here for a moment and address a dilemma many people, possibly even yourself, have encountered on their journey toward improving their lives, achieving their goals, and realizing their desires.

By now many of you have read a number of motivational, self-help, and inspirational works. Although there are so many emmenent and widely acclaimed authors who have been guiding lights in helping people to be all they hope to be, many are disappointed because, despite following and adhering to the advice they've received, their goals and aspirations have not been fulfilled. Indeed, some of the hopes seem farther away than ever. Some might be tempted to say, "I knew this stuff doesn't work". Others may think "I must be doing something wrong". What is the reason that these best efforts have not, so far, been successful? Is there a solution to this dilemma? Actually, it's quite simple: Drop your EGO!

When you're reading, observing, and then attempting to carry out the ideas and recommendations proposed, is God part of that plan? Edging God Out of your strategy will do you no good. If you are not spiritually prepared for your intentions to materialize, they may likely not happen. That's a heavy statement I know but you must keep in mind that IT IS GOD WHO ALLOWS CONDITIONS IN OUR LIVES. For many people this is a hard concept, if not impossible one, to accept.

When one reads a motivational book, they become aware of ideas, techniques, and hypothesis of the author in the anticipation of achievement of that which they want. You may have implemented - in some cases exactly - what was suggested. To no avail. In order to proceed with any expectation of success you must first strive to discern God's will for your life. *The only way you can accomplish this is by radical prayer.* The Holy Spirit can then impart on your heart the rightness of that which you seek. Without this impartation you are risking an experience you may not wish—a mild slap on the wrist or a severe misfortune. Or the unrealized objective.

The paradox is knowing when your will is in the service of God's. It is of the utmost importance to continue your quest with a positive expectancy—provided you are "at peace" with your intention—and in complete faith that it will appear in your life. Maintaining a defeatist attitude will block any attainment or good fortune from appearing. Not only must you "think" success but "feel" success. When you read of or hear about others who were able to "manifest" something in their lives, just go about knowing it was either God's will or He allowed it. *It can be no other way!* But you must do your part! There are those who use the phrase "I'm waiting on the Lord" and while this is sound reasoning when appropriate, it is not an authorization to not give your best effort to achieve your goal. It just may be that God is waiting on you!

Certainly, we need to have an optimistic outlook generally, and determination specifically, to achieve what we imagine. Without that faith, and absent that commitment on our part, God is unable to change our circumstances. Why? Because you've already made up your mind to live without.

Make no mistake—God's divine will is guided by love. Unfailing love. Jesus pronounced exactly this point in His parables about the lost sheep, the widow's coins and the prodigal son.

Before you become confused as to God's will and your having control over what you desire and then achieving it, let's go back to God's words to find His view: "Now nothing will be restrained from them, which they have imagined to do" (Genesis 11:6 KJV) Only you can control what you imagine, what you think. Researchers tell us that we have an average of 60,000 thoughts per day! 60,000 opportunities to think perfect health, abundance, realized goals, and God's favor. What are you doing with your thoughts?

The subconscious is in and of itself unable to manufacture a decision. That is one of the duties of the conscious mind. The subconscious receives orders but only responds and acts on feelings. It does not decide "Great idea!" or " this is not in our best interest." As soon as a decision is made by the conscious mind, done with emotion and sensory perception, the subconscious immediately begins to put into action the requirements necessary for the intention to appear physically. Thankfully your desires are delayed which allows you to consciously reassess the wisdom of actually materializing your goal. As Winston Churchill once observed, "You create your own universe as you go along."

Keep in mind that the stronger you try to avoid a feeling—not having a new car, living without the girl or guy of your dreams, whatever, you are expressing dissatisfaction with your corner of the world. Your focus is "I don't want to continue on without_______" and what you don't want will show up! Since this is where you focused your attention and feeling (don't wanting it) it can be no other way. This, my brothers and sisters, is "Free Will" in action.

You've noticed this propensity with money. People work diligently (sometimes obsessively) to earn it but will complain that they are always short no matter how hard they work. Being fearful of losing what you have—money, reputation, position, possessions, will set things in motion to make certain that you achieve your 'goal.'
Fear is an extremely powerful emotion. If you find yourself falling into this trap, simply take hold of your emotions by thanking God for all that you do have.

Another remedy that will be effective in stopping dependance—especially about money—is this: *give it away!*

Gifting money to anything worthwhile is not only commendable but empowering. It could be a charity, a fund drive, a building campaign, or a stewardship. Bestowing money through tithing acknowledges God's blessings in our lives as we've discussed. We abandon dependance, and trust that more will return. When Solomon wrote in Proverbs "Honor the Lord with your possessions, and with the firstfruits of all your increase; so your barns will be filled with plenty and your vats will overflow with new wine" (Proverbs 3:9-10) He was stating a truth as well as an affirmation. Remember that by going about God's business, you are assured of never-ending prosperity.

Be very discerning before making "money" your goal. There is no question that financial independence allows us a certain degree of freedom in the material world but making your goal to "have more money" to achieve your objective may be a bit short-sighted.

People sometimes think that it takes "more money" to reach a goal but that's not always correct. The truth is God is the one who knows the best way to realize an intention. Be careful that you don't get caught up with the thought "I want to be rich" because if you've not been exposed to significant wealth, you may be only countermanding what you say you want with the belief that you're asking for something that you'll never get. My experiences in assisting not only the wealthy but people who were "successful" in life taught me this: Those who had *the goal as their vision*, usually fulfilled that desire. Money appeared as it was needed to achieve that desire. In other words, they did not put as the goal 'money' in and of itself. This concept is extremely important. See the object of your desire, not the 'money'. There are no limitations in life only those of which you convince yourself there are.

"Let go and let God". How many times have you heard that phrase? This simple statement holds a great deal of significance. When we try to handle problems, objectives, or intentions on our own we place a great deal of importance on the outcome. "If I can't come up with the right answers on my application, they won't hire me." Catch yourself when thoughts of importance come up.

The reason worry and fear are two of the most insidious emotions is precisely because of the reactions they generate. Always remember—a perfect solution will come to you. Let me repeat—*do not attach enormous importance to your goal!* Proceed with confidence with the belief in its achievement and that God knows the perfect method to do so. Placing "life or death" significance on something, in someone, or with some outcome, places you in a position of doubting and through doubting you'll achieve your greatest fear.

Overcome this tendency with action. Do something to move toward your goal. Put your focus on the process of carrying out the work it will take to get there. When you are "in action" you are occupying your mind with doing, not fearing. Be mindful without worrying. Care without fearing.

Although it's easy to say (or write) not to worry or not to have fear, it's also important to keep in mind that these are natural emotions. Fear and anger are much more powerful emotions than happiness and delight. As I wrote earlier these sensations were needed by our pre-historic ancestors, through the "fight or flight" instincts, to survive. If they needed to defend themselves from danger a joyful attitude did not produce the necessary mind frame to do so.

Actually, our human species has been filled with hardships and impediments for most of its history on the planet. Until very recently, the last hundred years or so, human beings were repeatedly exposed to misfortunes of various kinds due to disease and plagues. It was not uncommon for parents to lose a child to any number of illnesses such as cholera, diphtheria, pneumonia and dysentery to name a few, but are treated with antibiotics today. The miracle of modern health care has improved our world in ways that could never be overstated. The quality of our lives has, from a physical standpoint, dramatically improved to where a man can now expect to reach 80 years of age and beyond. In 1800 that same man could expect no more than 55 years of life—if he were fortunate. When you question things to be thankful for, ponder the preceding.

The subject of "negative thinking" has been written about and discussed in so many books (including this one) as well as the general media, that today most people understand what "positive thinking" and "negative thinking" mean. Stress and depression also are maladies that we hear quite often.

Stress and depression seem to be pervasive in our world and it should come as no surprise when you consider that we are frequently exposed to bad news—wars, terrorist attacks, natural disasters, stock market fluctuations, panics and so on. The difficulty for us is when this unfortunate news becomes personal. By that I mean when we begin to identify with the outcomes.

When possible, strive to avoid fixing your attention on outside problems and unfortunate events. Abstain from the tendency of "picturing" yourself in the situation. Keep away from "living through" the problem. If you doubt the power of focus, the power of visualizing, lets go to Scripture: "Whatever things are true, whatever things are noble, whatever things are just, whatever things are pure, whatever things are lovely, whatever things are of good report, if there is any virtue and if there is anything praiseworthy – meditate on these things." (Philippians 4:8)

19

Feeding the Inner Self

The media plays a much more significant role than it's given credit for in keeping the ball rolling over negative events.

Whether it's a Soap Opera (where the viewer refers to it as "my story") or a primetime drama, there's always enough tension and histrionics to lock someone into placing themselves into the mania.

Newscasts are known to beat an upsetting story into ashes, accomplishing the same resonance in a person. Your average negative thinker is the one who buys the tabloid that reports catastrophes both real and fantasies. They know which industry is the one that just had a recent accident, where the latest world crisis is or who just got in trouble. The lesson here is don't get caught up in them! Don't become emotional about them by allowing these stories to live through you. It's toxic, radioactive, and completely destructive to leading the life God has planned for you. Be mindful without worrying. Care without fearing.

If you grew up in the 60s or 70s you may remember the song "Signs." The lyrics went something like this: "Signs, signs, everywhere a sign. Do this, don't do that, can't you read the sign?" Signs, labels, categorizations, and definitions surround all of us. It seems that we learn what-is and what-isn't to like or not like (or think) from such things. Unfortunately, we become induced to think or feel by using definitions. Worse still is that we tend to form opinions by the views of others when we haven't met the person in question or encountered the experience firsthand! Without doubt there are instances where the evaluation is accurate, but how often have you come to another opinion when you observed the matter first-hand or actually met, or got to know the person?

We lose a part of ourselves when we adhere to others (or the media's) viewpoint. As our minds constantly chatter it is convinced that only "logical" explanations can be correct. That everything can be intelligently explained. This essentially is what the secular world wants us to believe.

When you maintain a sturdy connection to the Holy Spirit the soul's voice can break through the mind's control, allowing the true self to be guided by God. Get out of your own way and experience the supernatural marvel that the Divine eloquence brings into your spiritual being. Our soul has the capabilities to speak to us when we simply ask ourselves "Do I feel peace about (performing, proceeding with, etc.) this?" as you become more comfortable that "this is not all in my head" you'll also be able to "feel" discomfort when you are being guided to not do, or move forward with something.

When a person picks a goal or objective or any type of intention, their mind usually muses "I really want this. I hope I can get it." Hope is a good thing when used in the sense of achieving with some degree of future certainty. *Hoping* needs to turn into *intending* then to *have* fairly quickly otherwise it morphs into "probably won't" and probably won't is what will come to pass. To reach your objective, faith and certainty need to be present.

When you are unsure about something, you usually tend to experience inner turmoil and confusion to a greater or lesser degree which creates stress - "How do I do this?" which then becomes doubt. Because you've made this particular goal or intention so important you become more and more frustrated which coalesces into disbelief. The tighter someone tries to control the scenario of how they think it should be done the more likely an outcome directly opposite of what they want, becomes. The mind becomes fearful, and worry begins to overtake the imagination. The mind starts to play the "What if I don't get it?" images and worst-case outcomes project onto the sub-conscious' big screen. If our leading man or lady adds guilt into the script ("I don't deserve happiness!") their lives now turn into a living hell.

So how does someone get off of this terrifying roller-coaster?

Take action!

There is a tremendous degree of freedom in taking action. You are no longer a hapless and haunted wretch, worried about what will happen next. You will have made a commitment to act, and that decision is *very empowering.*

Don't make the mistake of thinking about how you will achieve your goal. If your objective is challenging, in itself that line of thinking will nullify your efforts. For you to realize your goal take pleasure in thinking about it as if it were already achieved! When you allow yourself to move with God's direction everything falls into place as it should. Feeling comfort and peace in the objective you want to achieve brings about a tranquility that allows you to loosen the grip of importance.

What you will witness, what will transpire is a unity of your soul and your mind. You become calm and confident, negating worry, doubt, and fear. Isaiah exhorted us to be peaceful and confident because in these would come our strength. (Isaiah 32:17)

When you observe someone's walk it's fairly easy to see what their attitude is at that moment. An ambling, slow gait generally indicates a lack of enthusiasm. But when you see someone walking erect, with purpose and with determination you immediately spot confidence. There is an old adage—"Act as though I am, and I will be." Walk with knowing.

Confidence is really born of success, and an awesome attribute to behold. The greatest leaders are those who exude this quality. They seem to inspire faith not only in themselves but in those who follow them, infecting them with a "can-do" feeling. This of course is most obvious on a battlefield. A soldier feels they can rely on a confident leader to not only defeat the enemy but to get them out alive.

Confidence is said to be consisting of self-assurance as well as boldness. When you know your job, for instance, you feel certain about your abilities to perform it and proceed with fortitude. Know your subject matter, know your weak spots and work on improving them. This is the practical homework assignment you need to achieve the difficult. Educate yourself on the point in question. Stand high with character and do so with integrity. But most often experience allows someone to move forward with confidence. The more experience you have, the more confidant you become. And that confidence will *always* show.

Avoid—at all costs—the temptation to strut or boast. Confidence is not arrogance by the way. Let your actions speak for themselves. "A proud and haughty man—"Scoffer" is his name; he acts with arrogant pride. (Proverbs 21:24)

When you stop comparing yourself to others, when you stop feeling guilty, obligated, or dependent you will come to a place of genuine calm. Calm confidence in yourself is when your soul is in balance with your mind. You feel complete serenity. Practice, really work at, being in harmony with everything and everyone. People always welcome those who bring agreement and peace with them and when you are in unity with others you'll notice the tranquility that seems to surround all you do.

Too many of us have been in that place where we decide what we want, develop a strategy to obtain it, determined and confident we'll achieve it and convince ourselves we'll realize the goal. And nothing!

There is a way to succeed in our goal if resoluteness hasn't worked: *allow yourself to have!*

Engaging in hand-to-hand combat with yourself over a matter is pretty counterproductive. Why? Because you've built up such importance on the acquisition of your intention that worry and fear creep up which is then followed by doubt. You begin to anticipate that a struggle is ahead. Obviously in a life and death situation your alternatives are very limited but thankfully in 'everyday' life we're not faced with this type of challenge on a day-to-day basis. Release importance – I just cannot say this enough.

Enjoy the feeling of having it already. How? By simply daydreaming. Don't buy into that myth that you're being delusional by daydreaming. This is your imagination's day at the shore. It's fun and it's productive because you are giving your "self" the chance to feel what the realized dream will be. When someone says "that stuff doesn't work" think about the last time you had a nightmare, when you woke up terrified, full of panic and a pounding heart. Your body has responded to nothing more than imagination but was convinced it was true and authentic. More about daydreaming in a moment.

Enjoy the feeling of having it already. Loosen the death grip by losing the feeling of *"I gotta have this!"* and you'll notice the path to achievement becomes clear and barriers—free. Remember when your dad took off the training wheels from your bicycle? You were determined to ride that bike on 2 wheels. With little white knuckles you gripped the handlebars tightly, fear, excitement, and strong—mindness firmly on your mind.

The front wheel began to shake, then your mind shrieked "I can't" and the wheel shook even more. "I'm gonna fall" and you did!

After a few more attempts (and a few bruises and maybe skinned knees) you just knew you could go in a straight line. How did you "suddenly" ride straight ahead? *You relaxed and let go of doubt!*

When you're six, your mind is not concerned with how. It doesn't think of aerodynamics or continual uniform motion or probabilities. Logic doesn't get in the way. The 6-year-old mind allows. It just allows.

Might this simplicity and innocent demeanor, uncorrupted by the world, be the reason Jesus enjoyed being around children? My guess is it is. Their minds were uncluttered with deducting if heaven was for real or the conceivability of Jesus' words. They just allowed. Their innocence and trusting allowed them to accept the promise of joy and happiness without suspicion.

Another way of releasing importance: *Have a back-up plan. Insurance.*

As we've seen, when we want something so much, we put so much focus on the intention that it becomes an obsession. As you know by now, when we long for something we allow the fear of not receiving it to occupy our mind. It happens. Think of the last time you were so determined to have/do/ obtain something—"I need to get this or else!" Sound familiar? Here's how to handle that: *Have an alternative!*

When you have options your fear of not obtaining at least a portion of what you wish decreases dramatically and just the reduction of importance can be enough to accelerate belief which then can allow you to achieve.

When you take action toward getting your goal you reduce your anxiousness over it. The saying "just do something!" has meaning. But action without forethought is careless, however if thinking on your feet is your only option then do that. This is another instance where having a firm connection to the Holy Spirit is consequential. No matter how long you've anguished over achieving your goal, activity of some sort will negate the feeling of anxiety.

Despite your best efforts to avoid the feelings of fear or defeat, your 'logical thinking' mind will not allow you to eliminate those feelings completely. Consequently, the remedy for this reasoning is quite simple. *Allow the possibility of defeat!*

I know that until now most if not all of the motivational books you've read instruct you to think victory only. But realistically where has that gotten you?

Accepting possible defeat however does not mean abandoning your goal. What you do in this case is act from another angle.

Let's take an example. It's springtime and after months of being cooped up and stale air, we throw open the blinds, open wide the windows and breath in the fresh smells of the outdoors. Invariably however unwanted guests arrive. You know, the one's with the wings. Although the wasp comes in, he doesn't want to overstay his welcome. For hours he relentlessly pounds on the window trying to get back outside. If he would instead approach his goal from another angle, he would have found the open window space he originally came in through. Accepting the possibility of defeat doesn't have to mean giving up. It means seeking guidance to find a better solution.

Now we have arrived at that place in the road where so many of us get tangled up and confused: "If God wanted me to have it, I would have it."

The topic of God's impact on our lives has been written about for over 5,000 years. Throughout the ages and across the centuries religious scholars and laymen have attempted to interpret how we best can live a life—both devout and secular—in accordance with God's will. You're familiar with the phrase "You are what you think." by now and scripture is in accordance with that. If you feel like a failure, you are. If you feel unworthy, you are that too. The good news however is that if you feel that you can, you will! Let's look at what the Bible says: "He who doubts" wrote James "is like a wave of the sea driven and tossed by the wind. For let not that man suppose that he will receive anything from the Lord." (James 1:6-7) Reading those words leaves no room for mis-interpretation of what God put on James' heart. Notice how the word "anything" is used? It means "any thing whatever". This pronoun does not mean "some things" or "certain things". James' point was that when a person doubts not much is to be expected.

Jesus told the apostles to go to "The lost sheep of the house of Israel" to heal and comfort them and that "If the household is worthy, let your peace come upon it. But if it is not worthy, let your peace return to you." (Matthew 10:6-13) As in those days, we live among those who will always find fault when good things happen. This is another reason that a person should keep their personal business to themselves.

There are people who believe that they are helpless to circumstances. Today 'luck' has shined on them—they've gotten good news about something they've been waiting for. The medical report came back ex-cellent. The loan went through. They found a $10 bill on the sidewalk.

Then there are those who feebly believe that nothing is up to them. That "God willed it." They drift along the sea of life and smile when something positive happens and complain whenever a negative event is experienced. Taken to the extreme this attitude would have you believe that they should not be responsible to, or for, anything that happens in their life. Why wake up to go to work? Why study for an exam? Why do anything at all? It's obvious that this mindset would be ridiculous, yet there are those who expect (and demand) that very thing! Again, a misinterpretation of scripture may be the cause.

In Matthew, Jesus, in speaking to the multitudes, talks about not being concerned about managing your life, using the birds and flowers as example of God's nurture to them. But have you ever noticed a robin building a nest or pulling a worm from the ground? The lily converts water into carbohydrates along with carbon dioxide in order to produce it's nutrients. In fact, they both—the plant and the bird—go about their respective assignments of toil in order to experience life. Consequently, God provides and sustains them through His perfect will because they are doing their part.

We all know people who really do enjoy drama in their life. In their distorted view they are convinced that "life has beaten me down" and this is now the most comfortable space for them. Like my old buddy Paulie "Life is so miserable and it just keeps getting worse." he, and those like him can be right at least once in a while. These people sense a familiarity in their daily torment and have a distorted feeling of pleasure in realizing that the outlook they've always had is correct. When by chance they run into a patch of fortunate events, it doesn't last. People with this mindset look for signs that will confirm that happiness and enjoyment never last. World events and disasters of many kinds are a TV remote click away along with any number of dark thoughts and issues. The most dastardly result of all of this however is the vortex these people pull those closest to them down into. We may try to protect ourselves from such energy-drainers through avoidance and dismissal, but the single best way is making sure your own spiritual house is in such order that the contamination is limited.

The good news though (and there is always good news in most things) is that everyone has the capabilities of affecting the course of their own life!

Reality is in our moment-to-moment life, and every now and then we upset that moment by allowing an outside event to disturb our peace. It happens. Fortunately there is a way out of this labyrinth and it is really simplicity itself: *Whatever an event, negative or disappointing, disheartening or discouraging, depressing or unfavorable, whatever "it" happens to be—transform your attitude toward how you view it!* When you change the way you view an outcome, not only do you feel better, but despite walking the same path the negativist does, your view puts you on another path where a positive result occurs!

Please understand that I'm not suggesting you go through life with your head in the clouds, but I am suggesting that you weigh your response to the things that previously would have immediately upset you. The promotion you expected went to someone else—but now you're able to attend your child's baseball games. The house you were about to purchase was sold before you put in your offer but the "dream house" you really wanted is still out there waiting for you. She broke your heart, but you know God has the perfect one about to enter your life.

This is not about sour grapes but about transferring a stressed-out life to one of peace. As a bonus, your mind will have fun with the game.

I realize that this all is a bit unorthodox but what is better - wallowing in pity and anger or pleasure and the positive outlook? Besides in most cases you'll find that most misfortunes actually are blessings and I'm sure you've noticed that at times already.

Always keep in mind that God uses failures and disappointments to our eventual advantage if we keep a level head. David wrote "Why are you cast down, O my soul? And why are you disquieted within me? Hope in God, for I shall yet praise Him for the help of His countenance." (Psalms 43:5)

Most of us have a planned scenario as to how things should proceed toward achieving our goal. As soon as we experience any deviation in our scenario, we tend to view it as a negative. Our minds then push and pull, certain that since we are the expert as to what should happen, success is slipping away. Our tendency is to grab things by the throat (Desperation) before things slip out of control (Worry) and we lose our objective (Fear). As you can see, we set ourselves up and although we have prayed for His guidance, help and blessing we push God away, convinced our way is the only way. The mistake many of us make is to put God into a box telling Him how it should be done. Be assured - God has ways you never thought of. Notice how I have repeated this theme over and over? This is another proposition that just cannot be overstated.

So how do you overcome the tendency to not let go of your "well designed plan"?
On the spiritual level give God permission to help you. On the physical pragmatic level: Tell your mind he's fully aware of everything he just needs to view ANY development as positive! This works virtually every time.

No doubt this will take a radical change in your thinking. You'll need to prepare yourself and by declaring victory the very first moment you awaken helps to frame your mind to do. "Lord, thank you for this day. I always know you guide me and protect me. Help me to open my mind to your favor and thank you for the blessings in my life." Start your day in prayer, praise and thanksgiving and you won't help but feel empowerment in your life. Throughout your day think on God's name. Doing so you consciously maintain His presence within you. Things in your life will begin to create an auspicious change before you realize them. What you once viewed as set-backs will now become set-ups to achieve any goal.

Keep in mind that although your natural desire is to be in control, your life crosses the lives of other people who likewise are striving to be in control of theirs. Like you, they want their goals to be met, problems to be solved and their place in the sun. The good news is that now you know that by identifying your goal, working with integrity to achieve it and by allowing God to handle the details you are peacefully allowing events to work perfectly toward attaining what you wish. There is another step in this principle and that is "seeing" it. You know this as visualization, and we will visit that in a bit.

20

Just Imagine....

Your life experiences by now have validated the fact that in order to achieve and obtain most anything in life you must make an effort to do so.

You've heard the statement "work smarter not harder" at one point or another and what we're talking about here is something like that.

Certainly, you can revisit the thought "if God means for me to have it, I will." But taken literally you would starve to death! When Spinoza wrote "God helps those who help themselves" he was onto something. No one will be knocking on your door every day to feed you three meals. Your employer expects output of some sort by you to justify your salary. Expecting everyone to cater to your needs is decidedly farfetched. "There is a time to plant and a time to harvest" and each of these involves work. (Ecclesiastes 3:2 NLT)

Earlier I mentioned that many well-meaning Christians may feel that incorporating such activities as meditation, a feeling of expectancy, maintaining a positive attitude and utilizing mental suggestion is blasphemous and contradictory to Christian teachings. When Norman Vincent Peale wrote "The Power of Positive Thinking" he was ridiculed and rebuked by many for his "heretical" statements. Dr. Peale believed in a deep union with the Trinity whereby that very connection would bring about astounding results in our physical and emotional life. Peale believed in an intimate relationship with Jesus where that emotional bond with Him would naturally enable us to bring forth enthusiasm toward living. Having a mystical and emotional contact with Christ, Dr. Peale opined, meant that he actually lived personally in our hearts. Over 70 years have passed since the "Power of Positive Thinking" first appeared on bookshelves and the years since have produced studies and research that has now confirmed the soundness of Dr. Peale's composition.

Our minds contain powerful and dynamic mental capabilities. Within the mind are the senses, the will, and the consciousness. It is capable of a tremendous creative force. The real question here is—are you ready to have?

"According to your faith let it be to you" (Matthew 9:28). These words of Jesus are not empty but in fact charged with power. Our minds are inherently disposed to what is good. What is trustworthy. When Jesus preached in villages and in the countryside, those that had complete confidence and trust in His message were the healed, the renewed, the inspired. That confidence and trust in His assertions are as powerful and as alive today as they were 2,000 years ago. "If you abide in Me, and My words abide in you, you will ask what you desire, and it shall be done for you." (John 15:7) Notice once again that Jesus doesn't say "it might be done" or "there's a good chance it could be done". With the firmness that comes with conviction He says "It SHALL be done"! Doubt is common in human beings and without a determination on our part to move from the ordinary to the extraordinary we would go through life questioning and vacillating on most matters of consequence. "I need proof" becomes not only a mantra but an obstacle. We know a thought is real, but we can't see it or touch it. We know a soul is real, but we can't observe or touch that either.

Sometimes we get in our own way with being overly objective which in turn can cause barriers to form. Over time we become so settled in our objections that they become permanent. We become emotionally involved when something of importance appears and having made a determination that only tangible activity of some sort is the only course of action, we close our minds to any other way. Being overly emotional—putting in massive importance on outcomes—only delays or eliminates achieving your goal.

As you've also discovered, when we put too much importance on outcomes our thinking becomes a barrier—"What if I don't?" "What if it doesn't?" We end up suspending progress, if not outright eliminate, any progress. The really cruel result is when we don't want something to happen it happens!

What is false faith? We recognize that true faith is knowing—"I plant this seed of corn and soon a stalk will appear." False faith is present when you have to force yourself to accept belief. Forcing yourself to get excited. Forcing yourself to think what you're attempting is proper or virtuous. It's attempting to persuade yourself that something's true. Well then, what do you do? *Give up mind control.*

When you feel the need to force, direct or regulate you will, if you stay carefully attentive, notice the slightest degree of discomfort in your soul. *Trying to convince yourself is a sign that your soul is being guided by the Holy Spirit to avoid moving forward.*

When you "allow" you are relying on the Creator of the Universe to find a right way. When you try to force something, especially when you are internally uncomfortable, you are circumventing God's guidance over your life. Be assured that proceeding under such feelings, nothing good will come out of it. It may become visible quickly or it may be delayed but when we ignore His guidance, we ultimately atone for the failure to do so.

Dare to dream big dreams. Ask bold prayers knowing that God will "give good things to those who ask Him"! (Matthew 7:11) Erase the Hollywood theatrics from your mind—where the character pleads and begs. That image has been disabling due to a person walking away thinking that's how you get God's attention. Knock off the pauper mentality. Get rid of the feeling of lack. James continued to revisit doubt and disbelief, in his writings -"You ask and do not receive, because you ask amiss." the dictionary defines amiss: "to ask the wrong way." (James 4:3)

"Knowing" removes doubt. When you know something is true—"there are 24 hours in a day" you don't question or contemplate. Confidence is built through knowing.

You can now understand that your dreams and goals can be achieved with belief, with knowing the thing will be accomplished. God works where there is faith. God says "yes" but you also must say "yes". There will always be instances where you'll feel hopeless. Lost. Unsure. This is the time where you acknowledge your human limitation and cast your concerns on God, humbling yourself under Him so that He promotes you in His time. (Psalms 55:22)

If we lived in a fairytale world we would eliminate doubt, banishing it to the garbage dump never to return. But, we live in a world of what is, and doubt is hard-wired in our make-up.

You'll recall our discussion earlier on our hereditary markers left over from our distant past? Our Reflexive system is that part of the brain that is responsible for our emotions and feelings. It will push our analytical, logical thinking brain (the Reflective system) aside. Once we allow the feeling of doubt, which the brain translates to a type of fear, we greatly magnify that risk or fear. You're familiar with the term "when in doubt do nothing"? Actually, by following that advice we are able to "kick the can down the road" so to speak and hopefully deal with the decision or problem in a more "rational" way later.

Out of habit you'll find yourself doubting. You will start to "reason things out" with the scenario you formed as to how it should be done, then almost mechanically find fault with achieving the objective. But now you know how to catch yourself—"I know that with God ALL THINGS are possible." "If God is for me, who can be against me?" Prayer and meditation (where you go into silence) will help you greatly here.

There is an organized method to achieving your goals and it is not thinking about how to achieve it. It is taking your focus off the mechanics (where you rigidly hold to them) and acting. This does not mean to proceed without a plan but to be mentally flexible enough to allow for God's perfect guidance. Listen to your inner voice. The more often you do, the more you will come to depend on it. You will also notice how clearer; how sharper your senses will become over time. Have patience —it will happen.

"The thought is ancestor to the deed" as the saying goes. Now, through prayer, contemplation, and expectation you become a channel of Divine energy to realize your goal. Quoting Dr. Peale again: "Picturize, Prayerize, Actualize."

When we go about desiring a thing we immediately think of the likelihood of achieving it. "I'll never get that!" are four of the most disempowering words in the various human languages.

Now, let's pause for a moment and revisit the thought we spoke of a bit ago. Maybe you're of the conviction that you really don't need to do anything and things "will just work out". And you know what? You are absolutely right! Everything will 'work out'. The dilemma appears that when 'whatever way it works out' may not be the way you planned. Or wanted!

You see many people are like a little rowboat in the middle of the river. They allow the wind and the current to take them wherever it does. Tossed about by occasional waves, caught in sporadic whirlpools and eddies, and random patches of tranquil water, they move upward with the hope that God will take care of them. And really there is nothing that they should do differently if that's what they choose because *they've chosen* to live in this way.

How do we find our cozy corner of the world where the breezes are gentle, the fragrances sweet and living is easy? *Allow yourself to experience the occurrences.* To overcome doubt, worry, fear of never attaining, and anxiety *you need to simply enjoy.*

Enjoying means to take pleasure or satisfaction in something. Taking pleasure in something is a feeling that is either in the physical sense or through the ability to imagine. For our purposes we're going to traverse the mind's eye and how we are able to conceive, picture, dramatize, and create with it.

How many times have you been told "Stop daydreaming?" or "If she thinks she can do that she's daydreaming". Daydreaming has gotten a bad rap. It really is how many, if not most ideas originated. Vincent Van Gogh once said "I dream my painting and then I paint my dreams." Mark Twain observed "You can't depend on your eyes when your imagination is out of focus." And Michelangelo noted "I saw the angel in the marble and carved until I set him free."

There is something about the human condition that is activated when the mind is put before the reality. When we imagine we're in control of a situation for instance, we have the capability of reducing the neural process and activity in the part of our brain that processes pain, feelings, anxiousness and heartbreak.

When we use our imagination, we provide new stimuli which engages the Dopamine System. Although less than one thousandth of one percent of the 100 billion neurons in our brain produces the chemical Dopamine, that is enough to exert an enormous amount of influence and power over ourselves. When Dopamine neurons are activated, their signals rush over and through the parts of our brain that begins as motivation, which goes through the decision process and results into action. All of this happens in as little as as a twentieth of a second as the electro chemicals pulsate from the base of the brain to those parts of the brain that makes decisions. Since Dopamine is the "feel good" chemical, the knowledge that taking action motivates us to in fact take action, we do because it feels good to do so! Without the rush received from Dopamine early man would probably never have walked boldly and courageously out of the cave but would likely have starved to death. In short, we are genetically able to use our imagination to achieve our goals.

When we use our imagination, we in fact, are visualizing. Visualizing effectively is one of the most useful ways that we, ourselves, can bring our intentions to pass. To actualize our goal, eliminating doubt, worry or fear, we must view it from the end result. Although it's important to have a plan in mind we leave the "how" to God. Don't put any focus onto problems, confusion, trouble, or delay. When those weeds begin to sprout up turn it around by saying "Thank you Father for your perfect solution." God will line up the right people and put you in the right places at the right time. Isaiah wrote that God "Acts for the one who waits for Him." (Isaiah 64:4)You've already experienced (probably too many times) that when you get what you want out of the will of God you pay the expense. Give Him time. He knows how to get to the right places at the right time.

You know how to visualize by now but let's walk through a simple, but effective example in case you've not done so far a while: Close your eyes and relax for a minute or two. Keeping your eyes closed, mentally stand in the middle of your kitchen. Look around the room. Glance at the stove, scrutinize the burner. Then the oven door. Next, look at the cupboards. Notice the color? The knobs? See the refrigerator? The handle?

Turn your inner gaze to the countertops and what sits on them. See the table and chairs? Notice the floor and the light fixtures? As you inwardly take in the kitchen, you'll be able to mentally walk through the entire house surveying everything in it. This is visualizing and though you've done so many times we now want to affect it scientifically. This is specific work, but it is also time well spent.

From a biblical perspective, visualizing is a very powerful stimulus.

"... that the terror of you has fallen on us, and that all the inhabitants of the land are fainthearted because of you... and as soon as we heard these things, our hearts melted"

(Joshua 2:9-11). When Rahab relayed this information to the two spies of Joshua, she was confirming the effect that visualization was having on the people of Jericho. She also affirmed what we know to be true: Worst-case scenarios, when we dwell on them, usually come about. Like the inhabitants of Jericho, when the emotions of fear, worry and doubt are present we actually "feel" them. Before the event is realized we've already "picturized" the outcome. As we've seen, fear is part of our Limbic System where the "fight/flight" response resides. Trying to overcome what is genetically connected to our brain is near impossible. What is possible however is maintaining our Divine connection where we know that God can impart the energy and wisdom to think-and-act-level-headed. To calm us and give us peace and move forward thoughtfully.

To successfully visualize you need to put yourself in the picture. You cannot "view" yourself doing something, you need to "live" yourself doing something.

If your objective is to buy that new car in the showroom you need to see yourself behind the wheel, not looking at yourself sitting there but the view from "eyeball" level. You see the hood in front of you, the dashboard, the speedometer, the GPS, radio, and the glove compartment. You breath in the "new car smell" as you mentally drive on a sunny day. You actually squint because of the brightness of the sun. Then suddenly as you're "driving" along a sudden downpour appears. The raindrops are heavy at first and as the wipers clear the windshield the rain begins to stop and once again the sun appears.

You are the producer, the director, and the actor in this play and as the scriptwriter you are free to compose your own screenplay! Have fun with it. Enjoy the adventure. Smile. Laugh. Feel joyful because the more feeling you put into your motion picture the more you're preparing your "self" for the experience.

Don't allow negative thoughts to intrude in your play. Your job is not the "how". Your job is to enjoy the feeling. As you picturize in your mind, pray on the picture. Actualize it into your life. As you visualize what it is you want, pray frequently and affirmatively to discern God's will about your intention. Once you've determined that what you're pursuing "feels right," take practical steps to bring the goal to pass. Allow the Holy Spirit to lead you to what those practical steps are. Force nothing. Take your time. Run the drama over as if it were a memory. Already done.

The more you play the scene the more comfortable you'll feel, and things become "familiar". Worry will begin to disappear as will the feeling of being anxious. You will have dropped importance and you will have allowed yourself "to have". You'll be amazed as to the results as well as the ease and peace of mind where you allow the Lord to guide your steps.

As you now begin to question all of this (after all 'logic' eventually will burst through the door). I remind you again—*the proof is there in view of the reality that what you don't want continues to show up in your life!* This, until now, was when worst expectations occupied your conscious mind which in turn become a feeling of fear of not achieving and concentrating on that apprehension.

Loosen the death grip of importance with all its anxiety associated with not getting and simply focus on what you do want.

Don't panic and certainly don't give up because as you begin this new journey your rational, logical, left-brain will throw up roadblocks. After all, 'common sense' says you can't, you won't and you never will. Keep your eyes on the goal and remember to bring your compass— the Bible.

It is important to keep your own counsel. There is no need to tell people your hopes, dreams or your new way of conduct. "Prayer doesn't work" "You flipped" "You're crazy" or "I know a guy that tried that stuff and it never happened." These are just some of the negative, disempowering comments you'll hear. When you let people in on your plans you have to explain it and you have to defend it. Know when to keep quiet. Your intercessor is Christ. Put him on speed dial. Unfortunately, many of us have relied on acquaintances, associates, family and friends for encouragement and reassurance. Understand the simple but hurtful truth that not everyone we know wishes us happiness and success.

Before long you'll begin to notice "coincidences" such as opportunities presenting themselves "out of the blue", people eager to help, strangers being pleasant and initiatives launching with ease. You will think that luck has suddenly appeared in your life, but what most people call luck is in reality the favor of God. But be forewarned—expect the Deceiver to make a guest appearance. Just keep your wits about you but keep God closer. I just can't stress enough how important, how critical it is to put God in first place in your life. Not only will you sense His will for you, but you will be empowered to overcome difficulties and set-backs, knowing that difficulties are learning experiences and set-backs are really set-ups as I've said.

Remember to check your attitude at all times and when an event or thing looks negative accept the scenario as positive. In prayer give thanks for the experience and affirm your trust in God.

At the basis of all your dealings keep declaring "If God is for me, who can be against me?"

21

Ichi-Go, Ichi-E

In our lives we make lots of mistakes. Those mistakes can either destroy you or they can develop you.

Seneca wrote "Don't stumble over something behind you." Mistakes and 'failures' are part of the curriculum in the class of life. Embrace those lessons and be thankful for them because the knowledge gained from them are priceless. They are the currency you'll pay with for success. Each of the frustrations you've experienced until now - and will face in the future - will be used by God to promote you to greatness.

All human beings have undergone disappointments and reversals. It's what you take away from them that makes the experience a blessing or a blunder.

Avoid complaining about your past mistakes. Don't whine or reproach yourself because as you know, what you think about, you become. To visualize a future full of joy while keeping one foot on past mistakes and failures will do nothing more than guarantee more reversals, more sorrows, more anguish.

Now you know how to realize your dreams and how to avoid the barriers preventing you from reaching them. God's divine presence not only resides in unity with all of nature, but He also is made manifest in our spirit. We realize that presence through our constant dialogue with him.

When you visualize, do so with a lite touch. By that I mean don't take it too seriously otherwise you'll ramp up importance which will increase anxiety. Keep it simple and serene. Allow yourself time for the images to not only take root but to develop. The more you play your "movie" the more comfortable and natural it will feel. As I said a minute ago—be a part of the panorama. Feel the objective or intention. Allow yourself a few minutes to play your movie—without interruptions. "Imagination is everything" said Einstein "It is the preview of life's coming attractions."

Don't analyze. Don't rationalize or reason how it will come about. That is God's domain.

Continue being your best and doing your part. If your inner peace has encouraged you to move forward with your dream let go and let God. Don't begin to worry if when you begin visualizing you experience a degree of confusion or difficulty. Even impatience. Just remember— easy does it. All of this will become easier with practice. Again, I remind you, have fun and don't attach massive importance to the dramatization. Do not expect immediate results. Expect a delay. Remember you are abiding in God's time, ensuring His blessings over your intention. It's the devil's lie that if you don't get it now you'll miss out.

We've spoken about keeping your personal business to yourself, about keeping calm, keeping still and that silence is golden. But what exactly can silence achieve?

First and foremost being silent brings inner solitude. You also are not giving away your ideas, plans or decisions. You are reserving judgment and viewpoints and you are keeping your opinions to yourself. When people know that you are not given to being boisterous, they hold a special respect for you. Confucius observed that "an empty barrel makes the most noise." Unfortunately, we've all encountered empty barrels along our path.

You will recall that earlier in these pages I spoke of Asian or "Eastern" thought and practice. Most people's impression of Asian philosophies is one of deep religious immersion in the various beliefs found across the East. Each of us regardless of our religious beliefs have something to offer - and learn - from each other. If we, each 6 billion of us, strip away our prejudices and arrogance we find inspirational behaviors and proclivities from one another. So it is with meditation.

Meditation is frequently spoken about in the Bible; Joshua was told by God that by meditating he would prosper and realize success. (Joshua 1:8) David wanted only to meditate on that which God found acceptable. (Psalms 19:14) As he sat in prison, Paul encouraged the church in Philippi to meditate on that which is good, true, pure and beautiful. (Philippians 4:8)

Meditation is not only an opportunity to relieve stress but to become closer to our Creator. With this objective in mind allow me to introduce a form of meditation, which has proven to be uncomplicated and easily done. First taught by Siddhartha Gautama twenty-five centuries ago, what is known as Vipassana meditation has become a leading method of entering into silence. For centuries Vipassana - which means "insight" in the Pali language of India - was practiced due to its simplicity. For unknown reasons this form of meditation lay dormant for a period of time before being reintroduced within the past 30 years. Since then, there has been a resurgence in what was the fundamental nature of Siddhartha's teaching. Never advocating or espousing religion or philosophy, nor a system of belief, he instead concentrated on helping others to liberate themselves from misery. "Now as before" he said "I teach about suffering and the eradication of suffering." Soon he became known as "The Enlightened One"—Buddha.

Before proceeding it's important to consider a few thoughts.

First, although articles frequently appear in contemporary magazines regarding mindfulness and meditation, they usually are intended to be light reading: "take a deep cleansing breath. Allow stress to leave your body. Think about a pleasant spring day..." What you're about to read is loaded with protein-filled red meat. I would be doing you a serious injustice if it didn't.

Second, this in no way is blasphemy. Vipassana meditation *does not* involve chants, incense, idol worship, religious belief, or theological preparation.

Third, this section is devoted to calming our active minds, going inward where, Jesus said, we could dwell in the secret place with God. (Matthew 6:6) This place allows us to think about our lives, qualities, and character and Fourth, to inwardly discern what "mental detritus" accumulated over the years and how to go about uprooting and disregarding them.

If you've lived a full life, you've stockpiled numerous experiences. Our lives intersect with other lives and each of those lives, just like ours, have their own agendas, their own dreams and goals, and their own desires. In the world today it seems outdated to some to live by a moral compass. As a practicing Christian you already know this.

Sadly, the world has become a place where competition, individualism, impermanence, and anger are considered a sign of strength. Even pride. This is where Christians differ with the accepted normal. Kindness, gentleness, and love are where our focus is but above all what we seek is a relationship with God. A natural relationship that is both consuming and inspiring, feeling His love in a real and purposeful way. Ironically that type of Christian is being challenged by the social impugning that has now become common in society. As a society we can be mobile not only in our work and where to live but in our acceptance of what standards we want to adhere to. The choice is ours. What choice will you make? "Do not be conformed to this world, but be transformed by the renewing of your mind, that you may prove what is that good and acceptable and perfect will of God" (Romans 12:2).

By the sixth century the once great and powerful Roman Empire was eroding and splitting apart. As all great empires seem to have in common when their disintegration comes about, it develops from the decay that originates from within. The power of Rome which at one point stretched east to the Caspian Sea in Russia, across Europe and North Africa and to the west as far as Britain, now was broken into two separate realms. It was at this time that a Christian Monk, Benedict of Nursia founded a monastery devoted to preserving the tenants of Christianity amid a distressed and disintegrating world.

Benedict instinctively knew that the time had come to turn inward and inward would be the only means by which the one constant, the one foundation pillar that Christianity was built on could be found: Love.

Loving a virtuous life is neither easy nor in fashion, but we as Christians need this quality as part of our composition—now more than ever.

We cannot stop technology, nor should we want to. As fire allows a man to cook his food, it also can kill him if used improperly. Technology, especially social media holds the same capabilities—Cyber-bullying unfortunately, but discoveries and discussions to eradicate disease as well.

Turning inward where we cannot only rediscover who we really are but allow each of us to become transmitters of Divine tranquility, sending forth God's love to those we come in contact with.

It is said that prayer is where we ask of God, but meditation is where we hear Him. Turning inward we use this ancient technique as a kind of modern monasticism.

Contrary to what you may have been led to believe meditation is not the doorway to material objects, but a path of enlightenment. It is the serenity and peace of mind you'll acquire from going inward, the clarity of thought and the connection to God that will allow you to receive.

There are publications that give an in-depth explanation of Vipassana meditation, and I encourage you to investigate them. For our purposes we'll demystify the practice of this technique. If you've never sat in meditation previously that's great! You don't have any bad habits to overcome.

Where do you imagine your mind to be? The brain? No surgeon has found the mind there. Actually, the mind is everywhere.

The mind feels. Every atom of your body is mind. Your whole body is mind!

When your mind reacts to something it is either liking or disliking. Attraction or repulsive. This causes a kind of chain reaction of cause and effect. Whenever a "problem" arises it causes some type of misery reaction, but if you remain calm, to not react, there is no longer a feeling of misery. Accept reality as it is, but learning to free yourself from anger can happen if you view the anger objectively.

We all have met people who embrace their suffering. They allow it to control them and when they come into contact with someone who does not react to their despair, they get mad!

Observe yourself for the next few days, especially when a difficult situation comes up. Keep your mind balanced. By that I mean choose how to react. You will be taking action if you do because your action is mindful—and positive. Learn to act, but act with a balanced mind. By changing your habit of reaction to action—pro-action really—you will sense a freedom that perhaps you've never felt before.

In order to overcome problems, we first must realize that problems originate in the mind. When we are upset, it's the conscious mind that reacts. When we hurt our physical body in some way, hit your elbow on a steel table let's say, it's our conscious mind that processes the pain. In meditation we use a specific exercise to focus and purify our mind. Our goal in meditation has two very specific objectives—to develop tranquility and to develop insight. Taking control of where your mind goes is the foundation of becoming master of your mind.

You are about to discover how uncontrolled your mind is and has been for a long while. With time and patience, along with a definite of purpose (which I promise you'll need) you will not only manage your thoughts but uncover your Divine connection, transposing the verse "the peace of God, which surpasses all understanding" into a physical reality. (Philippians 4:4-7).

The practice of Vipassana meditation entails the most suitable and appropriate technique for discovering your inner self, your inner reality. This form of meditation engages the breath only. Buddha practiced this technique calling it "ĀNĀPĀNASATI," which translated means "awareness of respiration".

You'll recall earlier our discussion on the commonality we share with all living beings—that of breath. The early Hebrews believed that God's name was too sacred to pronounce, that the only acceptable manner to utter His name is by the sound of inhalation and exhalation of the breath. And it is by this method that we go inward.

For the most effective practice of meditation, it is best to sit in an up-right but comfortable posture with eyes closed. Dedicated practitioners of meditation sit on the floor, legs folded and without back support. This position will probably be uncomfortable at first so if you decide to begin to practice in this position (and have not sat cross-legged on the floor for a while) be aware that there may be some initial discomfort. As an alternative you can sit on a chair, feet flat on the floor hands touching sitting straight.

Now that you've ascertained the seating you found best, lets center on the technique: Think about your nostrils. Focus all of your intention on your respiration. On the air flowing in. Flowing out. Is it coming predominantly from your right nostril? Your left? Both equally? Ponder this. Concentrate on your breath. Feel it. Embrace the silence, eyes closed and do nothing but focus on your breathing.

That's all. These few minutes are devoted to you and God. When your mind wanders, you bring it back to your nostrils. You are simply retraining your attention. You will discover the reason for so much anxiety in your life—controlling your mind is not a habit you've developed. Yet. Like a wild monkey grasping each vine, jumping from one tree to the next, your mind jumps from one thought to another. The letter you want to send, the email you need to return, the dishes in the sink, the appointment you need to make, the concert you went to when you were 19! On and on he jumps around until you've forgotten to remain aware of your breath. Soon you discover who is really in control!

Relax and accept that this is nothing more than an ingrained habit. This is what you've done, without thinking, your whole life. Don't make too much of this. Be patient with yourself and bring your attention back to your breathing.

Along with mind chatter, you may find yourself getting drowsy. This is especially true if you lie down to meditate (which you should avoid if possible). You may find yourself making excuses not to meditate —your mind does not like constraints, and you are now beginning to retrain your attention. This is not about thinking 'no thoughts' or that your mind should be totally quiet. It is about noticing when your mind wanders and bringing it back to your nostrils.

Always start out with prayer. This is your alone time with God. Begin with a goal of sitting in silence for 5 minutes. Gradually bring your meditation duration to 20 minutes. You may want to consider practicing this awareness once in the morning and once in the evening eventually.

"When wisdom enters your heart, and knowledge is pleasant to your soul, discretion will preserve you; understanding will keep you (Proverbs 2:10-11).

When you rise above the usual and the mediocre you become enlightened by that truth.

Paying attention to your true self brings many advantages with it. Relieving stress is one burden that meditation can eliminate if done on a regular and consistent schedule. Stress is really a complex mix of physical, behavioral, and emotional responses. Your body can prematurely age caused by "aging defects" in your cells.

You've heard that focusing on the moment encourages you to notice things that you normally ignore. The author and Buddhist Monk Thich Nhat Hanh once observed that, "Life is available only in the present moment." Mindfulness is paying attention to the present and getting out of the way of the past and the future.

Being mindful means not only noticing your breath but the sensations of your body, the activities going on around you—the wind through the trees, a child singing, a fan humming, a baby laughing.

Focusing on the moment allows you to be grateful for what you have and to appreciate them. When you're mindful of your thoughts you notice the moments you become discouraged, disheartened, or depressed. When you're aware of your thoughts you don't get lost in them. The practice of mindfulness has been found to have an almost immediate calming effect. Calm breathing causes the parasympathetic nervous system to slow heart rate and reduce blood pressure—the opposite effect of the fight/flight response.

The Japanese have a saying "Ichi-Go, Ichi-E"—"Just this one moment, once in a lifetime." The awareness of the moment you're in now allows you to realize that you'll never be able to recreate this moment. How would you go about doing your work with that type of perception? How would you treat the people you meet? What would your life be like if you put your whole heart and mind into *everything* you experienced?

The next time you eat a piece of fruit, an apple let's say, relish the activity. Chew every bite fully and concentrate on nothing else except the reality of eating the apple for the few minutes it takes. Do this with everything you eat for just one day, putting all your focus on the act. You *will* find a new sense of presence and satisfaction.

As we discussed earlier, nearly all Eastern religions have strong philosophical foundations and it is from this basis, with no regard to religion that a Christian can practice an art or a concept without submitting to or accepting a religious doctrine. As human beings we share this earth with one another, regardless of dogma, creed, or beliefs. You don't need to be Chinese to enjoy a cup of tea even though it was discovered in China 2,700 years ago. We do not need to convert to Judaism to receive a Polio Vaccine even though a Jewish doctor, Jonas Salk discovered the treatment in 1953.

Meditation and mindfulness, research has shown, activates neurons in the left Prefrontal Cortex of the brain that helps you recover from upsetting events, work toward and achieve positive goals under perplexing, troublesome circumstances and suppress the upsetting negative emotions that commence in the Amygdala. As we achieve a greater level of activity in this left side of the Prefrontal Cortex, we seem to get less upset by scary scenarios. It's been found that Buddhist monks who spend many years practicing meditation have much higher levels of left Prefrontal Cortex activity that lingers long past their time of meditation. The purposeful habit of pushing away negative emotions seems to make room for and create, positive emotions.

The Prefrontal Cortex (also known as Brodmann's Area 10) is located on your forehead just above the eyebrows. Every time you take the time to meditate the neural circuits here are strengthened and gradually this strength becomes lasting. Just like strengthening muscle, the more hours you devote to meditation the greater impact it will have on your future life.

"Why" you may ask "are we talking about meditation in a work about motivation, inspiration and achieving intentions?" Actually, there is not one answer, but an explanation is relevant here.

To achieve anything worthwhile in life a person needs to be disciplined. It's easy to dismiss the significance of effort. It's common for spiritually-based people to think "If God wills it, it will be done". We've addressed this statement already. But let's look to the Bible for an example of the importance of effort.

For 400 years the Israelites toiled in the fields and mud pits of Egypt praying for deliverance from bondage. But it took one man, a prince of Egypt who discovered his destiny in the desert to work God's will to bring His chosen people out of slavery. "But Moses said to God, "Who am I that I should go to Pharaoh, and that I should bring the children of Israel out of Egypt?" So He said "I will certainly be with you." (Exodus 3:11-12)

God uses people *who relinquish their will in favor of His!* God, through the efforts of Moses, brought the Hebrews to the promised land. Moses was not only disciplined in his approach to Pharaoh, but persistent. To attain a goal, determination must also be present. How committed are you to obtain your objective? The steps contained throughout this book—to sit in meditation is but one—takes effort, determination, commitment, discipline, and faith. It also takes a new way of thinking. Embrace it. Honor it. Nurture it. You *will* be amazed at the results.

22 |

Everything Needs to be Coordinated

In the preceding pages you've been made aware of the truth that you are free to choose whatever you want.

You can choose to battle and fight for your place under the sun, but you are also free to choose to release frustration and struggle and just *have*. No matter how you go about your life—you get what you choose. Nothing more. Nothing less. You can choose the option of being a leaf in the stream, having no control or direction over your destination or you can grab hold of the wheel of the mighty windjammer, sails full, compass set and steer toward that which you intend to have.

True freedom from the merry-go-round that life is, with its ups and downs, is to release importance. You achieve that by adjusting your attitude toward the event. What most people call "bad luck" you see as an opportunity to learn. That is freedom. It will take time (and effort I'm afraid) to achieve this mindset. It won't happen that tomorrow morning you'll wake up forever changed, but once you have committed yourself to this idea you will begin to experience independance of dependance on outside events.

Things will come up to disturb your peace (Satan doesn't like letting go of a confused mind) and although it will be tempting to retreat to the way you used to handle things, don't despair and don't give up. In time you will end up in a gentle flow of a peaceful river able to consciously and proactively manage the provocations that come along. Remember and accept that there are other actors in your play, each with their own agendas, each wanting their dreams and goals to be realized regardless of their effect on you. But you have a powerful antidote and that is how you choose to respond and act.

To visualize, according to the dictionary means "to make visible: especially to form a mental image of". We as humans have, through our Creator, been given the gift of imagination and the ability to hold that image. We can play and replay over and over that image, branding almost, those images in our mind.

We visualize our wedding; we visualize a new home. We "see" ourselves on a beach or at the mountains on vacation. We know that worst-case scenarios happen, so that alone confirms the effectiveness of mental imagery. Visualizing something with passion, feeling and intensity will eventually come to pass. Whether we want them to or not. The goal here is to occupy our thoughts with what we do want and eliminate dwelling on what we don't. Let's look at a "worst-case" scenario.

John has been laid off from his job for two months. He's been submitting applications and even had one interview to date, but nothing definite has come about so far. Each week that's gone by John has become more worried that he won't find anything. His 'friends' have verified his fears with comments like "What are you going to do if you don't find a job?" "It's brutal out there. Nobody's hiring." and finally "What if you lose your house?"

As you can see (and maybe have experienced) his homeboys have asked disempowering questions that not only beget negative answers but conjure up nightmare situations.

As John contemplates these and other rhetorical questions he himself has considered, his heart rate increases, his breathing becomes irregular, his Cortisol levels rise and his blood pressure spikes, "What if *I can't* pay my mortgage? We'll lose our home!" Not only is his imagination running wild with terrible outcomes, but he now visualizes them with powerful negative emotions. Psychologically speaking, an abundance of activity is also mentally taking place.

John's Reflexive System is now reacting and responding to his feelings of fear. The portion of his brain, the Amygdala, responds to John's perceived threat without delay. The Amygdala is considered one of the brain's "fear centers" as you've read. It also releases neurotransmitters including Norepinephrine that triggers the adrenal glands to release adrenaline into the bloodstream which, in turn, increases John's blood pressure and heartbeat.

As John visualizes worst-case scenarios, the Hippocampus—the memory bank of the brain—will continually replay the horrific images provoking increases in John's fear and anxiety.

As adrenaline courses through his body and various other stress hormones are being released in John's body, a phenomenon is occurring that seems to "brand" these forebodings into his memory where they become lasting. Each of us visualize on a constant basis and what is certain is that we are "wired" to do exactly that. It is up to us as to where we want to put that gift. What slideshow we want to play.

Let's go back to Paul's definition of faith—"the substance of things hoped for, the evidence of things not seen" (Hebrews 11:1). Over and over the Bible talks about realizing goals and dreams. It is not blasphemous to strive and work and want and visualize these intentions. There is a key however, to your obtaining that which is "hoped for" and for you to realize what it is you want.

Have you watched children play recently? Children have an ability that every adult would be wise to emulate—playing. Children, especially toddlers, left on their own seldom get bored. Of course, mix them with grown-ups and they want to crawl out of their skin with boredom. Children can find something to occupy themselves with and seldom take anything seriously and if they do—when a toy is pulled away for instance—they rarely stay upset for long. Kids know how to have fun. The world holds endless fascination to them, and importance is not a tangible thought.

As we know Jesus loved being around children not only for their innocence but because they know how to laugh. There are no ulterior motives, no agendas. We as adults seem to get in our own way. Dissatisfaction occurs—"this house is too small" "this car is too old" "I never catch a break". Without a conscious effort to block them, jealousy, energy and resentment can silently take root which, if left unchecked, leads to fear and worry. We need to release dependence on things, think as a child for a moment and release the grip of importance. Worry and trepidation will disappear. You'll see.

There are various ways to discover if you've released dependence and importance in a thing. Let's take money as an example. How would you know that you've let go of being under the power of money?

By giving it away. By tithing.

"Whoever has," said Jesus "to him more will be given and he will have abundance; but whoever does not have, even what he has will be taken away" (Matthew 13:12).

This *sounds* like a very depressing statement. It's similar to the phrase "the rich get richer, and the poor get poorer." When someone has a right attitude about their finances and possessions, they need never worry that it will disappear. Right attitude here meaning they don't envy others who have more. They know that this is a blessing from God so they give Him their first-fruits. They do so because they trust Him completely. Never looking down on those less fortunate, they instead share their good fortune, without fanfare, with those less prosperous. What people like this are doing is releasing the chokehold on money, not putting a massive amount of importance on it because *they know* there will always be enough. There is a freedom here—a lack of fear and worry. I know we spoke of this earlier but the importance of this cannot be overstated.

Those who are without usually have fallen into a deep pit of hopeless despair "I'll never get ahead." There is a feeling of anxiousness that clouds the mind of a person like this. They never share with others because their mantra is "I never have enough." Can you really deny that as we think, so we are?

Worse than this attitude, is when this same person enters into a period of good fortune only to say "This won't last!" And it doesn't! It can be no other way. They've chosen their by-line and sooner or later that is exactly what will come to pass.

What you say is just as important as what you think. When you speak you need to invite God into your presence. Words have power as well as meaning. In Proverbs, it says "Death and life are in the power of the tongue." (Proverbs 18:21) Speaking negativity and defeat is more than just complaining. It's calling down misery, failure, and disappointment into your life. "I never get anything right." invites mistakes and misfortune. "Nothing ever goes my way" invites letdowns and discontentment. "I am broke. I'll never get out of this mess" invites insolvency and ruin.

And why would these results not materialize? You've chosen to acquire these afflictions. If you put as much imagination, expectation, knowing and feeling into what you do want, you would not get what you don't want!

Joel said "let the weak say I am strong" (Joel 3:10). This affirmation is as relevant and appropriate today as it was when Joel claimed it 2,600 years ago."Whoever calls on the name of the Lord shall be saved" (Romans 10:13) is a powerful confirmation of the mastery that God has over our problems if we call on Him.

You know that a thought, career, activity, or business has become mainstream when parodies are performed about them. For many years "Saturday Night Live" has been at the leading edge of skewering people and what they do. There was the "motivational speaker" Matt Foley, played by Chris Farley. There was also Stuart Smalley who Al Franken made famous due to Stuart's daily affirmation "I'm good enough, I'm smart enough, and doggone it, people like me." After the laughter stopped everyone seemed to know affirmations had become mainstream!

Affirming something on its own, I'm sorry to say, generally has a very small chance of success. I think you already know that. "I am losing 25 pounds now" may sound determined but you may have a hard time honestly believing it. Not that you could not lose the weight. You could if you believed it without any doubt. "I'm going to start saving money" sounds resolute but putting any actions off until the future is one of the least effective methods for achieving a goal. There is no commitment and there's too many variables that can appear between now and when you're "going to" do something.

For affirmations to be effective, they must be done with feeling and need to coincide with your visualization. Your "movie". Everything needs to be coordinated. This also means that the Holy Spirit has put on your heart the wisdom to proceed with your intention.

Many of the books on the market today discuss the "ways" to achieve your goals. Unfortunately, if these goals do not line up with God's will they likely will not be realized and if they are, you'll regret that they were!

You need to recognize this very important point: Without the guidance that what you are trying to accomplish is divinely attained you may visualize and affirm until doomsday and never fulfill your desire. You may have read some of these publications, did what was recommended and waited for results to show up, in vain. If you questioned why nothing appeared, or thought "I must have done something wrong" and asked yourself "Why not?" now you know.

Another factor, assuming they've prayed for direction and guidance, that most people who use affirmations err upon is that they may have already formulated how their desire should come about. Being (they think) intelligent folks, their EGO's (edging God out) have devised the path to victory, however at the first sign of obstacles, fear of failure comes brilliantly into view knocking any hope of realization into the gutter.

"See the end result, pray up the goal, realize the objective" as Norman Vincent Peale used to say. I know I've mentioned Dr. Peale earlier but his method of obtaining goals was ahead of his time.

Dr. Peale's approach was to imagine a desired goal being a form of mental suggestion that was common to religious science.

What exactly is metaphysical? Most of us, if we're familiar with the word at all, connect Metaphysical as another term affiliated with New Age. Actually according to the dictionary, the word means: "The philosophical study of the ultimate causes and underlying nature of things." It would be wise to keep this definition in mind, knowing that pursuing a goal from this base of understanding of how and why something is certainly attainable. Actually, this search is quite refreshing as it allows a person to look more closely into the rationale of pursuing, or desiring the intention to begin with.

Throughout the preceding pages you not only have been repeatedly counseled on these same themes but have hopefully come to accept that having a constant mental and emotional - as well as a spiritual - proximity to God is essential in order to discern the pursuit of any sort of goal. Affirmations, if honorable and right-minded, can immeasurably promote the success of achieving what you aspire to obtain. "I can do all things through Christ who strengthens me" (Philippians 4:13). Notice Paul wrote *all things*. Not "I can do some things" or "usually I can do this" or " there are some things Jesus is not able to help me with" No, He said ALL THINGS! Contemplate on the power of that sentence! Keep in prayer and dialogue with your heavenly Father - and do so continually. The "Jesus Prayer" that I wrote about earlier is simple, easy to remember and effective. Said with meaning, in other words dwelling on the utterance itself, you are calling Divine strength into yourself. "Lord Jesus, have mercy on me!" Our strength, our inspiration, our resolve, and our attainment can only come from one place and that is from our Creator.

Have an abundance mentality. "My cup runs over" David affirmed. (Psalms 23:5) Call down affluence, call down perfect health, call down peace and serenity into your life. Too many of us have a "slave mentality". We pray to just get by "Please Lord help me get the money to pay the rent this month" Sometimes we ask wrongly—"Why don't I ever get ahead?" Sometimes our affirmations are unsuitable: "I never get ahead." We need to ask boldly, and with confidence.

"Oh, that You would bless me indeed, and enlarge my territory, that Your hand would be with me, and that You would keep me from evil, that I may not cause pain!" (I Chronicles 4:10) This was from a guy whose name was "he makes sorrowful" in Hebrew. Even as he asked for blessings, he couldn't shake the guilt he carried with the name he was given, wanting to avoid hurting anyone. You know him by the name Jabez. Despite going through life with a name synonymous with misery and anguish, Jabez claimed victory with audacity. "So God granted him what he requested." Affirmations are a part of each of our lives. Begin now, if you haven't already, to pay attention to what it is you are affirming. Affirm God's blessings over your life and you will observe the good fortune that descends not only on you, but also over your family.

"For assuredly, I say to you, whoever says to this mountain, "Be removed and be cast into the sea," and does not doubt in his heart, but believes that those things he says will be done, he will have whatever he says. Therefore I say to you, whatever things you ask when you pray, believe that you receive them, and you will have them" (Mark 11:23-24).

Read this statement Jesus spoke again. Then re-read it. Continue to read it because as you do so it will germinate and grow within you.

There is no mention of begging in this teaching Jesus is giving. There are no "maybe's" here. No "hope for the best." Jesus does not say "you might receive them." He says "YOU WILL HAVE THEM" He doesn't say "some things" or "certain things" you ask for, but "whatever things you ask" Can it be any more plain or direct? This is an astounding quote from Jesus Himself.

"For assuredly, I say to you." The definition of assure is: to state confidently to, to make certain the coming or attainment of.

As you contemplate these words of Jesus, it would be wise to remember that He habitually spoke with clarity, depth and meaning. In other words: He just didn't say things to be heard. Consider also that when Jesus spoke, His words were not immediately written down. It is astonishing that they could be recalled years later with amazing accuracy due to the fact that His words were so indelibly stamped in the minds of His followers.

Each of us must, in the final analysis, ask ourselves "Is what I seek (or intend) in line with God's will in my life?" This I believe is why it's critical to be aligned with God in prayer. Not "give me" prayer or begging prayer, but dialogue prayer. We can state what we want "I intend to have...", visualize the end result (leaving the "how" to God as we know by now) and be expectant of that which you mean to have, all the while acknowledging God by stating "Not my will, but Thine be done in me and through me." It is my belief that this is where we fall short in achieving our goals—we put our will in front of God's. Jesus asserted that "whoever does the will of My Father in heaven is my brother and sister." and it is through discernment that we attain what we propose to have.

23

Knowing How To Ask

The 17th Century theologian and Cleric Jeremy Taylor observed the crucial and critical point "Our desires are not to be the measure of our prayers, unless reason and religion be the rule of our desires."

It is said that the greatest danger is not that we believe in prayer too much, but that we believe in prayer too little! Jesus taught that God's spiritual power had no limits set to it. Our problems in not achieving our goals arise from the belief that instead of faith being able to move a mountain our belief is in the faith that the mountain can't be moved at all! James confirmed that "The effective, fervent prayer of a righteous man avails much." (James 5:16) Jesus said, "If you have faith as a mustard seed, you can say to this mulberry tree, "Be pulled up by the roots and be planted in the sea," and it would obey you." (Luke 17:6) In speaking of a mustard seed, Jesus was using an example of one of the smallest seeds in the world. He always had a point, using profound statements, to make them. Like the mustard seed, even the smallest amount of faith—but with absolute trust in God—would allow us to achieve what would seem impossible.

This was not a sorcerer's tale, and Jesus wasn't advising His disciples to become magicians but instead that if one had faith, that God will reward that trust completely.

Have you ever noticed how, when asked about an event in someone's life (usually an event they'd rather not endure) a melancholy and dispirited voice will assert "it is useless"? With a heavy sigh they are resigned to undergo a joyless existence, looking anxiously for a sliver of hope. Yet the opportunity is always available. Rain will fall now and again in our lives and on our plans however we must not keep our concentration on misery and defeat but focus instead on fortunate events. "It is your Father's good pleasure to give you the kingdom" observed Jesus. (Luke 12:32) "Ask, and it will be given to you; seek, and you will find; knock, and it will be opened to you. For everyone who asks receives, and he who seeks finds, and to him who knocks it will be opened. Or what man is there among you who, if his son asks for bread, will give him a stone. Or if he asks for a fish, will he give him a serpent?" (Matthew 7:7-10)

But it is what Jesus says next that should eliminate any thought, any doubt, any anxiousness concerning God giving favor to those who make petitions to Him. "If you then, being evil, know how to give good gifts to your children, how much more will your Father who is in heaven give good things to those who ask Him!" (Matthew 7:11)

When was the last time you heard someone who received a blessing—received a massive financial windfall let's say—exclaim "This is to God's glory!" Or maybe someone who has been blessed with great health say, "Thank you Lord for my perfect health"? Most likely it would be infrequently, if at all. And yet these would be the probable times you would presume someone would offer up praise. Would they even praise Him through the storms that appear in their lives now and then?

"If you abide in Me, and My words abide in you, you will ask what you desire, and it shall be done for you." (John15:7) Jesus leaves no doubt, no room for compromise. He boldly states "Abide in Me... *it shall be done.* Answered prayer happens because by praying in Jesus' name to abide in Him, you will ask for nothing that is not in agreement with the will of God!

There it is!

By keeping Christ's spirit in your heart, your mind, and your body, you will never be led to ask for something not of God's will!

Bartimaeus was one of Judea's discarded vagrants. Living in Jericho with a handicap in the first century put you at a major disadvantage. However, unlike the lepers who were shunned and mistreated, a blind man may find an occasional act of kindness now and then. However not being able to work a steady trade, most times even the blind were forced to beg. It is said that with every misfortune a hidden blessing also is present and like most who have lost their sight, their hearing becomes acute, and Bartimaeus' hearing was excellent.

Despite the noise and congestion of the curious, Bartimaeus heard Jesus' approach. "This is my only chance" he thinks. Shouting out to Jesus brings only reprimands from the crowd. "Shut up you idiot!" "Be quiet you fool!" You can almost hear the taunts these many years later. "Not this time" he declares to himself. "They're not going to shut me up now!"

As he is shoved, pushed, and demeaned he shouts, "Son of David, have mercy on me." Sensing Jesus hasn't heard him, he screams above the crowd "Son of David, have mercy on me." Pausing in mid-step Jesus asks him to come forward. The Bible says, " and throwing aside his garment, he rose and came to Jesus."

Can't you imagine the excitement he felt? Nothing was going to keep him away from Jesus' side. "What do you want me to do for you?" "Let me receive my sight," answers Bartimeaus. Jesus, knowing the power of belief responds, "Your faith has made you well." (Mark 10: 46-52)

Free will allows us to accept God's path, protection, and power in our lives. Or not. We can choose to believe, accept and to avail ourselves of His favor, or we can choose to close off ourselves from that favor with neutralizing, cynical and counteractive thinking.

The people of Nazareth chose—chose with their God-given free will —to disbelieve that their native son was anything but an average man. However blind Bartimaeus and so many others throughout Judea knew that Jesus needed to "only say a word" and they would be healed.

We've all experienced the naysayer, the doubter, the pessimist, the downer. Someone once wrote "People who say it cannot be done should not interrupt those who are doing it." If you associate with negative thinkers, spend your time with complainers, keep company with discouragers, hang out with cynics and socialize with people who love doom and gloom your chances of becoming all that God wants you to be are slim. Be prudent and thoughtful in choosing those people you associate with. This is especially critical in determining (maybe a better word is discerning) who your close friends are. Some people just bring out our best. Others, by their very presence, can bring out our worst.

"You're crazy; you can't do that!"
"That's impossible!" "Everyone knows there's no way!" "You're wasting your time." "The only way people can talk to one another is if they're next to each other!"—until Alexander Graham Bell, a teacher of the deaf invented how in 1876.

"You can't get light out of a piece of glass!"—but using a burned sewing thread as a carbon filament in October 1879, Thomas Edison was able to.

"You can't hear voices through thin air!" Fortunately, Guglielmo Marconi didn't believe that when he patented the wireless transmitter in 1896.

"Only birds fly; men can't fly!" but they did when a couple of brothers—Orville and Wilbur Wright—proved you could on the shores of Kitty Hawk, North Carolina in December 1903.

"The world is flat. And the sea is full of monsters. You're insane. Your estimates are all wrong!" and then on October 12th 1492 Christopher Columbus discovered a New World changing the old one forever.

Jairus was a leader of his temple, the acting president of the congregation actually. Like so many throughout Judea, Jairus heard of the teacher who travelled with a small group of followers from village to village preaching and healing. Hearing that Jesus was nearby, he rushed to the Rabbi's side begging him to lay His healing hands on his little girl who was near death. Although Jesus was teaching to a crowd who'd gathered, He immediately followed Jairus to his home.

As they hurried toward where Jairus' daughter lay Jesus felt strength leave His body. Turning to see who touched Him Jesus sees a woman, timid, fearful and prostrate at His feet. Once again Jesus acknowledges the power of belief "Your faith has made you well. Go in peace, and be healed of your affliction," and 12 years of torture immediately disappears. (Mark 5:34)

Continuing the story "While He was still speaking, some came from the ruler of the synagogue's house who said, "Your daughter is dead. Why trouble the Teacher any further?" As soon as Jesus heard the word that was spoken, He said to the ruler of the synagogue, "Do not be afraid; only believe "Jesus knew Jairus' heart was breaking. The panic, the unbearable pain he is feeling thinking his little girl is gone is obvious.

Continuing "And He permitted no one to follow Him except Peter, James, and John the brother of James. Then He came to the house of the ruler of the synagogue and saw a tumult and those who wept and wailed loudly. When He came in, He said to them, "Why make this commotion and weep? The child is not dead, but sleeping." And they ridiculed Him."

What Jesus does next has profound meaning and implications for us today: "But when He had put them all outside, He took the father and the mother of the child, and those who were with Him (Peter, James and John) and entered where the child was lying. Then He took the child by the hand, and said to her, "Talitha, cumi," which is translated, "Little girl, I say to you, arise." Immediately the girl arose and walked, for she was twelve years of age. And they were overcome with great amazement. But He commanded them strictly that no-one should know it, and said something should be given her to eat." It is reasonable to assume that all twelve apostles were with Jesus when He encountered Jairus, based on Scripture. What is interesting however is that He chose only three of them to accompany Him to Jairus' home. Jesus knew that the slightest bit of doubt would prevent the mighty work He was about to undertake. Knowing this, Jesus bars the pessimists, the skeptics, the distrustful and the unbelievers. He allows Jairus in the room—after all it was Jairus' belief in Jesus' authority that caused him to seek Jesus out in the first place—the girl's mother and Peter, James and John. Five people who believed, trusted and who knew what Jesus could do. If there is any better testimony to who you should keep company with, as well as the power of belief, I don't know of it. (Mark 5:21-43)

Let's take a longer view of this story, however. Imagine if some of the disbelievers were allowed into the girl's room? "He can't do that!" Doubt would permeate the atmosphere. Chances are good that arguments would erupt between believers and the negativists. Chaos would likely ensue and nothing good would find its way to the room.

When we analyze it, if you associate with complainers you join in complaining, but when you associate with enthusiastic, inspiring, and motivated people you become energized with self-confidence and assurance. If you want to gauge where your life's perspective is right now, assess who your friends are and who you associate with. There is no better standard in appraising where you're headed than this self-examination. "Yea, but I can't just stop being friends with her!" "He's been my friend for years. I just can't dump him!"

Actually, if you're asking yourself those type of questions you already are aware of the toxic relationships you're involved in. To be all God has planned for you to be, your garden needs to be free of weeds.

The Gospels are replete with the narrative of Jesus' ability to not only teach but His ability to touch the life of every person He came in contact with. It was not hyperbole for John to write "There are also many other things that Jesus did, which if they were written one by one, I suppose that even the world itself could not contain the books that would be written." (John 21:25)

It's interesting to note that of the parables and stories Jesus chose to impart, He used the word "BELIEVE" (or variations such as Believing, Believed, etc.) 84 times and the word "FAITH" (including Faithful) 42 times—that's over 100 times that Jesus discuss' the significance of expecting with certainty.

These words were meant to not only encourage but to prevail upon His followers to trust in God's ability to affect their lives in extraordinary ways. Jesus' messages are timeless and as valid and appropriate today as when He spoke them.

There comes a story that, if it were possible to overshadow the previous miracles, does so. Jesus' ministry was nearing its completion and it is obvious that He is doing all He can to reveal the power of belief and faith through effective, sincere, and confident prayer to His disciples—and across these 21 centuries, to us as well.

The Gospels say little of the relationship between Jesus and Lazarus. Actually, what little we hear of Lazarus is found in John's Gospel and then in only two chapters. But it is clear that there exists a special connection between Jesus and Lazarus, and to his sisters Martha and Mary also.

When Jesus is initially made aware that Lazarus is sick, He is in the town (which is believed to be Bethabara) beyond the Jordan. This was a special place for Jesus as it was here that He was baptized by John and felt called to His tremendous ministry.

Although He is told the urgency of Lazarus' condition, Jesus chooses to stay in Bethabara another two days finally telling the apostles that "Lazarus sleeps" which is His euphemism for "Lazarus is dead". (John 11:11)

But what Jesus says next bears special attention: "I am glad for your sakes that I was not there, that you may believe." (John11:15)

When Jesus enters Bethany, it is with the full expectation that His divine power will be used to show His victory over death but, because of that very act, will lead to His crucifixion. Despite this knowledge, Jesus, a man obviously broken-hearted over His friend's death, exemplifies the power of faith, of belief and even through personal grief. "Jesus wept" as John wrote (the shortest verse in the Bible – John 11:35)—to teach us the effects of gratitude: "Father, I thank You that You have heard Me." (John 11:42) and knowing: "Lazarus, come forth." (John 11:43)

What can we make of the words that Jesus had spoken after leaving Bethany, at the final meal before the Friday that was anything but good? "Most assuredly, I say to you, he who believes in Me, the works that I do he will do also, because I go to my Father." (John 14:12)

Our intentions, in order to be realized, must be wrought through prayer in Christ's name and be to bring about glory to God. I know this runs counter to what most of us have read or been led to believe but it's best not consummated if these conditions are not present. No good thing will come of it if we work against God's will. By and through a relationship with God we will discern His intention for our lives, as well as distinguishing if our intention or goal is worthy.

When we acknowledge that Jesus never spoke idle words or used careless speech—saying one thing but meaning another entirely—we are left with a promise that is both amazing and astounding.

You may already be familiar with this reading found in Philippians: "Be anxious for nothing, but in everything by prayer and supplication, with thanksgiving, let your requests be made known to God." (Philippians 4:6) Notice Paul's declarations "Be anxious for nothing" meaning "don't worry" "Pray" and beseech. Be thankful for the results, although not yet in the physical.

24

Flexibility

When people think of a goal they wish to achieve, they "hope" they can attain it—that's how you *used to* think.

But doubt, maybe ever so slight, would appear and throw you off track because when doubt appears fear arrives directly behind. And you know now that fear and doubt are the ultimate party crashers. So, with this thought in mind let's explore the methods for allowing hope to become knowing and dreams to become visable fact.

There are two ways that a person can achieve something—the most common is to take physical action. This could be as simple as mowing the lawn or as complex as building a house. No matter how simple or complicated, taking physical action achieves something. Whether successful or not, energy was expended, but more importantly to our conversation, an illusion is created that this is the only way you can achieve anything.

The challenge with this option is that you can only work with what you've got which narrows your success considerably. Not only does this method cause stress which leads to other dilemmas as you've read earlier but can (and usually does) create an atmosphere of competition with others. This is how the idea "there's only so much to go around" takes root.

This is an idea that you need to throw out. There is no such concept as "I can but you can't" in God's Kingdom. There is abundance in His realm and competition need not exist. Imagine a world where competing is replaced by cooperation? As an adult, who has seen where "being nice" has gotten you, you can be forgiven for being somewhat jaded. But we as adults would do well to look, as Christ did, toward children for more virtuous examples of how to live as the following story illustrates.

In 1976 at the Seattle Special Olympics nine contestants, all physically or mentally disabled gathered at the starting line to await the beginning of the 100-yard dash. At the gun, all nine took off for the race of their lives. All of them but one little boy who tripped and fell.

As he rolled over and over on the asphalt he began to cry. Although all the kids heard the boy crying, two began to slow down and finally stopped. Turning around both of them went back to where he was lying while the other children struggled to the finish line. They picked their fellow contestant up and together the three linked arms and walked to the finish line.

It took over ten minutes before the stadium, now on their feet, many with tears running down their cheeks, stopped cheering.

When a person feels "I need to get mine first" he usually does so from a position of lack. "There won't be any left for me!" And we know worst expectations are realized.

Our man, in desperation to get his, rushes out the door getting behind the wheel only to find his keys are still in the house. Rushing back in "They were on the table!" he screams, then realizes he left them upstairs on his dresser so he would "save time" by keeping them with him.

Heading down the street he hits a red light. "Figures!" he grumbles and of course he's right. Not only is our hero hitting every red light, he's in bumper-to-bumper traffic which at this time of day is virtually unheard of. Pounding the steering wheel, he screams "I'm going to miss out!"

Finally, he enters the parking lot frantically looking for a place to park. Not able to control himself any longer he's just about in tears. "They're going to be all gone!" he yells to no one else in the car.

As he makes his way to the shelf the salesclerk sorrowfully declares "We just sold the last one!" We always get what we don't want when we don't want it badly enough!

If our man trusted more and believed in enough for everyone he would have the object of his desire this very minute. Unfortunately, his expectations were filled with doubt and his expectations certainly came true.

How you view your reality determines your comfort on this earth. Some people are naturally happy and grateful (you will rarely find one without the other). Others are bitter and jealous (likewise rarely one without the other). Life happens to those who assert "This is too hard." or "No matter what, everything works out for me in the end." They can say "The rich get richer, and the poor get poorer" (Jesus you'll remember spoke about this and we'll review it again in a bit) or they say "I can do all things through Christ who strengthens me." (Philippians 4:13) And either way they're right.

If you've read this far into the book, you've noticed many of the thoughts are repeated. This is purposeful. The concepts presented here may likely be new to you. With the goal of encouraging you to achieve all you hope for in this life, this continual dripping will, I trust, be helpful. You must accept – without doubting - that with God all things truly are possible. And perhaps as you've prayed for your objective to be realized, gotten a feeling of comfort and peace about your intention but still have not achieved your goal - fear not.

As a resident of the 21st century we want what we want now! We devise a plan and think we have the steps to achieve our goals. It is reasonable to develop a workable strategy before starting any type of quest. The problems arrive when there is a hitch in our plan. The moment something unforeseen comes up we begin to question the wisdom of the plan, maybe even the goal. The scenario changes and most people panic. The other glitch is when we think we're "doing it like I'm supposed to." You know this one because this was where you clearly stated your goal, you've claimed it and you don't think of it again. You've done that and *that doesn't* work either!

Unfortunately realizing goals—the "hard ones" in your mind anyway—is not so simple. The reason? Fear.

In the first situation we think if things aren't going along on the plan, we've developed to achieve the goal, it won't work, thus we sabotage God's work because our EGO's tell us "I got this." When we tightly wrap our hands around the throttle, we firmly believe we know better. *We must leave room for changes in the plan, not "freak out" when things change and maintain an attitude of trust. Still holding on to the mental picture of the accomplished goal.*

Visualizing your goal does help in imprinting the intention on your subconsciousness but sharing that objective with others can be counterproductive because it leaves you vulnerable to the doubt (and criticism) of others. Additionally, if you harbor any lack of confidence in achieving or obtaining that which you seek, your mind will usually reinforce loudly—"that's not going to work."

When you try not to think of your intention again, you usually think of your intention again—especially if it's important to you. If you were somehow able to not think of the objective, you would starve the goal of feelings—a major ingredient in achieving what you want. Allowing an intention to go into emptiness assures that the objective falls into empty space. Remember—faith without works is dead.

There is another way to eliminate doubt, fear and worry that your objective won't be obtained. This entails patience and endurance. This is known as "waiting on the Lord".

Although David was a man of God, "the apple of His eye" in fact, he knew the frustration of biding his time before God's perfection showed itself. After being anointed by Samuel to be the next king of Israel David was forced to wait years before ascending to the throne. In between those years he had giants to slay, music to play, and armies to conquer. It was while he waited that he learned how to lead men and command respect. As he remained in God's time he took action, refusing to remain idle. David knew that to be the best he could be and become the man and ruler God wanted him to be, he would need to rely on God's guidance. "Rest in the Lord and wait patiently for Him" he wrote. "Wait on the Lord and keep His way, and He shall exalt you to inherit the land." (Psalms 37:7)

As you wait for the goal you've decided upon let me remind you again you will need to fulfill one very basic requirement: visualize your already having whatever it is that you're trying to obtain or achieve! This sounds simple enough, but you need to accept that this method, though simple, requires patience.

Imagine going to your favorite restaurant and after being seated you're handed the menu. As you scan across the entrees you decide on the filet mignon. The waiter takes your order, hands it to the chef who then begins to prepare your meal.

After a few minutes you call the waiter back to your table and tell him that although you still want a steak, you'd really like a Porterhouse instead. As the waiter hurries back to the kitchen to change the order, you've grabbed the attention of another waiter and now ask him to tell your server you really wanted the Ribeye steak all along and now want that.

You've created complete confusion in the kitchen but now you would like the scallop potatoes instead of the baked. After that order goes in you decide that french fries would go better with the Ribeye (or was that the filet?). At this point the owner of the restaurant escorts you from your table to the door!

Life is like that. You can request what you want out of it, but you must be patient and clearly know what you want in order for it to be achieved. Just keep in mind the following:

Wait and learn to wait responsibly. In other words—live with integrity, always moving toward your goal with confidence in God's guidance.

Wait knowingly. God is in charge not you. Delay is often God's doing.

Wait obediently. Be submissive to God's will. As we know, this requires prayer and dwelling in the Lord.

Wait dependently. Rely on the right method to reach your goal by trusting the Lord fully.

Wait prayerfully. Prayer elevates us into His authority and potency. We rise above the conventional deliberations of our conscious minds and enter the spiritual domain of the Creator of the universe.

As David wrote "I waited patiently for the Lord, and He inclined to hear me." (Psalms 40:1) There is a certain wisdom in finding a chair to sit in silence and talk to God. When we commit ourselves to God we're able to hear Him speak to our heart. For some people it's more effective to keep busy, going about the day's work but staying ever vigilant to what God is imparting. Either option requires that you wait on the Lord.

Knowing that you're abiding in God's will brings a certain peace and it also provides you with a strength of character. " I would have lost heart, unless I had believed that I would see the goodness of the Lord in the land of the living. Wait on the Lord; be of good courage, and He shall strengthen your heart; Wait, I say, on the Lord!" (Psalms 27:13-14)

Before we leave the topic of submitting to God's timing, I'd like to share this prayer composed by the Trappist Monk Thomas Merton. Since waiting on God's schedule also involves trusting His purpose over our lives, we rely upon our intention of faithfulness to that purpose to impart the ability to endure the wait.

"My God, I have no idea where I am going. I do not see the road ahead of me. I cannot know for certain where it will end. Nor do I really know myself, and the fact that I think I am following your will does not mean that I actually am doing so.

But I believe that the desire to please you does in fact please you. And I hope I have that desire in all I am doing. I hope that I will never do anything apart from that desire.

And I know that if I do this, you will lead me by the right road, though I may know nothing about it. Therefore, I will trust you always though I may seem to be lost in the shadow of death. I will not fear for you are ever with me and you will never leave me to face my perils alone."

It is said that the greatest test of a man's character is not how he handles his success but how he handles his failures.

Muhammad Ali once said, "Only a man who knows what it is like to be defeated can reach down to the bottom of his soul and come up with the extra ounce of power it takes to win when the match is over."

Although no one sets out to lose, to be defeated or to fail miserably it happens to each of us. You'll recall our discussion earlier of how our attitude toward some thing or some event determines our reality, and based on that state of mind, that is how we experience our present moment. Failure can be debilitating, or it can be enlightening depending on your point of view. Henry Ford's opinion was that "Failure is only the opportunity to begin again, this time more intelligently."

Most of us enjoy, and are inspired by stories about success, achievement, accomplishment, attainment and so on. These ends are what we put our intentions toward, yet little is said about defeat, collapse, ruin, or disastrous outcomes. Our society seems to verify the saying "the whole world loves a winner but will not tolerate a loser" so we go about our lives doing everything we can to not make mistakes or suffer a bad result. As a matter of fact, most people lose sight of the blessings of failing.

We all pray for triumph in our efforts but now and then tragedy shows up instead. Most people end up blaming God for not answering their prayers but make no mistake—He did. You see, He put you on the right path to obtain the blessing, but the tragedy was just a part of the process to get you to the triumph!

How can you be in the winner's circle if you've never been in the contest? How can you be a conqueror if you've never experienced conflict? How can you ever achieve victory if you haven't been in a fight? How can you ever be an overcomer if you've never climbed the mountain? How can you ever have a testimony if you've never had a test?

When you face what seems like an impenetrable barrier don't ever forget that there is a power within you that no one and nothing can stop. No matter what gets thrown at you, God is your defender. He promised you that "No weapon formed against you shall prosper." (Isaiah 54:17)

There are times that favor is hidden in the middle of the storm and always keep in mind that when rains come things bloom. God is always in control of the time and the intensity of the storms in your life. He has a specific purpose for allowing them and they are designed to meet a specific need in your life so quit worrying and start worshipping. If someone tries "reasoning" with you that "God just abandones people" courageously say to them "Get behind me Satan." I love this quote from the singer Dolly Parton "The way I see it, if you want the rainbow, you gotta put up with the rain."

The consequences we face when dealing with failure are the ripple effects we allow to contaminate the actions, events and even the way we think. If your attitude towards the circumstance is one of total defeat—then allow yourself to feel that! Ruminate, mull it over and be happy being miserable. I know that must sound out of place here but just for a moment consider these: When we meet with failure the feelings above are usually present whether we want them to be or not. The stress is compounded because our emotions are lashed tightly to the outcome and the way we believe the scenario should play out. This is another instance where so much importance is placed on the outcome that fear and worry appear which interrupts, and usually prevents, what we want from happening.

The remedy is, of course, to release importance. Detach emotion from the outcome "I just have to have this, or else I'm..." and become an observer. An observer is one who calmly views the scenes as they transpire trusting that they've done their praying.

Additionally, by fighting those human emotions of disappointments most people begin to feel guilt for feeling them! They feel weak as well as miserable. Let yourself be you! Feel the disappointment—but allow yourself to feel that temporarily. Get it out of your system. Don't beat yourself up but instead realize these emotions are normal and that this is only a delay and not a defeat. God can shut doors to make certain you receive what He wants for you. He prevents you from getting less than what He has in store for you by allowing set-backs. What you take as a disappointment is actually a disguise of good fortune! Do your part by believing, by trusting!

25

Casting Your Cares on the Lord

We all experience a season when everything we hope for seems to effortlessly appear. This is what we remember when adversity comes our way—"Why is this happening to me? It always worked before." But it's always the failures that teach us our greatest, and perpetual, lessons. It's the collapses, downturns and downfalls that propel you toward your destiny.

'The Da Vinci Code' became a best-selling book for author Dan Brown, but before that happened Brown dealt with his share of disappointments and setbacks. He was, in some people's opinion, a serial failure.

His first career choice was writing pop songs, even recording a soft rock album! "I wanted to write songs about princes and queens and reading ancient manuscripts, but no one was interested. The album sold about nine copies. I'm pretty sure my mom bought all of them."

Brown didn't fare much better as an author initially. In 1998 his debut novel "Digital Fortress" appeared on bookshelves and at his first book signing for the novel he had "five pens at the ready, just to be sure." Three hours passed without a single person approaching him. "Finally, a man walked toward me, looking me right in the eye" Brown recalls "So I took the cap off my pen and was quivering with excitement, then he said 'Can you tell me where this restaurant is?' That was the only question I got all-day."

Susan Boyle began life in uncertainty. The youngest of 9 children, her mother had great difficulty delivering her (Susan was led to believe that she was oxygen – deprived because of it) but it wasn't until years later she learned that she was, in fact, autistic. Although bullied and tormented in school because of her appearance, Susan found her solace through her voice. First at church, then recording demos and finally on national TV.

Susan absolutely loved to sing and although decades would pass, she never abandoned that love. Now, years later, she decided to take a giant leap of faith with her life and boarded a bus to audition for "Britain's Got Talent" in April 2009. She had never traveled very far from her town in Scotland but now she was about to lay it all on the line.

Walking out onto the stage that night, the audience, as well as the panel, rolled their eyes. "What does this frumpy looking woman think she's doing?" Half with amusement and half in pity, the auditorium expected an embarrassing minute or two of screeching followed by a healthy dose of humiliation. The Washington Post felt that, in their opinion, the audience and judges were "waiting for her to squawk like a duck."

What they received instead was astonishment.

The resonance of sound that were transmitted from those Scottish vocal cords was nothing less than shocking, astounding and beautiful.

Since that night over 300 million viewers have watched Susan's performance on YouTube, and she has gone on to countless accolades across the globe.

God had something else in mind for Susan Boyle. She had the treasure He put there to show each of us that despite humble beginnings, despite appearances, despite low expectations, God never gives us a dream that He doesn't have the way to achieve it. Please – hold this knowledge in your heart.

How we handle adversity not only reveals our inner fortitude but exhibits our character to those closest to us. Your children will learn more about you from your failures than your successes. We have the choice of turning problems into promises and messes into masterpieces. Change your focus from the disappointments—which takes strong mental effort—to determination to grow in experience, turning that knowledge into a practical application.

As incredible as this may seem, there are times when God puts difficulties in your path to allow you to get rid of problems, even people —some who you always believed would be part of your life—freeing things up that would ordinarily hold you back. It's God's love for His children that causes Him to impart His favor that pushes back the forces of darkness as well as obstacles in your life. The same favor that held back the wall of water of the Red Sea. The same favor that tightly closed the lion's mouth. The same favor that caused the blind to see. No matter how big the problem, God is bigger.

Don't give up, don't give in and whatever knowledge you gain from this book, I hope it includes the pledge to never give your attention to defeat. Don't ever lose sight that the blessings of the Lord are always upon you. "Never give in, never, never give in" admonished Winston Churchill "Never, never, never, never—in nothing great or small, large or petty—never give in, except to convictions of honor and good sense. Never yield to force. Never yield to the apparently overwhelming might of the enemy."

The comic Steve Harvey is known today for his hosting duties on television's "Family Feud" and authoring the bestseller "Act Like a Lady, Think Like a Man." He's created a mega million-dollar industry with his talk-show "Steve Harvey" and hosting a syndicated radio show as well. But things for Harvey were not always so bright.

Starting his career in the late 80's, Harvey knew what the word "struggle" meant, living homeless for three years. "I lived in a car. I had nowhere to go." His address was his '76 Ford Tempo and surviving on $75 a week that he earned performing at comedy clubs. "When I landed a gig, they'd put me up in a hotel, but after, I'd have nowhere to go. I'd lost everything." Using an Igloo cooler as a makeshift refrigerator, Harvey somehow navigated a life but never gave up on his dream, "I just slept in my car with the front seat reclined, and I'd wash up in hotel bathrooms, gas stations or swimming pool showers."

Days became weeks and weeks months "It was so disheartening. A week is really the maximum you can do. This was three years! It was rock bottom. But even in my darkest days I had faith it would turn around." Through all of this Harvey's attitude focused on success and not defeat. Steve Harvey chose to keep his eyes firmly fixed on the One who can calm the storms and rise from the tomb. He lives with the knowing that with God, nothing is impossible.

Both devote Christians, Harvey and his wife Marjorie maintain an attitude of thankfulness for the favor God has given—and continues to give them. "At some point" says Marjorie "You gotta stop and see what God has already blessed you with."

When failures, setbacks, and disappointments happen, Satan will continue to remind you to keep feeling miserable, keep feeling defeated, keep feeling guilty. There may be consequences from your mess-up but those are from man, not God. Scripture says we may fall seven times, but that God will raise us back up. (Proverbs 24:16)

Have you ever noticed that when a disappointment appears in your life, especially one that leaves you stunned and bewildered, how you think your world has come to an end? Of course, this has happened to all of us. However, looking back at that "failure" after a few years you realized it was the best thing that could have happened. One day you wake up and suddenly realize that if whatever it was you were waiting on, working towards, or hoping for had come about you would not have been fulfilled. At the time you could not know how wrong it would have been. But now, with the passage of time you realize that God had your back all along. Despite the hurt, despite the tears, despite the disappointment you trusted Him.

As you know there are some people who just are not nice people. They are the ones who resent you and are jealous of you. They're the first to judge and the last (if ever) to congratulate. When you fall, they rejoice. Unfortunately, these folks can't seem to comprehend or understand the value of Divine guidance and protection. Subliminally they envy what you have, and they don't—peace. When blessings are given to you, they are the people who like to bring up your past. When you encounter these people just stay focused and determined. If God has blessed you don't allow anyone or anything to distract you from where He is preparing to take you. Silently ask God to bless them and go about your day. I know that sounds easy but if what these people have done or said is something that's not easily shaken, cast that to the Lord. Just acknowledge that this is too big to handle on your own and you need Him to handle it. Believe me—it works.

When you hit a brick wall, when everything just seems to fall apart, and you scream "I can't believe I'm going through this!" stop for a moment to acknowledge how right you are. You're "going through" not staying in. Stay in faith and continue to visualize what you're looking to achieve.

"Count it all joy when you fall into various trials." (James 1:2-3) If you think these are just "Bible words" think again. First, each word in the

Bible has been imparted by God but look intensely at these words—"be happy when things go wrong?!" Each time you face a trial of some sort, overcome it and pass through it and you come out stronger. Not once in a while, not every now and then. *Every time!*

Although you might not notice it at the time, God is remolding you. You achieve a greater capacity of resilience, a stronger resolve, and a new dedication. Trying and failing is not failure. Doing nothing is failure. Giving up is failure.

Never lose sight of the fact that God is right there beside you. Satan would have you believe you're alone, you're just a loser, but not for one minute believe that! You'll try to move forward but you'll hear "What's the use? You're just gonna mess it up again!" That sure is not God speaking!

When you feel overwhelmed, when you feel alone, pray bold prayers. "I don't see a way, but I know you have a way." Say that with conviction because it's true!

Thankfully natural laws are ones that we can actually see. They are nothing less than a reflection of God's authority. Nature endeavors to create balance in all things. High tide—low tide, birth and death, light and dark, good and bad. When atmospheric pressure drops it is balanced out by the wind. We observe the difference in temperature being counterbalanced by heat exchange. As we discussed earlier - whenever unbalance makes its appearance, you can be certain that natural law will begin to manifest itself.

Unbalance can be caused by putting too much significance, too much importance on an outcome. We've spoken about the emotions that present themselves when we "just gotta have" something. Fear and worry grasp your overwrought feelings with a death grip, creating an almost obsessive compulsion to have, to get –or else!

The antidote?

Calm down and keep a level head. Act impeccably in your quest but be an observer. Remove your emotions as much as possible. Know that by staying in God's will the perfect solution or answer will appear.

So now for the exciting news: If you've "failed" at something, you've been "defeated", or things are utterly and thoroughly horrible and un-nerving, start readjusting your attitude. Change your viewpoint to one of happiness and rejoice: When things seem horrible, when you think they can't get better, when your misery is so profound that you can hardly breath just KNOW that those same balancing forces of nature are going to balance out in your favor. God is going to compensate that misery with elation, sorrow with delight, melancholy with contentment and failure with success! Put another way you've been beaten, robbed and left bleeding on the side of the road and the next thing you know the Samaritan not only cleans you up, brings you to the inn, pays for the room but hands you a bag of money as well! The larger the misfortune, the greater the amount you'll find in there!

Keep the following in mind: Just as things can't be good all the time, neither can they be bad all the time!

God really does have a perfect plan for your life. His design for your life is *truly greater* than anything you can imagine. Open your consciousness to Him. This is done by asking - not begging, never begging - through dialogue prayer. Dialogue prayer is just that- talking to God. Asking for guidance, asking for answers, asking for wisdom.

The tests that you've gone through will become your testimony, not only to inspire others but most importantly to glorify God. *I stand witness to these words I've written and know them to be true.* There will come a day, when you will look back to the turmoils, the tragedies, the torments, and the tears and know that the strength you now possess came from them. Jesus told us that faith will move mountains so now it's up to you to live each day by faith, by trust, by believing and by knowing.

When it's all been said and done, we are given by God His greatest gift to we who are human—the gift of free will. As you know by now........choose wisely

26

Happiness

If I were to walk up to someone and ask "what would make you happy?" what answer do you suppose I'd hear?

Why would most people consider that money would make them happy (notice I didn't wait for your answer to the previous question?!)?

I do believe some people would say "being in a loving relationship" "Being healthy" "knowing my children are safe and are doing well." but I think it's fairly accurate to say that most people when asked "What would make you happy?" would, without hesitation, answer "money".

Throughout these pages, we've seen why, biologically speaking, we act and react the way we do. There is an abundance of statistical considerations and conclusions that have been compiled regarding inner joy, gladness, and contentment. We'll examine a few of them and how we can find true peace of mind and be unequivocally happy.

The tendancy for most people to equate money and happiness can be based on the physiological structure of the brain. When we compare our money and income to others, it causes us to feel good or bad. Actually, many different species form a type "status" level where those on the bottom level cater to the needs of those that are higher up.

Consider monkeys for instance, where the dominant members of the group receive grooming.

Unfortunately, those considered low on the totem pole show high levels of stress hormones in their blood and some have been found with enlarged adrenal glands where those stress hormones are produced. Our society rewards wealth, which in many ways is a false indicator of a person's character.

Being a dominant animal can allow the brain to release more dopamine (the "feel-good" chemical) into our system by as much as 20%! Envy and socially comparing ourselves to others is an instinctive trait and one that most of us try to suppress to some degree.

Happiness is a state of mind where we take a great number of factors into consideration, many times outside of ourselves, which impacts our mood at the moment.

Each of us seeks to be happy. Not only happy now but, if possible, continually. We know that rain will fall now and again on our hopes and plans but make no mistake—God did not put you on this planet to suffer. We learn through suffering and adversity, but we were not born to be punished.

We need to have purpose in our lives and to be proud of who we are and in the things we accomplish. We need to experience pleasure—taking time away from work, chores, and the daily efforts of living in a world that is instantly connected and rapid.

To begin to enjoy happiness, stress needs to be mitigated and replaced with joyousness. The basic needs—shelter, food and warmth must be covered, and we must lead a life of meaning.

Despite being considered poor, there are many people who live in countries with high rates of poverty and economic inequality that are happier than most Americans! In the U.S. it is common for people to compare their possessions with others. Sadly in our society, worth is based on how much money and how many toys a person has. In countries where the majority of people live with a lack of comfort and luxuries there is a sense of freedom. You no longer envy your neighbor because you are equally like-minded and are both on the same social scale.

According to the 'Gallup Healthway's Global Well-Being Index', Panamanians live in the happiest country on Earth.

Among the categories measured in their research were those measuring social support and financial as well as physical well-being. You could be excused if you thought this was an exception but in fact happiness is prevalent among Latin American countries such as Guatemala, Costa Rica, Puerto Rico, Chile, Mexico, and Belize—all in the top 10 happiest places on Earth. Gallop also measures how people live their lives with what's called the "Positive Experience Index." This index considers how people live their lives with qualities such as getting enough rest, laughing, and smiling, and feeling respected. They found the happiest countries were all in Central and South America. Despite political unrest and widespread poverty, Latinos maintain high levels of positivity.

To accomplish a goal, something that holds great significance and meaning to you, it must be viewed as already done. We've discussed the consequences that usually result from placing an enormous amount of importance on the intention. The fear, the worry that "I'm in trouble if I don't get this." that immediately accompanies such a feeling. You fear the worst and as you now know worst expectations usually appear.

Stress is a condition that a modern, goal-driven society reluctantly bears. Not knowing (or caring?) that there is a more suitable method to achieving an objective, people elbow, push and fight for their place in the world. You are now aware that there is a simpler and more efficient way to accomplish your intentions.

The happier someone is, the healthier and longer their lives will probably be. When you're happy you have relaxed the grip of importance and that happiness can enable you to not only increase your finances but to realize those desires you wish to achieve. There is a biological basis for this.

It's been found that people with greater activity in the left prefrontal cortex, that place in the brain that seems to generate happiness, produces more antibodies after a flu shot which suggests that the immune systems are stronger then we realize. Studies show that in both humans and monkeys, greater activity in the left prefrontal cortex is associated with lower levels of stress hormones throughout the body with these levels staying low all through the day.

When someone is out-going, an extrovert, they will usually have lower levels of a sugar-controlling substance known as glycosylated hemoglobin in their blood, which lowers their risk for diabetes and related diseases. There is an old saying in Italian that we should all embrace: "Vivi Bene, Ridi Spesso, Ama Molto"—live well, laugh often, love much!

This observation from John Lennon is priceless: "When I was 5 years old, my mother told me that happiness was the key to life. When I went to school, they asked me what I wanted to be when I grew up. I wrote down "HAPPY". They told me I didn't understand the assignment, and I told them they didn't understand life."

We've all experienced the terror of a nightmare as we spoke of earlier. We wake up with heart racing, panic-stricken and for a few moments at least, completely disoriented. That dream was as real as if it happened while you were awake, yet it literally was all in your head! The visions you saw caused physical reactions with no basis in fact. If a dream could cause such a frightening sensory response like this then we must accept that where the mind goes, so goes the body.

It's accepted now that our thinking also has a strong influence over our health and that same conclusion has found that our thinking has a powerful effect on the aging process as well. For instance, in 2002 researchers at the "Journal of Personality and Social Psychology" found that people who embraced a cheerful and positive attitude, regardless of age or socio-economic status and felt like life would continue to get better were living nearly eight years longer than those with pessimistic views!

On a personal note, I can attest to the power of living a life with purpose, positive thinking, physical activity, and "Joie de Vivre". My father's brother was riding his bike, driving his car, enjoying his freedom, and always exploring new places well into his 90s and all of that without medication of any type! When my son Geoffrey was getting married, my uncle—who was then 90—asked me if I knew any 50- or 60-year young ladies who would enjoy going out to dinner, accompanying him to the wedding and enjoy some quality time with him!

My Uncle Stevie celebrated his 100th birthday on January 28th, 2017! When I spoke to him that day it was as if I were speaking to a man half his age! Statistically, my uncle was one out of 72,197 Americans to reach the age of 100.

It is now without dispute that exercise at any age is beneficial. It does not only combat diseases but gives you the flexibility to do the things that bring you pleasure. In fact, vigorous exercise can actually slow down the aging process!

Analyzing 6,000 adults and by studying their physical activity and biological markers researchers found that on a cellular level, people were able to turn back aging by nearly a decade! Although you may be 25 years old it's important to understand that the earlier you incorporate strenuous exercise—running, jogging, weightlifting—the better. But age is no limit.

According to Time Magazine, where the report was digitally published, the researchers used DNA samples to measure the length of the participant's Telomeres, which are protein caps that protect the chromosomes similar to the plastic tips on shoelaces. Shrinking with age, Telomeres lose bits of substance every time a cell divides. One of the study's authors, Larry Tucker observed, "In general people with shorter telomeres die sooner and are more likely to develop many of our chronic diseases."

Researchers found people who vigorously exercised for 30 to 40 minutes a day, five days a week had longer telomeres—and this research took risk factors such as smoking, alcohol use and obesity into account. They concluded that exercising strenuously added about nine years of "biological aging advantage" over sedentary adults. People who exercised more moderately had a two—year advantage.

Physical activity could, researchers speculate, help preserve telomeres by reducing stress and inflammation. "We all know people who seem younger than their actual age" observed Tucker. "Exercise can help with that, and now we know that part of that may be because of its effect on our telomeres."

Another benefit of exercise is the effect it has on our bone density. It is a fact that as we age our bones tend to become less elastic, but according to researchers at the University of North Carolina School of Medicine—Bone, bone marrow fat plays an important role in bone health. Although bone marrow doesn't give us energy when we work out, physical activity causes this fat to be consumed for fuel, which leads to stronger and thicker bones in a matter of weeks.

When people think of a happy life they usually take their health for granted, yet without well-being and stamina no amount of money, no luxurious lifestyle, no loving relationships and no peace of mind can be enjoyed to the fullest. When we're young we think "I have plenty of time" however the time to begin living a healthful and active lifestyle is when we're young. The great news though is beginning a disciplined and focused exercise program begins to produce benefits at any age. 17

To avoid any misunderstanding concerning your body, your physical appearance, let me add this—you are not indulging in vanity by being your best physically and looking your best. Your body needs to be respected in the manner any of God's creations should be valued. In you rests the Holy Spirit. Your body, God's temple should always be cared for and regarded for what it is—His gift to each of us.

Dan Buettner, the explorer observed "The people you surround yourself with influence your behaviors." Each of us want to enjoy the pleasant things God has created for us and we want to surround ourselves with people that help us, lift us, and make us happy. But unfortunately, there are those certain people who will always find something wrong with most everything and will complain about anything that doesn't meet their particular dogma. These are the folks who can quickly darken a room and cause discomfort and embarrassment to those unfortunate enough to be nearby. When you associate with people, whether uplifting or depressing, for any length of time you often become the same way.

Although this is no surprise, what is surprising is that many people don't disassociate with negative people, usually because they "don't want to hurt their feelings". If this is you keep this in mind—they are not only disturbing your peace, disrespecting you and bringing you down but they are putting up brick walls, thick brick walls, that will prevent God's destiny for you. Are you prepared for that?

Learn to separate what is in your power to separate and what is not in your power to separate. By this I mean you can approach your life, and those in it, equally and tranquily. You owe nothing to those who continually bring you down. People do not have the right to cause turmoil, confusion, or agitation in your life.

You may have endured these people or this person in your life for years, but it is time to become mindful of the here and now. Maybe you've considered disassociating yourself in the past, but the past is no longer part of your life. You only have now. Think wisely. Your future is calling.

We all know people who motivate us, inspire us, and just make us feel happy to be around them. We also know those who bring us down as well as bring out the worst in us. These same people love to gossip about everyone and judge everyone. The musician George Harrison had a great quote, "Gossip is the devil's radio." and the worst part of it is people who do this, do this about you too!

One last thought before we leave this topic: We all have dark and negative thoughts. It really is ingrained in our DNA which helped our ancestors to be vigilant against predators as we've seen. To just sit around back then thinking happy thoughts constantly would not be conducive to staying alive. There had to be a lot of "what ifs?" "What if I get attacked?" "What if I fall and break my leg?" "What if I can't find food again today?" To stay alive then brought about dark thoughts. Fortunately, we no longer live in caves or fear that a creature will devour us. When a negative (or hurtful) thought appears in your consciousness do the following: Turn the thought into something else!

Have a few go-to topics that you could conjure up immediately. This could be a memory of a happy event with a loved one, a significant moment from that special vacation or the smile of your child. It could be anything that brings a feeling of contentment or happiness. Think of one right now. After you're done tuck it away for that moment something troubling appears in your mind. Before the hurtful or negative thought takes root switch to your "movie." It will take determination as well as a few practice runs but it works and works effectively.

Being happy is not a constant state of awareness for us. Life's experiences don't always bring euphoria or good feelings. In fact, if life only threw roses in our path we would most likely become bored and would definitely be unappreciative. It is the spontaneity of life, the novelty and the unpredictability of an emotion that makes life so special.

Growing up near the Falls of Niagara, seeing it multiple times a year, never dampened the wonder or sense of "awe" I felt when I saw them. Being awestruck is the word that comes close to describing the moment of amazement that carries with it the capacity to leave us speechless. This dramatic feeling has the power to both inspire us and to heal our soul.

The author Tony Robbins speaks about the necessity of "changing our state" when we're in the grip of negative thinking. When we are confronted with something greater than us, we are immediately altering our awareness.

Dacher Keltner who heads the UCLA—Berkeley's Social Interaction Lab describes the effect: "Awe is the feeling of being in the presence of something vast or beyond human scale that transcends our current understanding of things."

Some years ago I was in London, England for a conference. During breaks in the gathering I had the chance to explore the city a bit. Westminster Abbey was a spot I for years hoped to visit, and when I finally had the opportunity to do so, did.

As I walked into the church I stood in astonishment. Actually, I stood dumbfounded. The immensity. The enormity as well as the tremendous sense of history seemed to overpower me. Here walked kings and queens, the great as well as the humble.

What came to me at that moment was the awareness of silence. No one in the cathedral spoke above a whisper, such was the reverence and veneration felt by those of us walking through this majestic house of God. The Romans had a saying for what all of us that day felt "Omni Tempore Silentio Debent Studere"—"At all times cultivate silence."

When we feel a sense of wonder we realize we are part of something much larger than ourselves. We step out of our everyday existence if only for a moment. When you are in the course of observing something overwhelming you suddenly forget your cares, your worries, your "self". Not only are your emotions affected but physically you are too. Cytokine levels—markers of inflammation that researchers have linked to depression—are affected due to the positive emotions that most strongly reduce their state of balance in the body.

It's unusual to discover something that is actually right in front of us, but can you say that you don't take nature—more specifically trees, rivers, lakes, oceans, the mountains and so on—for granted? Many of us do. Being surrounded by nature allows our brain's command center— the Prefrontal Cortex- to rest and recover.

Happiness is not found in "things", it is found within. Within our minds, through our reaction to outside events—our attitude toward that event. It is found in our souls where God dwells. It is found in helping others. The Bible tells us that "A merry heart does good, like medicine, but a broken spirit dries the bones." (Proverbs 17:22)

God gave us the forests, the streams, the birds, and the flowers. Is it any surprise that we are renewed by them? It's been found that people recover faster in hospitals, perform better in school, and display less violent behavior when they have window views of trees and grass. Walking in a forest has been shown to lower anxiety by decreasing cortisol, the stress hormone, by 16%! But keep this in mind: be present. By that I mean enjoy and savor the experience. Be mindful of where you are.

Although we can enjoy those moments of peace and tranquility, the secular world will eventually intrude on the enjoyment once you're back into it. There are some methods to make the happiness last.

Planning an enjoyable experience—a vacation to the shore for instance—a few months in advance gives you something called "anticipatory pleasure." You visualize (there's that concept again) the sights, the smells, the sounds—even the weather—for weeks or months in advance. And each time you do you enjoy the experience. According to studies, conducted by the Dutch researcher Jeroen Nawijn and his colleagues the greatest increase in happiness was actually *before the vacation!*

When we're somewhere special we try to capture the special moments by taking pictures. We think that the more photos we take the more we can hang on to the happiness. Instead of loading up on photographs try committing the occurrences to memory. Describe the memories to someone else and you'll retain them even longer—which leads to a feeling of happiness.

Even though we want to be happy and we want to enjoy our lives as much as possible we have to make an effort to do so. Sadly, as I have continually been pointing out, the natural inclination of our brain is to think negatively. Our natural, biological proclivity is to survey our surroundings searching for threats and danger and looking at the dark side and the things we didn't want to happen. This produced a trait that, handed down these many thousands of years, requires our determination to change what comes naturally. But fortunately, we serve a supernatural God and we know that with dialogue prayer we can gather remarkable strength to do just that.

When asked late in life which year of his life he'd want to live over, Winston Churchill replied "1940 every time. Every Time."

Have you ever looked back on a particular event—a vacation, a project of some kind, the achievement of a goal and even a major life-changing occurrence—and what continues to impact your consciousness is the odyssey it took to get there? It is the passage, the journey that you now feel the most satisfied with. It was the effort to accomplish that dream or intention that now brings you pleasure and furnishes you with happiness.

When Winston Churchill spoke the words above, he was referring to the year that England stood alone against Nazi Germany and saw the beginning of round-the-clock bombing, known as "The Blitz", throughout Great Britain. France had fallen, Europe was under Nazi rule and Germany was planning the invasion of his country and of all the accomplishments and victories Churchill experienced throughout his life it was the year of his greatest desperation that he wished to relive!

Earlier I wrote about cold being nothing more than the absence of heat. In the same manner we could infer that the absence of happiness could include the feelings of sorrow, rage, and varying degrees of anger and anxiety. We could also add self-doubt, shyness, and low self-esteem to that list. But each of these are feelings not physical manifestations. Yet, left unchecked and unresolved these subjective perceptions can and most likely will become part of one's personality eventually.

2,000 years ago, the Stoic philosopher Epictetus observed that "Men are disturbed not by things, but by the view which they take of things." In other words, attitude.

Happiness then could be awareness such as love, laughter, joy, and moments of rapture. It could also be caused by the attainment of excellence or the experience of beauty. There is also a transcendent degree of inner joy, exhilaration, and contentment that we'll consider in a moment, but in order to fully compliment this matter for discussion we need to take the time to appreciate the beauty of life and that which is good in our life. Even if right now you just can't see it, it is there when you decide to look.

You'll recall that earlier I wrote that every day before you go to sleep you should write down 5 things that happened to you or for you that touched your heart and express gratitude for them. It might be the coffee someone bought you or the dessert they shared. It could be the compliment you received, or it could be the "thank-you" a stranger offered you. These courtesies and blessings are there when you open your eyes to notice. It is essential that you stay in the moment, in awareness and to savor each of them. By doing so you'll notice even the smallest favors that up until now you missed and will cause you to be grateful which in turn will attract even more to be grateful for.

Every human being looks for happiness in some way. We attempt to maintain that feeling of happiness for as long as possible and hopefully you have read some ideas in these pages that may help to make that feeling of happiness not only appear but to stay awhile longer.

Before concluding this manuscript, I'd like to leave you with, what I believe to be, the indisputable pathway to achieving lasting happiness.

Some years back a movie titled "Pay it Forward" made its debut at theatres. The story line centered around a twelve-year-old boy, Trevor, who as part of a class project conceives an idea to help others. By helping just three people in some way, who in turn each help three people and so on down the line, the world could not help but become a better place. Tantamount to a confirmation of this intention the following happened recently: A woman at an Indiana McDonalds drive-through noticed a dad with his children in the van behind her and paid the cashier on his behalf. The father followed suit and amazingly the pay-it-forward chain continued for hours. When it was over, 167 consecutive cars paid for the meal of the people in the car behind them!

When you are altruistic you lose sight of who you are. You become one with each of God's children. Helping others is a gratifying feeling because it involves intentional interaction with others—which Psychologists tell is the top key to happiness. By helping others, we innately are aware that we made a difference in the world. We know that because of our kindness we became part of that person or persons and therefore part of humanity itself.

When you impact another person's life in a positive and meaningful way you find significance to your own life and know that your life made a difference in someone else's.

Make a commitment today, now, this moment to do something good for 3 others each day. Whether it's taking someone to their doctor's appointment or to the grocery store, buying lunch or even paying the toll for the person behind you, you will be living in love, and we know that "God is love, and he who abides in love abides in God, and God in him." (I John 4:16)

And now you know—the greatest happiness is that which comes from helping others.

27

Final Thoughts

Most likely you have read various motivational and inspirational books and articles in the past. I know I have. A lot of them.

I'd try to follow the guidance offered in them—"think positive" "Say affirmations" "Declare it's yours and you'll receive it." I could go on, but you get the picture—probably because you did this too. Sometimes it worked, usually it didn't and when it didn't, I'd walk away saying "What am I doing wrong?"

Sound familiar?

As a stockbroker I would focus my mind on a goal and beat the door down in order to achieve it. I habitually Edged God Out because I "knew" I could reach my goal if I put my mind to it.

But that's not God's way as I learned over the years.

What you've read in the preceding pages is the compilation of experiences and knowledge - and discoveries - I've acquired over decades. I pass the "life lessons" I've undergone to you in the hope of shaving years off of your learning curve.

I cannot overstate the importance of living in the will of God. Prayer and supplication—petitioning —will provide you the opportunity to hear that still small voice. Please reread the previous sentence. It is that important.

Much of the information available today about accomplishing goals does not include adhering to God's will, hence your seldom realizing what it is you intend to have. God gives us free will and we either use that freedom by going about things on our own (where God may or may not allow the goal to be reached) or we can trust Him to guide us in our efforts and energy toward achieving the objective, knowing that we put our heart and mind into the endeavor while adhering to what He wants for our life. Personally, what I found after many years of earthly education is that my Creator can direct my life better than I can!

Maybe it takes being broken (for me anyway) to then ask God to put you back together—reformed, remolded and restored into who He wants you to be. For some of us the tests came about in order to give a testimony.

Throughout these chapters, you've clearly seen the necessity of maintaining faith. You'll recall that Matthew related the parable of the talents in Chapter 25.

Jesus once again explained the role of faith and the belief we should have not only in God's guidance but in ourselves to do His will. Two of the servants had faith that they could increase their assignments but the third servant, not having faith in this belief, failed in his responsibility. The lesson we take from this of course is that we need to live with courageous faith.

Having faith does not mean expecting a miracle. This doesn't mean a miracle cannot nor will not appear, but it should not be completely depended on. You must do your part in conformance with God's Divine Laws.

The Holy Spirit will guide you when you call Him but will not do your work for you. He will, instead sensibly direct you and assist you in achieving the intentions you have. He will do this by placing impulses of thought in your mind which will enable your plans to be carried out through the most logical and suitable way possible.

Be determined and know definitely what it is you want, however be very cautious in how you think, what you ponder and what you put your focus on. Thoughts, like physical movement repeated over and over and over become a habit. Deeds, as you are aware, follow thought and thoughts mixed with emotion become manifest in your life. It makes no difference in what thoughts you maintain—fear, hate, greed, worry, doubt, despair, anguish as well as hopelessness or on the other hand desire, faith, enthusiasm, success, achievement, joy, optimism, and peace of mind—your subconscious doesn't know the difference and will act on the strongest emotion. We already know this to be true because – once again - worst expectations usually are realized and what we don't want keeps showing up in our lives!

This however is exceptional news because we have the choice of what to think and to put our focus on!

Over the preceding pages we've talked at length of the importance of adhering to the will of God, but how can you know His will? The answer:

Do the next thing He tells you to do!

Be sensitive to the still small voice. When you hear that voice, don't over-analyze the message. By being perceptive and obedient you'll notice dramatic changes begin to happen. Things begin falling into place, doors previously closed begin to open and even those who were unfriendly, argumentative, even hostile towards you become congenial (Proverbs 16:7). Small acts of obedience lead to great blessings.

Beware however—negative thinking prevents accepting God's favor. God cannot do His work when all you do is argue with Him.

I recall an incident some years ago when "the voice of reason" was causing me to question what I inwardly felt lead to do: I had considered transferring my broker's license to another securities firm and had interviewed with that company. The company was based in Boston and at the last minute I rejected their offer as I was just not ready to move there.

Some time had passed, and I learned that now they would be opening an office in Buffalo. I heard that soft, humble voice encouraging me to reach out to them but all I could think is, "They won't want to talk to me. They're probably offended that I turned them down earlier." But the urge to call was incessant.

The next day I followed that guidance, made the call, and spoke to the vice president of the firm (who I had initially interviewed with) who, upon hearing from me said, "I am so glad to hear from you! We wanted to talk to you but somehow misplaced your paperwork. I was hoping you would call!"

I went on to a very enjoyable and rewarding career with the firm. This was another lesson in not ignoring that voice even when it seemed illogical!

For those who think God doesn't speak to them, I would ask you to consider this: If you decide to do something—*whatever that may be*—and get a feeling not to do it, but do it anyway and then feel guilty afterwards—that was God talking to you.

The world will say "that's just your guilty conscious!" but that's because there are those who refuse to honor God (and they have free will not to!)

The Holy Spirit, indwelling in us, constantly guides us if we let Him, but God will *never* override our will. The more we are open to receiving His guidance however, the more appropriate promptings we receive.

Always remember to thank God for the smallest of things and He will multiply the big things as well. Never let a day pass where you didn't acknowledge His kindness, mercy, and grace.

Throughout the book, we've spoken at length about the role fear, doubt and worry play in obtaining what we want. When panic sets in we form scenarios of what life will be like if we don't reach our goal. But now you've learned the "trick" to achieving what it is you intend to have and that's by lowering importance. And having a back-up plan as well.

Plan your strategy in how to proceed realizing your goal with "seeing" the end result, but also loosening the grip as to how it should be done. Stay the course but be flexible enough for changes in the route to get there. In other words, relinquish the wheel to God.

Scripture holds an interesting narrative that exemplifies this point fully.

Naaman was known as "a mighty man of valor" and he certainly must have been that because not only was he the commander of the Syrian army and a favorite of the King, but He was also a leper!

As we know, lepers were not only considered repulsive and hideous but were shunned by the populace, it speaks to how respected and highly thought of Naaman must have been in Syrian society.

After being told that there existed someone who could cure him, Naaman immediately sets out to find this man living hundreds of miles away in Israel.

It doesn't take much to imagine Naaman's excitement as he rushes to find Elisha the prophet who will finally rid him of his grisly disfigurement. "I'll bet he will pour oil over my head and sprinkle some over my body. He'll have incense burning and we'll sing and dance by the fire and then—finally—I'll be clean! I'm so excited, lets just hurry up and get there!"

We can relate to Naaman's eagerness and impatience, as well as his pre-conceived ideas as to how he'll reach his goal.

Out of breath he pounds on Elisha's door "I'm here to be healed!" and from the back of the house he hears someone shout to the house-keeper who answers the door "Tell him to go jump in the river. Seven times! He will get his healing then!"

"What?! You gotta be kidding?" he must have thought. Naaman, according to the Bible "became furious "and went away and said "Indeed, I said to myself, He will surely come out to me, and stand and call in the name of the Lord his God, and wave his hand over the place, and heal the leprosy."

"The Jordan River? That cesspool? We have two beautiful rivers in Damascus, clean, blue, and sweet, Why can't I go there?"

But showing love and concern, Naaman's men gently say "You're here now. If Elisha would have told you to do something spectacular to be healed would you not have done it? Go now and try what the prophet said."

We can almost see Naaman dipping his foot in the Jordan, smell and all. "I can't believe I'm doing this." The first time he immerses himself in the brown water nothing happens. A third time, a fifth time. Even a sixth time—nothing.

But now, doing what Elisha instructed, knowing "he said seven times" and now with faith and expectancy, Naaman plunges into the water one last time and emerges "restored like the flesh of a little child." (II Kings5:1-14) Our ways are not God's ways, as Isaiah said. (Isaiah 55:8)

We mortals are limited in our knowledge and compared to a boundless Providence who spoke worlds into being, we could not possibly comprehend, or indeed compose the perfection of the Divine Path to realizing a goal.

Maybe you read this book in the hope that by doing so you could discover an effective method to attain your goals, objectives, and intentions in conjunction with your Christian principles. My prayer for you is that it served its purpose. Choose, believe, and acknowledge that what you conceive in your mind you can achieve. Act in accordance with God's will and your corner of the world will be filled with sunshine, joy and peace of mind.

Whatever your goal may be—a new home, a car, perfect health, a loving relationship—be aware of the responsibilities that accompany the realization of the intention.

It's conceivable that you've read this book with the desire of improving your finances, having more money. With this objective it is essential to be mindful of the definite reasons for this desire and what you will do with it once you attain it. It is absolutely necessary that you know how to manage it and to be psychologically prepared for the experience of being affluent. This blessing, once obtained, should never be taken lightly and needs to be considered with forethought.

What truths do you hold in your heart? What do you believe them to be and after you've thought about them what value do you place on them?

Do you have a personal creed that you live by? In other words what core beliefs do you hold within your heart?

Regardless of what others think of you, what do you think of yourself? Are you satisfied with what you know of yourself, of what you've discovered about your values?

Write down what *your truths* are. They may be things like faith, character, integrity, honesty, and courage or whatever accurately describes your convictions. Devote time to this exercise.

Now write down all the falsehoods, fabrications and lies you've been told—to yourself, by yourself as well as by others. Like your truths, you know—and God knows—the distortions, misrepresentations and untruths spoken by, and about, you.

Let whatever truths you discover about yourself become the cornerstone of the new foundation you will build for yourself going forward.

Carry these truths with you—put them literally on an index card—get past your failures. *And then burn the lies.* Actually, put those falsehoods in a fireplace, stove or fire pit and burn them because from here-on they are no longer part of who you are. You are now called to a higher purpose—to be a shining example of God's love and glory.

If you think God can't use you, consider who He used in the past. You may recall that Jacob was a liar, Joseph was arrogant, Moses stuttered, Rahab was a prostitute, Gideon took a lot of convincing, David was an adulterer—and a murderer as well, Isaiah liked to preach naked, Job went bankrupt, Peter denied Jesus three times, Zacchaeus was too short, and Paul persecuted Christians. No matter where you've been or what you've done, God will turn your struggles into successes if you let Him.

Hold your head with dignity. Live with honor. Be above reproach. Live your life with a clear conscious. Be noble. Say what you mean and mean what you say. Be honest and straightforward but not intentionally hurtful.

Be humble at all times but never be a doormat. Receive compliments with gratitude and grace. When you are asked something meaningful and serious, take the time to consider it thoroughly.

Pray unceasingly—for clarity, for guidance and for wisdom.

Always envisage on "What would Jesus do?" before proceeding.

Never gossip and have thick skin because in life most others will never hold to your standards. Allow for criticism and negative comments that will be thrown your way and use them to grow.

Never stop learning and be open for new challenges and adventures.

Do not put yourself down—even jokingly—but don't take yourself too seriously either.

When you say no, make that firm and final but when you say yes honor that.

Contemplate on scriptures that hold something special for you.

Speak sparingly but also be engaging and friendly. Be no-one's fool but never be unapproachable.

Be sincere. Create core values and never abandon them.

Love and honor your family. Love God with all your heart and love your neighbor as yourself.

If you are serious about breaking out of the old life you knew, moving forward into a new way of thinking and applying the concepts found in these pages—then you must be all in. There can be no half—measures —"I'm gonna give it my best" "I'll try". If you're not at that place where you can accept and believe that God *really does* have an amazing and incredible life planned for you, I urge you to spend quiet time in prayer and edification.

As human beings we are not able to be on top of our game 24/7. Perfection unfortunately is not in our capabilities. Other than one man who continues to influence us in profound ways these past twenty centuries, we all fall short of the glory of God.

Thankfully however we can choose to pick ourselves up, dust ourselves off and continue running the race, knowing that we are constantly being reconstructed and rejuvenated by the Holy Spirit. (II Timothy 4:7)

Being part of a faith community enables us to share and gain strength from one another. Dr. Billy Graham once said, "Amazing things happen when the family of God bands together." Coming together in a church allows us the joy of praising and worshipping God but the experience and presence of the Lord are also found well beyond it's walls.

If through prayer and meditation God inspires you to reach for what you hope to have, you now know how to achieve every dream, every goal, every objective, and every intention.

Each of us as Christians are representatives and emissaries of Jesus Christ. As such I am reminded of the following words of St. Francis: "Preach the gospel often, when necessary, use words."

Now it's time to go where your hopes, your aspirations, and your desires can be realized. A place where not only possibilities reside but a place of knowing, a place of choice. Prayer must be part of your life going forward. You will however need to possess a spirit of belief, knowing that with God *all things are possible.*

There are no accidents and God has a purpose that He's calling you to if you will devote the time to hear Him. Once again, in those words of Solomon - "Trust in the Lord with all your heart, and lean not on your own understanding. In all your ways acknowledge Him and He shall direct your paths."

Finally, in closing allow me to leave you—in love and with my encouragement—the following from Numbers 6:24-26:

The Lord bless you and keep you;
The Lord make His face shine upon you,
And be gracious to you:
The Lord lift up His countenance upon you,
and give you peace."

1. Known as the Intracardial Nervous System, this group of nerves has been confirmed to have a mind of its own.

2. Jutting into the Aegean Sea, this peninsula is located in Northern Greece. Mt. Athos is home to dozens of Orthodox Christian Monasteries. Mt. Athos stands as a giant shrine to the Virgin Mary and was granted sovereignty by the Byzantine Empire in the 9th Century. There are no drivable roads connecting Mt. Athos to the rest of Greece and is only accessible by boat or helicopter. First broadcast on 60 Minutes on Easter Sunday, April 24th, 2011 the program is an amazingly, spiritually – moving look at Mt. Athos. Go to cbsnews.com/news/mount-athos-a-visit-to-the-holy-mountain/

3. Given shortly after the fall of France, Churchill delivered this speech before the British House of Commons on June 4th, 1940.

4. The Mayflower reached landfall in November 1620. After spending a month in the harbor in what is now known as Provincetown the ship made its way west across Cape Cod landing in Plymouth in December. Accounts vary – some list the date the Pilgrims landed at Plimouth (as it was then spelled) on December 21st other accounts list December 26th, 1620. 41 men aboard ship put their signature to a document known as "The Mayflower Compact" agreeing to form a government and to obey its "just and equal laws" They elected John Carver as their governor.

5. Unfortunately, history seems to have forgotten Henry Allen Ironside which is sad, given Dr. Ironside's dedication to Christ. Given up for dead at birth, Ironside's pulse was detected 40 minutes

later! He started a Sunday school at the age of 11 and unable to locate an adult teacher began teaching himself to dozens of children and adults each week. At 16 he was preaching full time giving over 500 sermons a year. Dr. Ironside was also an author and theologian. He became pastor of Moody Church in Chicago after preaching under the direction of the Bible Institute of the same name. Henry Ironside who died 1951 at 74 is considered one of the most prolific Christian writers of the 20th century with over 100 books, booklets and pamphlets to his credit.

6. This quote, taken from the Timeless Classic "The Impossible Dream" was first heard on Broadway in 1965 in the play "Man of La Mancha"

7. This poem was written by Charles Osgood of CBS Radio Network and read by him the day after the game, which was played in Buffalo, January 3rd, 1993. Houston had gone into the Locker Room at halftime with a 28-3 lead before increasing the score to 35-3 in the 2nd half. 'The Comeback' as this game came to be known, remains the largest comeback in NFL postseason history. At the Final gun the scoreboard read – Buffalo 41 Houston 38.

8. King Xerxes 1st is known to us by his Biblical name - Ahasuerus. In 479 BC, after punishing his wife Vashti for refusing to nakedly display herself to the royal court, Xerxes/Ahasuerus held a nationwide beauty hunt throughout Persia (roughly present-day Iran) to find a new wife. He chose the beautiful Esther.

9. The New King James Version of the Bible contains 66 books within it. The Catholic Bible contains an additional 7 books. The Greek Orthodox Bible includes the 7 Catholic books plus 5 more.

10. Anger causes an immediate burst of adrenaline which causes a fight or flight response in our nervous system. This spike leads to an increase of cortisol, the stress and anxiety hormone, keeping us on constant edge. Not only is this detrimental to our health but it's been observed that rage begets more rage. Letting go of

anger, in the case of a personal relationship or relationships, gives us the opportunity to forgive. The journal 'Cross-Culture Research' conducted a study based on the input of close to 42,000 participants from 30 countries. The study identified how people prioritized forgiveness across the globe. On a list of 18 values, people ranked forgiveness eight over-all, higher than virtues such as ambition and obedience but below love, honesty and responsibility. But the researchers found that the rankings varied country to country. *The US sample rated forgiveness more highly than did most of the other countries it studied!* The benefits of becoming a forgiving populace were encouraging. Analysis showed a positive link between the ranking of forgiveness in a country and the average well-being of its inhabitants.

11. Mites were too small copper coins. Together the widow's two mites were worth about 1 penny.

12. When young Albert Einstein debated with his professor concerning the existence of evil, it was his way of explaining that God doesn't "Make" bad things happen to his people. Einstein was trying to explain evil in the context that the room full of students that day, and the professor, could identify with and understand. In the Hebrew, which Isaiah spoke, he wrote in Chapter 45 verse 7 "I form the light and create darkness; I make peace and create evil: I the Lord do all these things." Evil in this passage seems to be a retribution from not doing what is right. Evil is in the world because Satan is still allowed (by God) to be the prince and power of the air and the fallen nature of humanity. We humans have free will and when we separate ourselves from God, are inclined to follow our fallen nature. The book of James (1:13) talks about God not tempting because He cannot tempt. But we need to realize that each person is carried away by their own lust.

13. Agnostics are those who believe that the existence of God is unknown. Deists believe in human mortality and the use of reason rather than divine revelation. Atheists deny the existence of God.

14. George Washington's inauguration that spring day took place on the steps of what is now Federal Hall located at the foot of Wall Street in New York City. New York City became the nation's first capital in 1785 and remained so until 1790 at which time it was relocated to Philadelphia. It remained in that city through the following 10 years as the newly designated area along the Potomac River was developed. The city of Washington became the nation's permanent capital in 1800.

15. This cross is formed by the White House to the north. The Jefferson Memorial to the south. The location of The United States Capital to the east and the Lincoln Memorial to the west.

16. The Romans divided the twelve hours between 6 PM and 6 AM into four equal parts. These were called 'watches'.

17. For a more complete explanation of exercise, health, anti-aging and nutrition see my book: **"Unchained and Unbroken: Life Lessons and Strength Training from a Jailhouse Gymrat"** available through Amazon as well as fine bookstores. This is a protein-filled book for those interested in developing a no-nonsense workout program, as well as for those who are advanced weightlifters, workout enthusiasts or anyone looking to become Jailhouse Strong. Included in the text are stories, anecdotes, and life experiences I lived through in nearly a decade in the Federal Prison System.

Shortly after entering prison in the fall of 2011, I began to immerse myself with material that would fortify my spirit. Prison is a dreadful place; however, the sense of dread is not only intense but magnified in those first days and months into a sentence.

The library at FCI Elkton, in Ohio, where I was first sent that autumn, had an extensive collection of reading material all very well organized. Most of the inventory had been collected since the facility opened in 1997. Other than magazines and newspapers the inventory comprised of donations from the inmate population from books sent them over the years.

As I related in the Introduction, when I found a passage, thought or idea enlightening and informative I wrote it down. Because we were restricted in having more than a few items in our locker, cell or cubicle it was not possible to maintain anything that would take up space, books included. Punishments were harsh for those who did not adhere to the prison regulations, and I was not interested in adding to my misery. Even the paperwork I did maintain, although neat and organized was routinely confiscated by over-zealous staff. Shakedowns were constant throughout my bid and sadly much of what I tried to save was destroyed. That this book – which was completely hand-written - was left untouched was, to me, a bit of a miracle. Adding to this confusion were my transfers – referred to as 'Diesel Therapy' - to several different facilities in my nearly decade in prison where more of my personal possessions were routinely taken. Due to these constant upheavals, I may not be giving credit to those authors who imparted their wisdom to me and of which I possibly share with you. Furthermore, I had no thought of writing any type of meaningful book during those first half-dozen years. Wherever possible however I do quote and acknowledge who I could. Should there be someone, somewhere who I overlooked crediting a passage, thought or idea please write me, and I will certainly acknowledge them. In editing Chrysalis, we scanned the material to ascertain any degree of plagiarism and found none. I ask for your indulgence and understanding, however as I wrote, please let me know if I can give credit where credit is due.

There are over 60 English-language versions of the Bible today, of which the NIV (New International Version) and NLT (New Living Translation) are very popular. In writing Chrysalis, I wanted to use a Bible that most closely followed word-for-word the Aramaic, Greek and Hebrew texts originally used to write God's Holy Book. The King James Version (KJV) and the New King James Version (NKJV) are both word-for-word translations of the Bible.

The King James Version, named after James I, King of England who commissioned the English translation of the Bible in 1604 (published 1611), used what's known as "Early Modern English" - that language commonly used in England at that time. For instance, in Proverbs 21 verse 28 the KJV proclaims "A false witness shall perish; But the man that heareth speaketh constantly." In 1982 the NKJV of the Bible was published with the goal of incorporating the modern English we speak today while still retaining the purity and stylistic beauty of the original KJV. It was this version, the New King James Version, that I relied upon for the majority of the scriptural quotes. Where appropriate I used another version but each of those are identified where used.

KJV – King James Version   NIV – New International Version

NKJV – New King James Version   NLT – New Living Translation

Guy W. Gane, Jr.

Guy William Gane, Jr. had the privilege of serving his clients for 34 rewarding years both as a stockbroker and Registered Investment Advisor, eventually owning his own firm with multiple offices throughout the US. In keeping with his commitment to give back to his community, Guy, for many years, served on numerous boards, donated his time to various charities, and as well, to provide military personnel from Western New York, where he lived, the opportunity to call their loved ones during the Christmas holidays.

There is a saying that "One's best success comes after their greatest disappointments" and Guy stands as a testament to that statement.

On a beautiful early spring morning in 2008, and toward the end of his career, Guy's world came crashing down. Charged with Money-Laundering and Mail Fraud, Guy, despite vehemently proclaiming his innocence (as well as passing two separate Polygraph tests), was eventually given a 13-year sentence in Federal Prison.

In order to reconstruct a structure, be it a building, a company or a life, you must first break apart the old, existing one. Guy's tortuous experience accomplished just that. Although already a Christian, it took living in a living hell to fully hear the Lord's voice to become one of God's staunchest ambassadors. Literally being the guy who in every sense has 'been there, done that', it was put on his heart to write a book that would reveal the method to achieving every objective, fulfill every dream and reach every goal, through Divine obedience. 'Chrysalis: Awakening to God's Path, Protection, and Power in Your Life' is the result.

Today, Guy through his company Gane Wisdom (ganewisdom.com), is a much sought-after Speaker, Author, Certified Life Coach, and entrepreneur. Guy, who also authored 'Unchained and Unbroken: Life Lessons and Strength Training From a Jailhouse Gymrat' created the mentorship program known as Prisoncology (prisoncology.com), where his full story can now be told. This organization, which is partnered with the Christian community nationally, provides not only pre-entry guidance and preparation to those about to enter the prison system, but to their families as well. Prisoncology is also at the forefront of prison reform in the United States.

www.ingramcontent.com/pod-product-compliance
Lightning Source LLC
Chambersburg PA
CBHW050458160726
48003CB00001B/65